FRED BEAR

Other Books About
FRED BEAR

FRED BEAR
A Biography

CHARLES M. KROLL

THE FRED BEAR SPORTS CLUB PRESS
Gainesville, Florida

ISBN 0-9619480-1-9

Dedicated to all who appreciate the
Earth's creatures and enjoy the great outdoors.

CONTENTS

FOREWORD

If Fred Bear had been born a hundred years earlier, he might have been one of the mountain men scouting the Rockies on hunting and trapping expeditions. He could have been one of Jim Bridger's or Kit Carson's men, or, more likely, he might have crossed the Cumberland Gap with Daniel Boone. If he'd been born in Quebec in the early days, he would have been a voyager roaming the Great Lakes, the Mississippi and the Northwest Territories.

He was born too late for all that, but not for pioneering in a field that he himself did much to establish. In moving to the peak of success in his vocation and avocation, this shy farm boy became part of the great American tradition of free enterprise and the self-made man.

Over the past 50 years literally hundreds of articles have been written about Fred Bear. They have appeared in small local newspapers with circulation in the hundreds and in major national magazines reaching millions.

On the occasion of Fred Bear's 80th birthday in 1982, a surprise party was held in his honor in Gainesville, Florida. Scores of his old friends flew in from around the country to be with him for the celebration. The evening was the subject of a piece written by one of America's foremost conservation writers, John Mitchell, Field Editor of Audubon Magazine and appeared in the pages of Field and Stream Magazine. It seems an appropriate way to begin this story.

Papa Bear

PAPA BEAR
by John Mitchell

"A heavy Floridian rain was slicking the windows of the Gainesville Hilton the last time I saw him. It was March and under such unseasonal circumstances, one might have guessed he would be out of uniform. No battered Borsalino hat with the felt pinched tight at the front of the crown, no camouflage bowhunting togs, no scuffs on the boots. Just that topknot of silver hair and the chiseled face grinning above a blue business suit and a bolo tie with a Kodiak bear embossed on the clincher. The mufti fooled no one, for a bear was the clincher. It was Fred Bear — the Papa Bear of the great outdoors, the archer emeritus, the patron saint of bowhunting in America, the elder statesman of the field sports — come now to receive the accolades of 150 friends and admirers gathered to celebrate his eightieth birthday. As he came through the door of the ballroom someone shouted,"Surprise!" The Bear looked stunned. His head wagged side to side, eyebrows arched high each time he spotted another familiar face from a faraway place — from California and New York, Nebraska and Pennsylvania, Texas and Connecticut, Arkansas and Michigan. Faces remembered across the campfire years, faces from the memory book of a lifetime afield."

"So," one ungracious fellow asked the guest of honor later on, "how does it feel to be a senior citizen?"

"How would I know?" said Bear. "Call me an old man, but not a senior citizen. That's almost as bad as the word 'retire.'"

"And well said, for Fred Bear at eighty appears no closer to retirement than most men a generation younger. He is still chairman of the largest archery company in the world. Still a doodler at the drawing board where, for half a century, his razorhead inventiveness hit upon a string of technical innovations that would help substantially to wrench bowhunting out of the dark ages of sport. Still, perhaps the nation's most respected spokesman for adherence to a code of outdoor conduct and the rules of fair chase. And still the hunter — "the finest natural hunter I've ever known," a veteran Alaskan outfitter once said of him — though nowadays, the sated Bear seems more content to prowl the woods unarmed, functioning as den leader to the younger cubs of the hunting party."

They remembered all of it, that night at Gainesville, or possibly less, for there was so much to remember…Bill Wright of San Francisco, bagging his world-record moose on Bear's Little Delta hunt in 1959; Bob Munger, from brook-trout country, U. P. Michigan with memories of the ice off Point Barrow and of Fred and the no-show polar bears. Astronaut Colonel Joe Engle, fresh from his flight aboard the space shuttle *Columbia*, recalling an Alaskan adventure in 1972, in which the Bear seemed to spend "every minute of his waking time making sure that everyone else was having a good hunt." And, Merrill L. Petoskey, deputy director of natural resources for the U.S. Department of Agriculture and former director of the Michigan Game Division, paraphrasing the ecological philosopher Aldo Leopold by proclaiming: "There are some people who can live without wildlife and some who cannot. Fred Bear is one who cannot."

"And here, too, was Bill Boyer, for many years head of the Air Transport Division of General Motors Corporation, but now retired and not liking the word any better than Bear does. Boyer is the one who owns that fabulous whitetail commissary called Grousehaven, deep in the oak woods of Ogemaw County, Michigan, where he and Bear have hunted together for a quarter of a century; though more and more they tend to sit by Boyer's blastfurnace fireplace, swapping the lankiest tales you'd ever imagine. Even now, in Gainesville, Bear was at the microphone confessing to be "the last of the liars," and adding, "Never go into the woods with a rifle or bow unless you're prepared to come out with an awful good alibi."

"What's wrong with Fred?" Boyer was asking later in the evening. I said I hadn't noticed anything wrong.

"Maybe so," Boyer allowed. "I just have a feeling something's not right and I'll be damned if I can put my finger on it."

"For my own part, I had been looking for something not right with Fred Bear the first time I saw him. And it was raining then, too — a soft September drizzle against the windows of his office in the old Bear Archery Plant at Grayling, Michigan. This and the imminence of his company's move to Gainesville—some 1,200 miles south at the sunbelt end of Interstate 75 — had drawn out some pretty long faces in Grayling, including Fred Bear's. He seemed not much enamored of palm trees and black bass. His heart was up here at the edge of the north woods, hard by the dry-fly Au Sable and the prospect of frying-pan trout."

"In a figurative manner of speaking, I suspect I had come to Grayling looking to bury Caesar, not to praise him. At the time, I was one month into a yearlong assignment, a series of articles (and later a book) exploring all aspects of hunting in America. The question being: Was it an honorable tradition, or a dishonorable shame? I think I went into it leaning toward the latter. I had hunted a bit as a youngster, had drawn away from it more by circumstance than by disfavor, drifted gradually into a circle of acquaintances who by and large regarded hunting as an activity falling somewhere on the far side of abomination. And I had just come down from Michigan's Upper Peninsula, having observed there a shabby no-show bear hunt replete with CB radios and jack-pine savages in Cadillac sedans. Now to the lair of this man whom Cleveland Amory had dubbed the "Grand Dragon" of the bow hunt. I was loaded for Bear. Or so I thought."

"We talked for more than three hours, Bear and I. About what I was up to and how he perceived the motivations of anti-hunters and why one could learn more about deer in one week with a bow than in a lifetime with a rifle and where he had traveled to film his classic hunts and what he had shot; and whether, indeed there would be any hunting left over when the corporate farmers got finished plowing their fields to the borrow-pits of the county roads and all the Earth's wild places had gone down the drain of development, or been shot up to hell by the lawbreakers. I was loaded for Bear, all right — and totally disarmed by him. It was not so much what he said, but how he said it: openly, undefensively, sometimes humorously (and then, at his own expense), often with perception and sensitivity; and always, it seemed to me, with such a large measure of humility for a man so tightly hitched to the practical business necessities of self-promotion. Disarmed, outflanked and won over and then Bear saying that the whitetails were running down in Ogemaw County and why didn't I join him there at Grousehaven for a bow hunt in October. I told him I didn't hunt, much less with a bow. No matter, he said. There'd be time to continue the conversation. And we did that."

"We did that four years in a row — three in the bow season and one in rifle (when I did go armed, if only to put an ambiguous punctuation mark at the end of my story). Mostly, I just moseyed over the acorns with the old hunter, sponged up his yarns and savvy, watched him spend his time making sure, as Joe Engle would testify, that everyone else was having a good hunt. I had never before been in the woods with such a lucid observer of the ways of nature. And I don't just mean his knowing where the deer might run. I mean his sense of place, his appreciation of light and color and where the wind was blowing and what a certain cloud might bring. "The finest natural hunter I've ever known," the pro from Alaska had said. "A practicing ecologist," Merrill Petoskey would say of him in Gainesville. "A catalyst...toward helping the American citizen better understand the out door life as we believe it should be understood — wonderful, awesome, sometimes cruel, but always dynamic and revealing of truth to those who do understand."

"After the first two seasons at Grousehaven, my official chores as questing scrivener of the hunt were finished. I had covered the beat from Texas to Alaska, from Montana to Michigan and had met and talked along the way with scores of hunters and anti-hunters, game biologists, public officials and professors of this-and-that. So where, an occasional critic wanted to know, where had the moment of truth come to me? Who, of all the respondents along the way had touched me with the stoutest staff of wisdom and turned my preconceptions about hunting into a better understanding of the outdoor life? And always, without hesitation, I would have to make reference to this lanky archer and that rainy day in Grayling and the days with him that would follow, afoot in the acorn woods of Ogemaw County. It was as if the Bear had loosed a razorhead at my prejudice — and skewered it clean. Requiescat in pace. I buried that gizzard at Grousehaven. For that alone, all praise to the Bear in the famous Borsalino hat."

"So much has been written about the life and times of Frederick Bernard Bear — and not so little by him — that I am not about to effort a full chronology here. Except to wonder what key events or achievements might have tickled the corners of his mind that night in Gainesville as he moved among his friends with a winning smile and a ready hand. I can only guess. I guess there might have been a private moment long enough for him to remember the Cumberland, the Pennsylvanian hills of his earliest home, the bow of his canoe cleaving the mists on Conodoquinet Creek, a mink in the muskrat trap, his first .22 (a swingbolt Quackenbush), chestnut trees before the fatal blight, squirrels in the stewpot and venison steaks and his papa, Harry the tool maker, coming home from the shoot at Carlisle with his .32/40 Winchester match rifle in one hand, a prize ham in the other. He was indeed one of the finest shots in the state, that Harry. Father to son."

"Or perhaps there was a moment to recall Detroit in the 1920's, the turn-over jobs as auto-plant pattern maker, the basement workshop where he tinkered with gunstocks and the crudest of bows. He had discovered this book by Dr. Saxton Pope, the bowhunting protege of Ishi (alas, poor Ishi — the last of the Stone Age Indians, the first of the museum ones). He had seen the silent film of Art Young, first paleskin ever to stalk the Kodiak bear and the Kenai moose with a bow and arrow. As things turned out, it was almost as if Pope & Young had been stalking Fred Bear."

"Surely, with the presence in Gainesville of so many archery colleagues, there must have been fleeting thoughts of his company's growth over the years, workshop to rented garage to Grayling to Gainesville; the first target model made of osage orange with a bowstring of Irish linen; and always the new ideas at the doodle board — the first-ever shooting glove, the first quiver attachable to a bow, the first bowfishing reel, the first modem arm-guard, the first take-down bow, the first use of laminated fiberglass, which would revolutionize both industry and sport. In one lifetime — from longbows no different than those used at Agincourt to this newfangled Bear Delta V, a fast, flat-shooting bow with its high-strength alloy wheels, interchangeable speed blocks, multiratio nylon cams, power grip, pylon design, platinum hue and satin finish."

"Or did the guest of honor's memory drift now and then to the far-off hunting places, to Mozambique and the thornbush lions and the elephant as big as the Ritz, to India and Sher-Kan the tiger, to the Kispiox River and the silvertip grizz, to Dry Creek and the Little Delta in Alaska? What an incredible travelogue he had made of his life. And what an unperishable record. Almost always it was for the record, the cameras humming, the pencil by lantern-light skipping across the pages of his field notes, the films (more than twenty-five) and the books (three), the trophies and artifacts accumulating at last in the Fred Bear Museum. Always pushing himself, pushing his pro ducts, pushing his sport. "I don't know how I did it," he told me our last time together at Grousehaven. "There must have been something driving me to run like that — just running around the mountains. But gee! It was fun."

"Now, in the ballroom at Gainesville, after the chow and the speeches and the tendering of gifts, the celebrants began to gather themselves for goodnights and goodbyes. I watched Bear moving through the crowd, a Lincolnesque face with eyes the color of glacial tarns. They had seen so much, those eyes. They had seen the mountains of Pennsylvania and the cedar swamps of Michigan before POSTED signs. They had seen farms good enough to tolerate coverts in fencerows, before bib overalls gave way to pinstripe suits. They had seen the day when a twelve-year-old boy could behold a recurve bow without asking his father, "Hey, Pop! Where are the wheels?' The AuSable, before fly fishers were run down by bumper-to-bumper beercan canoes. The road north to Mackinac, before bumper-to-bumper blazeorange vans on Opening Day. "There are so many people," he had told me at Grousehaven. "And so little room left for the game."

Still, the situation couldn't be all that bad up in Ogemaw County because here was Bear now, lecturing a small audience of deer camp cronies about the possibilities of the upcoming season. I moseyed over and overheard him to say:

"Gentlemen, in spite of a rather severe winter following a light crop of acorns, the deer herd at Grousehaven seems to be larger than ever and it becomes imperative that something be done to reduce the herd to range carrying capacity."

"Well, now," said one of the visitors. "What the hell are you going to do about that, Fred?"

Bear said, "Bill Boyer has selected me to chair a committee to come up with the answer to this problem. Following several stormy sessions, we think we have a course of action that might produce the desired results."

"And what course might that be, Fred?"

"It has been decided," said Bear, screwing his face into a mask of great sadness, "to hunt the area with bow and arrow."

"Oooooh noooo."

"And we are now in the process of rounding up volunteers who might be willing next October to sacrifice themselves for this most distasteful task."

"What a pity," the straight man said. "Where do we sign up?"

Then I spotted Boyer, the grand duke of Grousehaven himself, standing apart from the group. He was shaking with laughter. I went over and said to him, "Did you just hear what I heard?"

"I didn't hear anything," Boyer said. "Been too busy figuring out what's wrong with Fred Bear."

"And that's *funny*?"

"Hell, he *looks* funny," Boyer said. "Been trying to figure it all evening and what just now occurred to me is — I don't believe I ever saw Fred dressed up like this. I mean, in a *suit*."

CHAPTER 1

The Cumberland Valley lies in the heart of Pennsylvania. It extends some 40 miles from the Susquehanna River toward the state's western boundary. The valley, comprising most of Cumberland County, is bordered on the north by the Blue Mountains and on the south by the South Mountains, off-shoots of the great Appalachian system.

Two centuries ago, this historic county was the doorway to the western wilderness. Its first settlers were Scotch-Irish families who came into the valley in 1720, cultivated friendly trade with the Shawnee Indians and established permanent communities on the present sites of Carlisle, Big Springs and Boiling Springs. Prior to 1750, numerous mills and distilleries were in operation and the area soon became a major military center and depot for the shipment of goods and supplies to the western frontiers. The many Indian raids and massacres that occurred between 1753 and 1763 reflected the influence of the colonial wars, but these incidents abated after the negotiation of European treaties.

Since early frontier days, the Cumberland has been richly endowed with quality wildlife habitat and rural traditions, which combine to form an ideal setting for the outdoorsman. Within the valley are many crystalline limestone streams issuing from artesian springs. Boiling Springs, near Carlisle, is the state's largest, with a daily yield of some 24 million gallons of sparkling pure water. Other spring creeks famous for their purity and steady flow are the Letort, Yellow Breeches, Big Spring Run, Trindle Spring Run and Green Spring Run. All are rich in aquatic vegetation, insect life and husky trout, offering an angler some of the finest fishing to be found east of the Mississippi.

Thickets, glades and coverts that edge the Blue and South Mountains are home to deer, bear, wild turkey, grouse and a variety of other small game such as squirrels and rabbits. More than 40 miles of the Appalachian Trail cuts across the southeastern reaches of the county.

The fertile soil of the Cumberland Valley has, from the time of earliest settlers, supported a thriving agricultural industry. Immigrants were of varied stock, including German, French and English. The Quakers, Mennonites and Amish also found refuge in the Cumberland and their descendants are still there today.

Two of the families settling here during the nineteenth century were the Bears, of English, German and Swiss extraction and the Drawbaughs with

English-Dutch origins. This story of challenge and adventure begins with the marriage of Florence Drawbaugh and Harry Bear.

Harry Leon Bear was a skilled machinist. He would be known today as a toolmaker. He worked at the Landis Tool Company in Waynesboro, Pennsylvania, about 30 miles from Carlisle. Harry and Florence's second child, following the birth of a dark-eyed daughter, Aileen, was a son. Frederick Bernard Bear was born at the Bears' home in Waynesboro in 1902 during the worst blizzard of the winter. On that wild March evening, the doctor had to buck the snowdrifts with his horse and buggy to reach his patient; the youngster he brought kicking and squalling into the world during the height of the storm that night was destined for a very special kind of fame and adventure.

There had been evidence of genius in the family line. Florence Bear's uncle, Daniel Drawbaugh, was reputed to have been the original inventor of the telephone. His company fought the Bell Telephone Company for seven years over the patent rights, going all the way to the United States Supreme Court, where a decision was finally handed down with a majority of one vote in favor of Bell.

J. Edward Hyde, author of "*THE PHONE BOOK*," published in 1976, said about Fred's great uncle, Daniel Drawbaugh:

"Ever since 1879, the Bell Company had been in court. In fact, Bell would be involved in nearly 600 lawsuits during its first seventeen years of existence. The company won every one of these lawsuits, but a few decisions were uncomfortably close. The closest Bell ever came to losing in court was a suit filed by one Daniel Drawbaugh of Pennsylvania in 1888. Mr. Drawbaugh's suit contended that he had invented the telephone in 1867. He had a score of credible witnesses on his side of the case and actually won the lower court decisions. Naturally, Bell appealed these decisions. But only by a narrow 5-to-4 decision in the Supreme Court of the United States did it prevail. The minority report of Justice Bradley is historically interesting because it shows that not everyone was ready to accept the Gospel of the Bell Company:

'We think that Daniel Drawbaugh anticipated the invention of Mr. Bell... It is perfectly natural for the world to take the part of the man who has already achieved national eminence. So it was with Bell and Drawbaugh... We think Bell's patent is void by the anticipations of Drawbaugh.'

This close call, following Drawbaugh's victory in the lower courts, gave credence to the rumors that Bell had bribed someone on the High Court bench. But of course, they were only rumors."

Fred's paternal grandfather, Abner Bear, lived with his second wife in Mechanicsburg, a small town eleven miles east of Carlisle. Because his sons, Harry and Charles (Fred's father and uncle), had not gotten along with their stepmother, they were brought up by Abner's Mennonite sisters, Sarah and Elizabeth, who lived on a small farm in Plainfield, five miles west of Carlisle. Consequently, both Harry and Charles considered the aunt's place their home and since Charles never married, it was the only family home he ever knew.

When Harry was about twelve or thirteen years old, he was separated from his brother Charles and the good life with the aunts, to again live with his father and stepmother. Abner had moved to Barnum, West Virginia and apparently needed the help of his older son in setting up a small sawmill business. He traveled to Pennsylvania to visit his sisters and take Harry back to his new home.

The record does not show whether Harry stayed in West Virginia until young adulthood or came back to spend a few more years with the aunts and his brother. Fred, however, remembers his father saying how unhappy this disruption in his life made him. A letter Harry wrote to Charles soon after their separation bears this out:

> Barnum, W. Virginia   April 9, 1888
> Dear Bro. I will now write to you and tell you about our new home. We passed through Kerrsville, Newville, Chambersburg, Matinsburg, Cumberland and Piedmont. We had to stop at Cumberland and wait 20 minutes until another train passed. There was nobody on the train but ourselves. When we got to Bloomington, we got into a two-horse wagon and came to Barnum. The road was rocks the whole way and it was the roughest ride I ever got. We had to walk about 1/2 mile down the tramroad to Mr. Watson's. When we got there, they were eating supper, so we had to wait until they were done. After supper, Mr. Sauers, Papa and I went over to the house and there was a nice, warm fire and carpets laid down, bedsteads up already for the bedclothes. Papa and I are making a chicken house and we had to carry the boards from the sawmill.
> On the north side of the house, there is two windows, one in the sitting room and one in the kitchen. From the kitchen window, we can see the river dashing over the rocks. The railroad is about 15 feet down the bank. Mr. Watsons men started up to the coal mine, but

they only got about 6 feet till they broke down. Papa is welding some bandsaws. I have not commenced to work in the sawmill yet because I have so many little jobs to do around the house for her. I went up to the Dr. to a place named Shaw, which is 3 1/2 miles from where we live. I thought it was about 10 miles instead of 3 1/2. I had to walk up the railroad, for that is the only way to get there. My next job after I finish this letter is to wash my hands and you know how well I like that. I will close for this time hoping to hear from you soon.

Your brother, Harry

Although young Fred and his sisters, Aileen and Elizabeth, called them "the aunts," Sarah and Elizabeth were the children's great aunts. They were in their late fifties and early sixties at this time. Both aunts regarded Fred with great affection and as a result his early life was influenced nearly as much by them as by his parents.

Aunt Sarah was the older aunt and while not domineering, she was more or less the leader. She read the weekly newspaper and subscribed to numerous magazines, keeping well abreast of things and was interested in people and all of nature. She was an excellent cook also and at one time Sarah worked with Mr. Milton Hershey, who became famous for his chocolate, reputedly helping cook and test his recipes in her farm kitchen.

In contrast to Sarah, Elizabeth, affectionately called "Aunt Lib" by the family, was quite introverted and took to the background when the sisters were together. When she was not cooking or cleaning, she was content to spend long hours in her upstairs quilting room occupied with the art in which she excelled. Both Sarah and Elizabeth wore the Mennonites' traditional dark gray dresses and white lace caps. Out of doors, they wore starched gray sunbonnets. None of the family ever saw them in any other kind of dress. They lived their religion every moment of the day, but they neither spoke of it nor tried to impress it upon anyone else. They rarely left home except to attend church and, in Sarah's case, the market. Nonetheless, they greatly enjoyed entertaining company, which gave them an opportunity not only to visit with friends but to display their considerable culinary skills.

The two-story, wood frame house on the aunts' farm was elevated from the roadway and bordered by a low stone wall topped with a white picket fence. The walk from the front gate to the house was surfaced with scrap leather cuttings from the shoe factory in Carlisle, laid down to a thickness of several inches. The leather trimmings, soft and rust-colored, made an attractive walkway that gave off a pleasant, leathery aroma.

Fred Bear as an infant, with his parents and sister, Aileen.

At less than two years, Fred showed a fascination for firearms. In this picture, taken by his Uncle Charley, Fred examines his father's Stevens .22 caliber match rifle.

The drive leading into the barn and vehicle shed passed through an ornamental, mechanically operated iron gate that Abner Bear had installed. It was reinforced with iron bars and when the wheel of a buggy drove over a twelve-inch iron bar, the upright was depressed, moving the bottom hinge off-center, causing the gate to swing open. Another bar inside reversed the process and closed the gate. It was necessary to keep the ground bar slots free of snow and ice in winter and sand in summer and one of Harry's chores (and a generation later, also one of his young son, Fred's) was to maintain the smooth operation of this gate.

The heart of the aunt's house was a large kitchen and dining area. There was also an offset summer kitchen, a living room, parlor and four bedrooms upstairs, two of which had balconies overlooking the gardens. Large quantities of apples, potatoes and cabbages were brought into the cellar for winter storage through sloping, ground-level doors.

In the east wall of the large kitchen, an enormous fireplace was once used for heating and cooking. In Fred's time, no longer used for warmth, this area was filled with racks for drying apples and corn.

An oversized stove now warmed the kitchen and bedrooms upstairs through registers in the ceiling. One fortunate enough to lie abed mornings could hear the pleasant sounds of the aunts at their work and savor the wonderful aroma of breakfast coming from below.

The house, garden and orchard occupied about one-quarter of the twenty-acre tract. The remaining fifteen acres planted with wheat and corn over shadowed the luxurious vegetable garden Fred toiled in all summer. However, cultivating, weeding and harvesting the endless rows of asparagus, peas, celery and tomatoes, left him with time for very little else.

When Fred was still quite young, his parents moved from Waynesboro to Plainfield, a mile from the aunts' farm. Harry Bear was employed at the Frog and Switch Manufacturing Company in Carlisle and raised White Leghorn chickens as a hobby. His wages as a skilled toolmaker enabled him to lay aside a tidy savings with which he set himself up in the chicken business. Harry's father-in-law, George Drawbaugh, a carpenter, lent an able hand in constructing the necessary buildings.

The venture was a struggle from the start and after three years in Plainfield, the Bears sold the business and made yet another move to the small town of Elliottson.

The failure of the chicken business had a sobering effect on Harry. To recoup his losses, he took on the job of assisting the aunts in running their farm. A third child had been born by this time, a warm, sunny little girl named Sarah Elizabeth, honoring the two beloved aunts. Fred was now nine years old.

Sarah and Elizabeth Bear — the aunts.

Aileen and Fred at an early age. Note mechanical bear brought from New York by Uncle Charley.

Following the move to Eliottson, Fred was old enough to assume family duties other than small chores. At the farm he fed the stock, cleaned the stable and helped in the garden. His most disagreeable summertime task on the farm during this time involved an acre of asparagus. The delicate green stalks grew so fast that two cuttings a day were required to keep abreast of it. After cutting, it was tied in bunches and set in pans of water to keep fresh for market. On the evenings before market day, Fred loaded the spring wagon with asparagus and other vegetables and by 3:00 a.m. was hitching up the horse to the wagon for his and Aunt Sarah's trip to Carlisle, five miles away. They reached town before daylight, transferred the produce to the family's market stall, unhitched the horse and led it to the livery stable. By 10:00 a.m. the market was usually sold out and they would be back on the farm by noon to start the whole routine over again.

Eventually, the aunts moved to Carlisle, leaving the farm to Harry where Fred followed his marketing procedure with a neighbor, the Wainricks, for which he was paid twenty-five cents a day.

Fred, Elizabeth and Aileen during the chicken farm days.

Fred, his dog and sister Aileen on horseback, attended by their mother, Florence Bear.

During the early summer, Fred augmented these earnings by gathering dandelion greens and selling them from a corner of the market booth at five cents a bunch. They were popular with Pennsylvanians wilted with bacon fat, vinegar and sugar. However, Fred realized little or no profit from this enterprise. With an aromatic bakery stall near the Wainrick booth, his assets quickly dissolved into fresh, hot cinnamon buns.

Another of his responsibilities at this time was to drive the aunts to church in Plainfield in the horse and buggy or sleigh in winter. Years later when his father owned a car, Fred drove that to church during the summer.

Usually he attended services with the aunts, although he was not required to do so. The church was very plain, with no heat and no music to accompany the hymns. The men sat on one side and the women on the other, on hard, uncushioned benches. In the winter, one had to dress warmly, as it was often colder inside the church than out. The services lasted about an hour and the sermon, delivered by one of the church members, seemed endless. After the service, Fred was obliged to be patient while subdued visiting took place out-of-doors before they could go home.

In those days, the old Pennsylvania Blue Laws were in full force. Sunday was a day of complete quiet and contemplation. Neither work nor recreation were allowed — no fishing or hunting, no running about or shouting — even pounding a nail was prohibited. The young people were expected to refrain from playing, keep their clothes clean and look respectable all day. Of course, Fred and his friends slipped away whenever they could for a little skinny-dipping in nearby Conodoquinet Creek.

A regular allowance was unheard of in Fred's youth. Young people were expected to pay their own way, earning spending money and buying their own clothes. Fred solved this problem by trapping muskrats, skunks, mink and an occasional fox in the winter. His major trapline was along Conodoquinet Creek and its feeders. He acquired an Old Town canoe for making his daily rounds before school. This required rising early, before sun up. After dressing with half-closed eyes, he'd strap on a light belt axe, hunting knife and Stevens single-shot .22 pistol, whistle for Scot, his collie and take off for the creek. Scot was a constant companion on these trips. He sat in the middle of the canoe, where he served admirably as ballast except when a duck or other game was spotted, at which time he would jump excitedly around, resting his paws on the gunwales, to the discomfort of his master trying to hold the light craft stable.

Scot, a natural retriever, was also taught to catch chickens on the farm.

Harry Bear displays his leghorns at the County Fair.

Once he understood which bird was wanted for Sunday dinner, he would chase and catch it, holding it down with one foot until it was picked up.

Muskrats were the chief products of Fred's trapline. He put out about fifty sets and sometimes caught three or four of the animals in the course of one night. This was quite a coup, as the skins brought $2 to $3 apiece. Sometimes mink were taken in a muskrat set. They brought the princely sum of $10 or $15. Skunks were not so prevalent, although they brought in $7 each. During the summer, if Fred found a skunk in his traps, he simply turned it loose. But eventually it occurred to him that he was wasting time letting them go only to have to trap them again in the winter when the furs were prime. So he set up his own "skunk farm." When he found a skunk in the trap now, he slipped a gunny sack over the little creature and carried it to the canoe. The skunks often took exception to this and although the burlap strained out some of the resulting resentment, enough of it got through to give the young trapper a commanding presence. Many mornings in school, he was surrounded by a ring of empty seats.

For his skunk farm, he rigged up an unused wire enclosure with wooden nest boxes and straw. At times, his domesticated skunk population rose to eighteen or twenty animals. They grew so tame that it became almost trau-

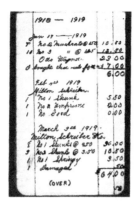

"From young Fred's trapping ledger."

matic to dispatch them for market toward spring.

There were very few other trappers in the immediate area, so Fred had no competition and ran his trapline over as much territory as he could handle. The opportunity to earn what was then good money, plus being in the great outdoors, was irresistible. He sent for and thoroughly digested books and magazines devoted to trapping techniques, his favorite volume was Harding's *Tracks and Tracking*. From these, he learned such things as how to boil his shiny new traps with walnut hulls to stain them brown, making them less conspicuous as well as resistant to rust. Fred also kept his own field book (still in his private library) filled with sketches of tracks and other notations. His trapping experience taught him a great deal about the habits of animals and their environment.

Fred skinned the pelts at night out in the barn then stretched and dried them on cedar shingle forms. He sold the cured skins to New York fur buyers who advertised in trapping magazines. Most farm boys were pretty much at the mercy of the fur buyers, who graded the pelts upon receipt and paid whatever prices they chose. However, Fred had a contact in New York: his father's brother, Charles Bear.

Uncle Charley was a Spencerian penman for the Metropolitan Life Insurance Company. Wills, insurance policies and other important documents were hand scrolled then by expert calligraphers, of whom Charley was counted among the best. He investigated some of the fur merchants to determine where his nephew might get the best prices. Fred eventually became expert enough at fur grading to tell in advance about how much each pelt would bring. In the spring, he tagged the furs, wrapped them in heavy brown paper or burlap and sent them off by insured parcel post. In a week or so, a check would come back and be deposited in his account at the Carlisle Bank & Trust. His total profits for a winter's trapping would net him around $100.

Formal education for Fred began in the rural, one-room Bear School, located about half a mile from the farm. The neighboring youngsters all walked to school regardless of the weather, except when there was enough snow for good sledding. One of the Mennonite families, the George Bears (there were several other unrelated Bear families living in Cumberland County), had three youngsters about Fred's age who owned a big, good-natured mule named Pete. In winter, they put a collar and singletree on Pete, hitched their sleds to it and rode to school. Along the way, they picked up other classmates, among them Fred and Aileen, who tied their sleds in tandem until the procession lengthened to seven or eight sleds. After reaching the schoolhouse, they would hang the singletree over Pete's collar, slap him on the rump and head him for home.

Waterproof footgear was scarce, so wet feet and colds were common occurrences. Fred was quite susceptible to head and chest colds, a condition which held both an advantage and a disadvantage for him. The advantage was that since he was sick, he couldn't go to school (but somehow seemed able to go hunting). The disadvantage was his mother's home remedy for sore throats, a collar of sliced onions rolled up in a cloth tied around his neck. The cold and wet onion ring probably didn't contribute much to his recovery, but it was a burden to be borne for the opportunity to get out in the open.

Fred spent the sixth and seventh grades in the two-room Plainfield School, a mile from the farm. One of Fred's friends here was Norman Brice.

Norman was an orphan who had been adopted by a neighboring farm family. Both boys loved to run. They were inspired without a doubt by Jim Thorpe's (the great Sac-Fox athlete) performances in track meets and football games at the Carlisle Indian School near their homes. Fred and Norman were not particularly fast, but they had staying power and could keep up a good pace for several miles. The improved physiques and increased lung capacity that resulted served Fred well in later life.

Norman also loved to work with watercolors and encouraged Fred to join him. All one winter they met to paint as soon as Fred's chores were done. It was the year the *Titanic* sank and their portfolios dealing with the catastrophe have probably never been exceeded in volume or range of view. The *Titanic* hitting the iceberg, the *Titanic* listing to port, rolling to starboard, sinking at

Fred Bear, age 12, with his dog, Scot, returning from a successful rabbit hunt.

the bow, or sinking at the stern, plus the launching of lifeboats.

That winter's endeavor ended forever Fred's absorption with the arts, but Brice went on to become a successful artist, doing illustrations for such magazines as *Colliers* and *The Saturday Evening Post*.

It was also during this period that Fred's attention was first focused on girls, one in particular, a very pretty little schoolmate named Rosamond Finkenbinder. Fred carried her books and, in his bolder moments, held her hand. But things had not gone beyond these preliminaries when disaster struck.

One of the two grocery stores in Plainfield was owned by Rosamond's father who occasionally hunted with Fred's father. Directly across the street from the store was the Finkenbinder home, a fine residence with a full-length front porch.

At this time, the Bears owned a former racehorse named Prince that had come from the aunts and lived in semi-retirement on the farm. His only chores were to pull the wagon to market or a small cultivator in the garden. He was a spirited horse and since the family had an English saddle, Fred rode him from time to time.

Standing: Abner Bear, Aileen and Fred. Seated: Florence holding Elizabeth and Harry Bear.

One warm summer evening, Mrs. Bear needed something from the grocery, so Fred put the saddle on Prince and started for town. On the way, he thought of Rosamond and hoped she might be sitting in the rocker on her front porch. If she were, thought Fred, the situation would be ideal to display his equestrian competence. Despite his age, old Prince still liked to run and Fred's strategy was that by walking him to the edge of town to save energy and then urging him with his heels, he could roar into town on a cloud of dust and, under Rosamond's admiring eyes, slide to a stop at the hitching post in front of her father's store.

But this ambitious plan backfired. As Fred drew near, Rosamond was, in fact, sitting on the porch. Sinking his heels into Prince's sides, he began his gallant ride. He had neglected, however, to take into account that Prince had not been worked for several days and had a bellyful of green pasture grass. The agitation of these intestinal contents caused by the sudden violent exercise generated a remarkable amount of gas…As Fred and Prince approached the house, the inevitable occurred; the volume increasing at an alarming tempo. The youthful rider wished fervently that the earth would open up and swallow both him and the horse. But since this was not likely, he kept right on going until he reached the second store at the other end of town, got the needed groceries and returned home by a circuitous back road. The romance never fully recovered from this embarrassing episode.

Another lasting memory occurred in the spring before the aunts left the farm. One of Fred's regular chores was to help Aileen prepare feed for the stock. Their father had mounted a shear at the small end of a wedge-shaped trough and it was Fred's job to feed bunches of hay into it, compressing it in the wedge and shoving it under the shear wielded by his sister. The resulting short lengths of hay were then mixed with bran, water and molasses for the horse and cow.

One morning, more consumed than usual by the boredom of this task, Fred started to tease his sister by jerking the hay back just as she came down with the shear. Aileen, keen on getting the chore finished, was not at all humored by her brother's behavior. Inevitably, Fred shoved a clump of hay a bit farther than he should have and the shear came down quickly on one of his fingers along with the hay. The blade was extremely sharp, as were all of Harry's tools and it cleanly clipped off a small section of the third finger of his right hand.

Upon realizing he was minus the tip of a finger, Fred suffering in frenzied panic, made a couple of turns around the barn at high speed trying to think

Fred's first love, Rosemond Finkenbinder (on bicycle) with Fred's sister, Aileen.

of what to do. He knew his father was out at the chicken house and thought he'd better report to him first, but as he neared the door he saw that Harry had a visitor. Not wanting to interrupt them, he made another fast turn and headed for the house.

The aunts were in the summer kitchen when Fred burst in bleeding uncontrollably. The good women were immediately equal to the occasion. One of their country cure-alls was a lily leaf soaked in rosewater. Aunt Sarah stemmed the flow by binding this over the end of the finger and holding it in place with a bandage. This was, of course, a temporary expedient. The situation called for a trip to Dr. Van Camp's office in Plainfield. The doctor was perhaps the most respected and important person in the community and one didn't visit him in a disheveled condition. While Sarah was finishing the bandaging, Aunt Lib worked swiftly with washcloth and clean shirt.

With time running out, another problem arose. In those days, sleds did not have steering gear and one changed course by dragging his toes. After months of winter sledding, Fred had worn holes in the toes of his shoes. During his fast footwork around the barn, one black stocking had worked out and protruded some two inches from the shoe; to his consternation, Aunt Lib simply picked up a pair of shears and neatly snipped it off, hoping to save face in front of the doctor.

Following the accident, Fred was allowed to spend a week convalescing at his Grandfather Bear's home in Mechanicsburg. His memory of Harry's stepmother — Abner's wife — was never very clear, although he remembers getting along reasonably well with her. She was a demanding woman, however and perhaps this was why Harry and Charley preferred to live with their aunts.

Fred's memories of his grandfather, Abner Bear, on the other hand, are very vivid. Abner was outgoing in nature and prepossessing in size, being well over six feet tall and weighing more than two hundred pounds. He sported a sandy handlebar mustache and always wore a Stetson hat and gray suit, with a gold watch chain across his prominent midriff. Fred recalls that, as a boy, he seldom saw Abner when he was not wearing a coat.

Abner's gregariousness and humor aptly suited him for his work as a salesman for the Henry Disston Company, a manufacturer of sawmill equipment. He also sold farm machinery and it was his demonstrations of the latter that most impressed his grandson. One stunt in particular used to show the power of the traction engine (forerunner of the tractor) was spectacular. To exhibit this power, Abner erected a ramp some 30 feet long and rising at a 30-degree

Fred's grandfather, Abner Bear, on the right, was a salesman for Disston Saws.

Johanna Bear, first wife of Abner Bear and grandmother to Fred. Johanna died at the age of 26 from tuberculosis.

angle to about 10 feet at its high end. He ran the traction engine up this incline, where assistants chained the cleated, ironshod rear wheels down. Then, by putting the steam engine in gear, he could raise the front end to an almost vertical angle. This was a very popular event at state fairs and never failed to draw a crowd.

Although he was not exactly affluent, Abner earned a substantial salary and lived a very good life. He never tried to advise his grandson on worldly matters, leaving that to the boy's parents. He would on occasion, however, reward Fred with a nickel for doing headstands and back flips to encourage him in athletics.

CHAPTER 2

Although Abner Bear was so highly regarded by his grandson Fred, the hero of his formative years was his father. Harry was over six feet tall and carried about 175 pounds on a husky frame. He had black hair and dark brown eyes whose crinkled margins were evidence of a ready sense of humor. He was a first-class sportsman and hunter, an excellent wing shot and undoubtedly one of the finest rifle shots in the state at that time.

Despite what one might think, it was not then common for all farm boys to take to hunting. Usually only those whose fathers or older brothers were so inclined showed more than a passing interest in guns other than the ubiquitous .22's and air rifles.

Some of Fred 's earliest recollections are of his father coming home from a Saturday afternoon shooting contest in Carlisle with an assortment of prizes; generally smoked hams, turkeys or a hindquarter of beef. The Carlisle Rifle Club was a well-established organization with a clubhouse and both rifle and trapshooting ranges. One of the favored rifle calibers of the era was the .32-40. Harry owned a single-shot Winchester match rifle in that caliber. It had iron sights with a rear peep and was heavy barreled, weighing about 12 pounds. In addition, he placed a 5-pound chunk of lead on the muzzle to add weight and stability for offhand shooting (standing and without a rest). Match shooting was generally from one hundred yards at a four-inch bullseye and a competitor had to group his shots quite tightly to be in the running. Ammunition for the match shooting was all hand loaded.

Harry also did a great deal of trapshooting and shooting at live pigeons, which was popular at that time. Fred often accompanied his father on pigeon shoots and would get behind a large tree down range to have his turn at missed birds.

Harry Donson, the sporting goods dealer in Carlisle, was one of Harry Bear's hunting companions and for several years was Pennsylvania state champion in shooting at both clay and live birds. The two men often staged a nip and tuck battle on the target range and frequently it was an even match.

When Fred was six or seven years old, he was allowed to accompany his father on hunts for small game, such as rabbits, squirrels and quail. For a year or two, he was limited to a BB gun, but when he was eight, his father presented him with a .22 rifle, a single-shot, swing-bolt Quakenbush. It was the pride of Fred's life and under his father's tutelage, he became an expert shot. Harry

Harry Bear returning from a hunt in the valley.

stressed the responsibility that went with owning firearms and, concerned about safety, forbade him from pointing even a cap pistol at anything, "you wouldn't want to shoot."

Harry once bought a muzzle-loading shotgun for thirty-five cents at a farm sale. Later that week, Fred, spotting an English sparrow perched on a neighbor's slate roof, "borrowed" the gun and shot the sparrow. Unfortunately, in the process he mowed about 4 or 5 feet of slate off the roof and was punished both for damaging the neighbor's property and for taking the gun without permission.

Fred and his friends, like most country boys, made bows and arrows, crude weapons with little accuracy or power. The bows were carved from tree limbs and the arrows made of reeds, some of which were tipped with nails. Fred once fashioned a bow from umbrella stays, binding them tightly with cord and gradually tapering them at each end. This performed considerably better than the wood bows, but the only thing Fred ever shot with it was a cow.

The nail-tipped arrow didn't penetrate very far, but it hung where it landed, flopping around as the unfortunate animal raced home. Fred headed in the opposite direction when he saw that he was not going to be able to recover his arrow. No real damage was done to the cow, but after a bit of discussion between the animal's owner and Harry Bear, Fred got the final word concerning bows and arrows.

With homemade slingshots, however, he became quite accurate at short range and knocked off a lot of tin cans set up for targets. He also stalked pigeons in the big grain elevators at Elliotson, but that was long-range shooting and he rarely scored. These experiments with bows and slingshots were temporary diversions, however. His father, an expert with the rifle, was regarded by his son as another Daniel Boone and at that stage in his life Fred was a dedicated gun man.

At the age of thirteen, Fred marked three milestones. First, he was considered old enough to wear long pants, a sign that he was grown up. The second milestone had to do with school, for although he might earnestly have wished it, life was not all roaming the woods or paddling the rivers in his canoe. To be eligible for high school, students had to pass an entrance examination at the Lamberton High School in Carlisle. While still in seventh grade, Fred, probably anxious to get his school days behind him, decided on the spur of the moment to accompany the eighth grade students into town and take the examination a year early. He passed it, skipped the eighth grade entirely and entered high school with the class ahead of his own.

Fred Bear, age 12, with a family friend, George Farthing, after a day of hunting around the Bear farm near Elliotson. Fred's gun is his 12 gauge L.C. Smith double, circa 1914.

Also, at thirteen, Fred hunted deer for the first time. His father belonged to a group of Cumberland farmers and businessmen who hunted together on South Mountain ridge about five miles from the Bear farm. Their early camp, a shack formerly used by a road construction crew, had no bunks; the hunters simply spread their bedrolls on a thick layer of corn shucks in the loft. Later the group bought a small farm on the edge of the mountains and the farmhouse became their clubhouse. That was a much more comfortable and picturesque hunting camp and was desirable in summer for picnics or weekend outings.

The country had been cut over and the secondary growth, largely oak, was very dense. Hunting in groups proved more successful than hunting alone since noisy ground cover made still-hunting and stalking impractical much of the time. Most of the deer were secured by drives.

When Fred first started hunting, the hills were full of large chestnut trees that produced heavy crops of wonderfully sweet nuts, ideally suited for deer food. But the 1915 chestnut blight swept through the country and hunting dropped off noticeably. In the early years of Fred's deer hunting, the camp could fill its quota of six deer in two or three days. After the blight, camp members might wind up the early December season with only two or three deer to be divided among them. Pennsylvania's deer population declined rapidly at this time because of inbreeding and lack of winter food.

The annual deer-hunting seasons were among Fred's happiest times. He looked forward to the trips all year, despite the fact that he was the youngest of the group and thus subject to considerable hazing. From the start, however, he was able to maintain his share of the hunting. His first deer, taken on the opening morning of the season, was the group's total for the first three days.

While teaching his son to hunt, Harry instilled in him a deep respect for the woods and waters and a knowledge of the need for moderation in taking game. Hunting at the camp also taught Fred important lessons in getting along with people. He had to learn to take the constant practical joking (much of it instigated by his father) with good grace.

The hunters did not allow drinking during the hunt, but in the evening, after one or more of them had bagged a buck, they passed a bottle around. One season there was a Baptist minister in camp. He didn't drink, but when the bottle was passed, he would pour a little liquor into his palm and rub it on his bald head to prove he was not critical of their imbibing.

When the season was over or the group had killed its six deer, whichever came first, there was a day of skinning and butchering. After the meat was divided as evenly as possible, the portions were stacked side by side on a table. As one of the group pointed to various stacks of meat, another stood with his back to the table and read the camp roster at random. A fair and unique method of sharing the meat, agreeable to all.

The Bears did not have beef cattle on the farm. Nor did they have a lot of money to buy meat. Fred was twenty years old before he tasted his first steak. The family lived very well, however, on pork and chicken plus a large variety of game and fish as well as garden produce. The Cumberland Valley was a sportsman's paradise. Wild game of all kinds was eaten all year by its farmers.

This was the golden age of small game hunting. Natural habitat and food for small animals was plentiful. Plowing was done with a team of horses and, consequently, four or five feet of cover was left along fence lines. No lands were posted; one could hunt anywhere he wished without asking permission.

But this fact didn't keep Fred and Harry from asking permission to take a nongame item on one occasion. During a pleasant morning in early autumn, they were hunting rabbits with Harry's beagles and came upon a fine patch of ripe cantaloupe along the edge of a cornfield. Across the road was a

Fred's first deer, marked with an X. Taken at the Pennsylvania hunting camp when he was 13.

farmhouse. The Bears walked over and asked the farmer if he would mind if they ate a melon or two. The farmer replied that no, he didn't mind. So Fred climbed the fence and collected an armload. The farmer furnished spoons and a salt shaker and all three had a great feast on his front porch. After they had finished eating, Harry asked the farmer how much they owed him for the cantaloupe.

"You don't owe me nothin'." the farmer replied. "They aren't mine!"

During these years, neighborhood frog hunts often took place of a summer evening and on one occasion, coming home, Harry Bear felt called upon to show off his frogcatching prowess. Emptying his sack on the kitchen floor to impress his wife, things soon got out of hand with bullfrogs hopping in every direction and Florence up on a chair. She usually enjoyed such teasing, but this time he had gone too far. She refused to come down from the chair until every frog was back in the sack and Harry had restored her floor to its usual unsullied state.

Fred Bear, Hugh Burgett, Guy Young and Bill March at the South Mountain Ridge Camp.

At another time, a cousin was subjected to some of Harry's humor. She had gone fishing and stowed her catch in the trunk of her Model T Ford coupe. When she got home and took the fish out, she failed to notice one that had slid under the spare tire. It came to light in a couple of days, however, when the hot summer sun and lack of air had done its work! Cousin Katherine scraped out the remains and scrubbed the trunk vigorously. But the odor persisted, so she asked Uncle Harry what to do about it. His terse reply was, "Throw a skunk in the trunk!"

Butchering days on the farm were festive affairs, especially for the youngsters. At such times, the family made arrangements with a neighbor who had meat processing skills and who also had large copper kettles, grinders, scrapers and other necessary gear. He came to the farm with all his equipment on the afternoon before butchering day. It was the farmer's responsibility to have water boiling in the kettles by daylight, when neighbors or relatives arrived to help with the work. The men and boys took on the heavy work of hauling

Harry Bear's Maxwell - the same vintage as Jack Benny's famous radio show car.

wood and keeping the fires going. The women made sausages and prepared the hams besides cooking the big noon dinner for the crew.

Most time-consuming, but of prime importance on these days, was the 'pudding,' a staple on every farmer's table during Fred's childhood. Pudding was made by boiling odds and ends of meat in the kettles. The cooked meat, forked into a sausage grinder and poured into gallon-size crocks, served as a tasty spread for pancakes when heated on frosty winter mornings.

Next, cornmeal was stirred into the remaining rich meat juices and when the mixture was seasoned and cooked to the consistency of mush, it was poured into bread tins to cool and solidify. This was called ponhaus and was delicious sliced and fried to a crusty brown. This product is still sold in Pennsylvania markets as Philadelphia scrapple.

Another special day was Thanksgiving, which fell in the middle of rabbit season. Fred and his father rose early on this holiday and spent the morning afield. At noon they joined the family and guests for a traditional goose or turkey dinner.

To share in the Christmas celebrations, Uncle Charley came on the train from New York, bringing a large box of gifts from the big city. Although he himself didn't hunt or fish, he brought such presents as a Daisy BB gun for Fred and a fine, heavy-barreled .22 match rifle for Harry.

It was young Fred's job to find and bring home on his sled a suitable Christmas tree, usually a five or six foot juniper, that would be held up-

The Cameron Road deer camp, 1915.

Fred Bear near the Cameron Road camp.

right by a wooden stand in a corner of the parlor. The white cotton arranged around its base was surrounded by a small wooden fence. Family members decorated the tree with strings of popcorn, colored-paper chains and tinsel rope. Christmas morning, their stockings bulged with rock candy, nuts and fancy sugar cookies. Oranges, seldom seen at other times of the year and considered a rare treat, were also included.

Other than the presents Uncle Charley brought, most of the gifts were strictly utilitarian: gloves, boots, woolen caps, mufflers and underwear. One Christmas when Fred had saved a little money, he decided it was time to put something under the tree besides necessities. His love for music prompted him to purchase a phonograph for the family, which he carried home in his arms on the electric interurban that ran between Carlisle and Newville.

Easter was looked forward to for weeks. When the children were quite young, Florence would send them outside in the morning to find colored eggs under bushes and in other hiding places selected by the Easter Bunny. Following these early morning activities, all the neighborhood children gathered, rain or shine, at some designated spot in the woods, where they boiled eggs over a campfire and held an egg-eating contest. Baseball games took up the afternoon hours, but on Easter Eve, church services were attended by the entire family.

As Fred grew older, he was too committed to outdoor life to have much to do with girls. There was no time for sports either, since he had to get back to the farm after school to do chores. He enjoyed watching sports, however and took a special interest in baseball and track.

Fred's second deer was taken in 1916 at the Cameron Road Camp at South Mountain at age 14.

At one point, to get extra cash, Fred sold The Saturday Evening Post and for winning the prize in a contest, received a set of boxing gloves. His friend Jacob Bear, to whom he was distantly related and who lived nearby, showed an interest in the sport and became Fred's sparring partner. They boxed in the furnace room of the greenhouse on Jacob's farm. Although the latter was two years older and several inches taller than Fred and won nearly every round, their friendship endured throughout the years.

For the Bears, the final year of World War I when Fred was sixteen years old was conspicuous by an untimely death and a move away from the farm. The nationwide influenza epidemic spread into the Cumberland Valley and large numbers of people died. There were no immunization shots or special medicines to combat the dread disease and among the casualties was Fred's older sister, Aileen.

Because of her calm and self-effacing temperament, she suffered her illness without noticeable complaint. Her brother did not realize how delicate the situation was until the grim evening when the doctor came downstairs to announce that she was gone. Fred, shocked and disbelieving, was stunned by

Fred and his father hunting in the fields. Bear homestead in the background.

the loss. He left the house in silence and dealt with his grief alone. Aileen was buried in the family plot in the Carlisle cemetery.

Later that year, the Bears left the farm and moved to Carlisle. They held a big farm equipment sale to help pay off some of the debts incurred during the chicken farm breakdown.

One of the items for sale was a car that Harry had bought used in 1914 for $150. It was a Maxwell (the same model Jack Benny later made famous on his radio show), complete with leather hood straps, wooden steering wheel and gas headlights. It was a dependable vehicle and easy to care for.

The Maxwell, still in excellent condition, had to go. In order to prove its worth to prospective buyers on the soggy, rainy day of the sale, Harry and Fred constructed a 'track' of cornstalks over the muddy ground so the car could be demonstrated. The venture was successful, resulting in the sale of the Maxwell for $156.

Carlisle provided the Bears with a wealth of activities. The Carlisle Rifle Club was in the nearby fairgrounds. Saturday evening concerts, at which Sousa marches and other military tunes were popular, took place on the courthouse lawn. Harry Bear played cornet for the Greencastle Adult Band during this time.

Also on Saturday evenings, there was an old-time medicine show with a pitchman selling snake oil from the tailgate of a fancy, paneled, horse-drawn

Fred rode 5 miles to school on his bicycle while in the 9th grade.
In the 10th grade, he rode a motorcycle.

wagon. It was usually preceded by music that would gather a crowd — music that included the first ragtime jazz the young folks had ever heard.

But nothing, perhaps, exceeded in importance the Fourth of July holiday in Carlisle. Some of the buildings still carried scars from British cannonballs during the American Revolution. The war had divided the town then and during a meeting on the square, the matter was settled according to legend, when British sympathizers lined up on one side and Revolutionary patriots on the other.

Naturally, the Fourth was celebrated with all the gusto and hoopla that could be mustered, including military band concerts, parades and fireworks. To liven things up, Harry would fire his gun a few times or even set off a stick or two of dynamite. Although fireworks were legal at the time and Fred enjoyed them as well as anyone, he saved his hard-earned money for other things. He made up for this sacrifice years later, however, by supplying the town of Grayling with Fourth of July skyrockets for many years. And, since his home was on the outskirts of town, few birthdays and New Year's Eves passed without a fusillade from his own considerable supply.

The Bear's home in Carlisle.

Carlisle had an opera house that showed movies in the summer and staged minstrel shows several times each winter. The Boiling Springs amusement park and picnic area was a few miles away and could be reached from Carlisle by an open-side streetcar. It was a favorite recreation site and the pleasures available there ranged from riding the merry-go-round to boating on the lake.

The big September County Fair in Carlisle was one of the highlights of the year and lasted for nine days. In addition to horse and harness racing and judging of livestock and produce, there were bands, a Wild West Show, game booths and side shows.

Fred Bear, high school sophomore, with his motorcycle and some of the results of his trapping endeavors.

CHAPTER 3

During his first year at Lamberton High School Fred had excellent marks, was at the head of his class in English and was on the honor roll. But well into the second year, things had changed drastically.

He had purchased an Indian motorcycle for $35. It was barely running at the time. He took the engine apart, repaired it and reassembled it. It had no gearbox, so in order to start it, he had to put the stand down and pedal to get the engine going. Then he would kick the stand up, pull back the clutch lever and take off, classes at school forgotten.

His friend, Chester Eppley, also had a motorcycle, a Reading Standard and together they toured the countryside. This pairing proved to be providential, as one would often end up towing the other back. There was very little traffic to contend with but the sandy roads caused many a spill.

Chester and Fred also participated in hill-climbing contests. In one event, Fred's motorcycle caught fire and the flames spread in the dry brush of the mountain, burning a large area before they were contained. He came through the mishap without harm and soon had his machine repaired and running again.

Mechanical ability ran on both sides of Fred's family. His mother's brother, Will Drawbaugh, was generally considered a genius along these lines—particularly after he built a complete automobile that was probably the first car on the streets of Carlisle. Sometime later, out for a spin, Will met up with a Stanley Steamer that the owner was unable to start after the engine had stalled. Drawbaugh, intrigued with the prospect of penetrating the mysteries of a steam engine, traded his operating vehicle on the spot for the bulky steamer, fully confident that he would soon have it running again.

Young Fred unwittingly picked up considerable mechanical knowledge from this man throughout his early years. One incident concerned the seat of his motorcycle. The nut had come loose and Fred went to Uncle Will for a wrench to tighten it. The threads squeaked under the wrench and Will told Fred to apply oil to them. Fred demurred, thinking that oil would encourage the nut to come loose again but Drawbaugh assured him that by lubricating the threads the nut would be drawn tighter and therefore less likely to give trouble.

The only paved road in the area at that time, outside the main town streets, was the Walnut Bottom Road from Carlisle to Chambersburg and over the

The Cameron Road Deer Camp group that Fred and his father, Harry Bear, hunted with. On Sundays during deer season, the camp members sometimes enjoyed a picnic with their wives. Because of the Pennsylvania Blue Laws, they could not hunt on Sundays.

Blue Mountains to McConnellsburg. Here, Fred and Chester could open up their motorcycles to top speed.

To keep from burning their legs on the hot engines, the boys wore leather puttees purchased at an army warehouse in Middleton. By opening the exhaust pipe and bypassing the muffler, they created a very impressive roar in the machines and established themselves as early hot-rodders. They had to tone things down when approaching a team, however, for the noise caused horses to rear up in panic.

Their "hot rodding" also served a good purpose on holidays, when they set out for McConnellsburg to visit a pair of the hotel keeper's lissome daughters. Not many "sports" comparable to Fred and Chester on their thundering motorcycles were in the running for the attentions of these young ladies that summer. This association went far in bolstering Fred's normally shy attitude toward girls.

As Fred was growing up, he was influenced both ways by the two men in his family — the life of an outdoorsman and hunter by his stable and home-loving father and the life of the New York business world by his Uncle Charley. The two brothers seemed to understand and respect the other's viewpoint and it was left to Fred which way he would go.

As it turned out, he went both ways. His fame in the world of outdoor sports can be laid straight at the door of Harry's hunting lodge and his ability to charm audiences from the speaker's platform and his success in business came unerringly from Uncle Charley.

For quite some time, Fred had been talking about striking out on his own to try his wings and, of course, Charley would have liked to have had him in New York. But New York was too far from his hunting grounds, so Fred's interests turned in the opposite direction — west to Detroit — that was reasonably close to the forests of northern Michigan. Neither Harry nor Charley interfered, but Charley, anxious for his nephew's future, enlisted the assistance of a friend in the motor city, Clarence Zahrant, who offered to help when the time came to get the young man situated there.

Meanwhile, Carlisle, which had contributed a great many heroes to both the Revolutionary and Civil wars had a vigorous National Guard unit that Fred wanted desperately to join. A volunteer had to be at least eighteen years old unless he had his parents' consent. Fred's parents gave their permission and he joined the unit on his 16th birthday.

After two months, the Carlisle National Guard was converted from an infantry unit to a cavalry unit. Fred, who'd had enough of horses and stable cleaning during his years on the farm, was keenly disappointed. But the experience was utilized several years later when many of his greatest hunts could only have been accomplished by pack train, which entailed riding a horse.

Two years later, a massive and disorderly strike developed in the state's coalfields and the Carlisle National Guard was mustered into the regular Army to help contain the situation. Guardsmen were on active duty for about six months in the Cherry Valley near Pittsburgh — the task was to prevent the strikers from destroying the mines and the army managed to do so without a great deal of violence.

Fred reported the situation in these letters to his Uncle Charley:

"*July 31, 1922, Burgettstown, PA.* I don't suppose I will get out to Detroit as soon as I expected. I was called out for patrol duty in the coal regions of Western Pennsylvania and at the present am located at Burgettstown and don't expect to get home for some time."

"*August 7, 1922*...Now to start at the beginning. I was notified while on my way home from work Thursday eve July 20, to report at the Armory at 7 o'clock that evening. I did and we were issued full equipment and spent the remainder of the night loading our gear and horses. We did not know where we were going. When we asked the officers, they would say with a grin, 'To Mt. Gretna.'

Our train pulled out at 5 o'clock Friday morning and went to Harrisburg but from there we did not take the Mt. Gretna road but instead went the opposite direction up through Bellwood, Altoona and Pittsburgh, where we were issued ammunition and told to load our guns and turn out the lights as it was about 2 o'clock in the morning. We then proceeded about 20 miles where the engineer sidetracked the train and would not move until they had placed guards on top of all the cars.

I was one of them and believe me that was some ride up among those mountains, around sharp turns where you could almost shake hands with the engineer, through tunnels with nothing but fire from the smokestack to see by, which was only three cars away from me... My eyes were full of cinders. Outside of that, nothing happened and we pulled into our destination that morning which was a small mining town called Cokesburg, probably because they have about two miles of coke ovens there. It is situated on the side of a hill — there is nothing but hills in this country — we would call them mountains back in the valley.

Our camp was pitched on the side of a hill overlooking the town and believe me, that was some place. We went 8 miles for water that was not fit to drink and slept in little pup tents. If you didn't watch yourself, you would slide clear out of the tent at night while asleep. From Thursday until 10 o'clock Sunday night, I got about four hours sleep.

Our lucky star was shining, for on Thursday, our troop, a squad of machine gunners and 6 big army trucks loaded with equipment and supplies left for this place, which is a paradise compared to that. The town is probably the size of Newville and we are encamped about 1/4 mile from it. We're on an old Fair Grounds with plenty of water and 1/3 mile racetrack that comes in handy for working out the horses.

We get up in the morning at 5:30 and clean up the camp, water and groom the horses and clean up the picket line. We usually drill on horseback about three hours in the morning. It is about dinner time then and so we water, feed and groom the horses again and then fall in for grub. Dinner time is usually about 3/4 of an hour. In the afternoon, we have different work most days. Sometimes we go to the rifle range, sometimes to the pistol range and often get instructions on map sketching, range finding, signaling, gas attacks, they use gas masks for demonstrating gas grenades, smoke candles (for making smoke screens), skirmishing, patrolling, sharp-shooting, entrenching, disarming people, boxing, wrestling and lots of things in the line of military training.

"We got an issue of gas grenades, gas masks and smoke candles the other day. The grenades can either be shot from a gun or thrown, the fuse is a three second one and when it goes off, the gas just boils out of it. It is called tear gas because it makes tears stream out of your eyes and you are blind and helpless for awhile. But it is all over in a short time. The idea is to be as lenient with the strikers as possible and the gas grenades are to be used before the gun or sabre in dispersing a mob. We have a few large ones, too, which are about 8 times as strong and will lay one out for quite awhile — they are to be used as a last resort. I will have to close this letter now or I will have to send it by freight. Sincerely, your nephew."

"*September 13, 1922* — I suppose you know that we are home again. Arrived here Saturday morning about 9:30 a.m. and found the town and folks just about the same as when we left them…About all the excitement we had on patrol was one night when someone tried to break through the guard line that was around camp. About fifteen shots were fired but I suppose they were all misses as a thorough search around camp failed to reveal any signs. Everyone in camp was wishing for excitement, but I suppose it is best as it was because there would probably have been losses on both sides and I don't suppose fighting among themselves ever did any country any good.

"I haven't written to Mr. Zahrant (in Detroit) since I have been home as I would like to have your opinion before I do whether you think it would be advisable to ask him to make the arrangements for a later date. Until I have taken the bear hunt I have been promising myself for the last three years…I would love to have a bear added to my trophies before I go because I don't suppose I will get much hunting done for a few years after I get there. Ever since I carried a gun beside my father for the first time and since the time when I was thirteen years old, for two years (in order to get a hunting license) I have looked forward each year to the time when there would be only two more pages on the calendar and I would put them all down as

Charles Bear, the New York dandy and his brother Harry Bear, who preferred the Cumberland Valley.

red letter days in my memory for that year. So, if you think it is not asking too much of Mr. Zahrant, I would like to lengthen what I call my boyhood for a few months.

Awaiting your reply,
Sincerely, your nephew, Fred"

The time lost from school due to the Guard activities proved of little consequence to Fred, who had set out to fail all his classes in any case. Since his earliest outdoor days, his secret ambition had been to go to the Canadian wilderness and trap such exotic game as wolves, lynx and otters, of which he had read so much in his hunting magazines. He calculated that having flunked out of high school, he would be free to take off for the north woods without parental interference.

Dropping out of school was not as serious then as it is now. The great majority of farm-raised boys never completed grammar school because they were needed on the farm. Farmers' sons couldn't be in school in September anyway, when they were cutting corn and harvesting other crops and in spring they were needed for plowing long before the school term ended. Most dropped out of school after the seventh or eighth grade.

Having Fred quit high school before he'd finished was a distinct disappointment to Harry, but he did not try to force his son to continue. After all, Fred had gone farther than most farm boys did. But Harry was adamant in his belief that if his son didn't want to continue school, he would have to learn a trade. Without bitterness or recrimination, Harry simply faced the fact and came up with the solution he believed best, which, as it turned out, was a good one.

It was not difficult for Fred to get a job in the drafting department of the Carlisle Frog & Switch Manufacturing Company (railroad) where his father worked. But drafting proved too confining for him, so after six months he found another job with a sash and door company, where he set up and ran machinery. He liked this type of work better than drafting but one balmy autumn day as the leaves were turning gold and the hazy sun warmed the air, he was gazing out the window when a crow lit on a nearby pole and began to caw.

It was too much. He took off and went hunting, consequently losing his job. When the hunting season ended however, he got a job in the wood pattern making department of the railroad shop.

He seemed to have a natural aptitude for pattern making and did very well.

After about a year in the Frog & Switch pattern shop, he transferred to their foundry pattern shop where a greater variety of detailed work was done. His wages at that point were 17 cents per hour.

In this work, Fred finally found something that suited him. A draftsman was akin to an artist. People looked at the work and admired its detail and there it ended. But in pattern making, the worker fashioned objects that were useful. He had to be a skilled mechanic as well as an artisan because he must create an article from lines drawn on paper. And while the railroad shop dealt with somewhat large, crude models such as railroad crossings, the foundry shop turned out finely detailed and highly accurate patterns.

Fred learned a great deal there and enjoyed his work. The woods still drew him, however and vacation trips took him into the wilderness rather than to an adjacent city. His desire was not so much to avoid people as simply to live an adventuresome life in the open. But, very slowly, almost unnoticeably, he grew out of his burning desire to go to Canada and his restlessness was temporarily quieted.

There was a certain amount of fun in this new job. An example: Fred and his father ate their lunch in the toolroom separated from the electrician's room by a cement block wall about twelve feet high. The Bears' lunches usually included apples and occasionally one would mysteriously disappear from the box. One day, when he noticed this shortage, Harry Bear quietly placed a ladder against the partition, looked over the top and spotted an electrician eating his apple. He got one of the toolroom men to go over and engage in conversation with the culprit. The emissary casually mentioned that Harry Bear had been bothered by rats that were eating the apples in his lunch, so today he had brought one laced with arsenic. Now it was missing and he just hoped no one had gotten it by mistake. Harry's confederate reported that the miscreant turned blue and suffered near apoplexy. The apple poaching ceased from then on.

The brothers, Charles and Harry Bear, were very close although their lifestyles as adults were quite different. Charles, aesthetic and unafraid of breaking the bonds of their childhood upbringing, fled to New York at an early age never again to live in the valley. This saddened Harry, who was equally determined never to leave the valley. He went to New York a few times to visit his brother but there is no evidence that he enjoyed himself. Charley kept in close touch with the family, however, returning to spend most of his holidays and vacations with them.

Charley was another Bear who never married. The family knew very little about his life in New York, but that he was "doing well" had to be presumed. On his frequent visits home, he joined in the simple pleasures with a zest that belied the sophistications of his city life. But one thing never changed, whether he was in the mountains of Pennsylvania or the marble corridors of the Metropolitan Life Insurance Co., his dress was the same — well-tailored, vested suits, white shirts and high starched collars.

In those years of scanty communication, word did not get back over the mountains as it would today telling of Charley's work and achievements in New York. After his death, however, some light was shed on the riddle of his life through the pages of a scrapbook he left behind. Here he preserved letters from people in high places concerning the scope of his life. The letters told, among other things, of his efforts in the cause of World War I.

In June of 1918, the following item appeared in a New York newspaper concerning fundraising for the war effort. It pertained to a document inscribed in Charles Bear's exquisite hand and decorated lavishly with scrolls and flowers in red, blue, green and gold:

> ...And then there was the $55,000.00 which Cleveland H. Dodge paid for President Wilson's autographed Red Cross Proclamation, knocked down to him at auction, after the dinner amid a perfect gala of enthusiasm, the climax of the patriotic feeling which made the affair one of the most notable in many years.
>
> "Onward Christian Soldiers" has assisted at many exciting episodes but few more dramatic than when to its strains, played by the orchestra, sailor Cameron bore the framed proclamation (Charley's) through the crowded grand ballroom of the Waldorf Astoria escorted by a detail of soldiers and sailors.
>
> "This is the only proclamation outside of state papers that President Wilson has signed," cried Mr. Day. "What am I bid for this document that will go down in history as the original copy signed by the President?"
>
> "Fifteen thousand dollars," said a voice. It was Cleveland H. Dodge. Mr. Day looked pained. "Now I know," he said, looking over at Mr. Fox and J.P. Morgan, "there is more money in this room than that."
>
> "Twenty-five thousand." Mr. Fox responded obediently.
>
> "Twenty-six thousand." cried another voice.
>
> "Fifty thousand dollars." came the deep voice of J.P. Morgan. But

Fred Bear on his cavalry mount.

Fred Bear at left.

Fred at the right.

104th Cavalry unit at site of coal mine strike. Western Pennsylvania, 1922.

the courtly Cleveland H. Dodge, with whom, by the way, President Wilson had dined while in New York the week before, couldn't bear to see the proclamation slipping away from him.

"Fifty-five thousand dollars." he bid from the speakers' table and was heard to say as Mr. Breed handed him the document,"...I predict that one hundred years from now, my great grandchildren will estimate its value at $1,000,000.00."

A short time later, Joseph P. Day wrote to Charles Bear:

"...I very much appreciate what you have done for me and the Red Cross, by engrossing President Wilson's Proclamation...It must be gratifying to you to know that I sold the (proclamation) at the Waldorf Astoria on Monday night, May 27th, to Cleveland H. Dodge, for $55,000.00..."

In 1936, the letters were still coming — from Russia, Paris, Switzerland and shipboard, all praising and thanking him for beautiful works of art. One writer summed it up for them all: "It is just like you to want to do something of value for your friends without pay." Charley was not interested in pay and seemed to do these things for the love of creating beauty and sharing it with others. The letters thanking him came from individuals, Masonic Lodges, the Metropolitan Life Insurance Company, churches, Hadassah, Trust companies, law firms and college fraternities. "Congratulations on thirty eight valuable years at the Metropolitan Life Insurance Company..." said one "and many more years ahead...but most especially for your unstinted devotion to mankind, for which your real friends know you best..."

One wonders if Charley ever dreamed of the fame his pen would bring him when as a young man he graduated from the Zanerian Art College in Columbus, Ohio.

Fred's skills with drawing tools showed up early according to an old letter he'd written to his uncle on February 13, 1916 (Fred was then 14).

Dear Uncle Charley:

I received the book several days ago and I thank you...I am getting along fine with my drawing at school. I made 94 every month this year...95 was my last month's mark in woodwork...

During his youth, Fred made a few trips to New York to visit Uncle Charley. The latter was anxious to indoctrinate the young man into the opportunities offered by the great city. Fred traveled by train and was met at the station by his uncle who made the most of the time they had together.

To the young man, his uncle seemed to be the height of self assurance, knowledge and success. His easy ways with the doormen at the hotel where he lived, cab drivers and waiters in the fine restaurants filled his nephew with awe and admiration. There were times when part of him almost weakened — life in New York and growing up like Uncle Charley would certainly have some merit. Charley took him to the Automat where the wonders of depositing a nickel in a slot and receiving an instant, delicious sandwich bordered on sheer magic. They went to the Museum of Natural History spending hours of such fascination that Fred remembers never wanting to leave. One night, Uncle Charley took him to the Ziegfield Follies and another time to the Metropolitan Life Insurance Company building where he worked. Passing through a large office with many people at many desks, everyone stood up as Charles Bear entered the room!

Once home in the valley, however, with neckties and polished shoes back in the closet, Fred realized that life in the open was what he really loved. The fresh mountain air after the city canyons of New York filled his lungs with life-giving strength. Charley had taken him to visit several of the fur dealers Fred had sent pelts to and it wasn't long after this that he determined on his own the houses he wanted to do business with. Charley understood his nephew and realized, finally, that Fred would not thrive in New York.

Fred's early days in Detroit. Fred is on the right, with Charlie Lockwood and his wife.

CHAPTER 4

Fred and Uncle Charley kept in close touch through the years and on April 22, 1922, Fred wrote:

"Dear Uncle Charley:

I am getting anxious to go to Detroit and would like to know if you have seen your friend from there and what success you had. I would not like to go before the first of the year you know, (hunting and trapping season) but rather than miss the opportunity I would go almost any time.

"I used to think of building bridges, dams and other engineering jobs and sometimes do yet but I have learned that opportunity doesn't often rap and when it does one should be ready. Being a pattern maker all my life does not appeal to me but I believe I would like this job of learning the auto business clear through and maybe I could use my head to a good advantage for I think there are improvements to be made on them...Maybe sometime I will be able to repay you the favors you so kindly have done for me and the interest you take in me..."

It was Charley who helped Fred get a start in Detroit. In those days, young men from careful families did not leave home without a 'place to stay' and a job. Charley provided both through his friend, Clarence Zahrant, who was there. Mr. Zahrant, a carpet salesman for the automobile factories, not only got Fred a job as pattern maker in the experimental department of the Packard Motor Company but also offered him an extra room in his home.

So in 1923, a few days after Fred celebrated his twenty-first birthday, he left the family home in Pennsylvania for the large and distant industrial city of Detroit. This was a big decision for one who had been raised on a farm and spent his entire life, to that point, in an area of limited population and a strict lifestyle.

The Zahrants took Fred into their Detroit home as a member of the family. They polished his social graces, encouraged him to take courses at night school, nursed him through scarlet fever and even taught him to play Auction Bridge.

Fred lived with the Zahrants for two years and his letters indicate they were busy ones.

The formal training period for a pattern maker was four years. Fred had studied only two years before arriving at Packard and his stock of tools was relatively crude. Nevertheless, he stoutly maintained that he was a finished pattern maker and was accepted as such because of the quality of his work.

Fred found those first years in the Motor City enjoyable and educational. He soon completed credits for a high school diploma and attended night school at the Detroit Institute of Technology studying English, public speaking and mathematics.

Packard was building Liberty Aircraft engines at that time, a project started during World War I. Some of the big engines they turned out were also used for many years by Gar Wood in his *Miss America* speedboats.

Fred was still worrying about his future, trying to assure himself that he had gotten all the education and training necessary. He rebelled at the great amount of overtime expected of employees in the automobile factories and in his letters even touched on the vagaries of romance that came his way.

"Detroit   May 9, 1923
Dear Uncle Charley:

I put in 9 hours of overtime last week. The reason for it was to get the three racing cars finished in time for the big race at Indianapolis May 30. Last Thursday night, I worked all night making a pattern for a manifold for the cars. Packard will have three of the finest cars on the track and three of the most popular drivers, I think. Ralph DePalma, D. Vesta and Joe Boyer. Ralph DePalma has been here since April 8 and the cars are being constructed under his supervision and from his own blue prints. So with that and Packard Motor Co. behind them, I think they should make a grand cleanup, don't you?"

September 1924

"Dear Uncle Charley:

I have not come to any definite decision about what I am going to do. What do you suggest besides staying at Packard and without spending 4 or 5 years at school? I spend a lot of my spare time trying to map out my future but the more I think the farther away I get. Sometimes I think I will just ride along and grab the first thing that turns up but I am afraid nothing will come my way.

I attended night school last winter. After taxing my brain all day figuring out blueprints and patterns, I then went to school the evenings that I did not have to work — there is not a pattern maker's job in Detroit that does not call for overtime. I had to study Sundays to make up for the time I lost when I had to work.

While at school I studied the characteristics of my associates and tried to find someone who was somewhat like myself. About 9 out of 10 said they studied because they liked to...If I could get as interested in school as I am in an Outdoor Magazine, I would be on top all the time...If you can figure this out for me, I wish you would and tell me just what you think.

Sincerely, Fred"

Fred's struggle between an inner sense that he should adequately prepare himself for life and the irresistible urge to be free to spend time in the woods was quite apparent in these letters. It would seem that he wanted his uncle to make a pronouncement either that he continue taking courses to further his education or that he should forge ahead with the status quo and somehow make his dreams come true.

(The irony is that fifty years later he receives letters from young outdoorsmen asking him for advice in the same vein. He feels compelled to tell them to finish school but his heart aches for their yearning to take shortcuts which will free them for the wilds.)

The record of this period ends with an account of Fred's first car and Charley's final advice about women:

"...I am sorry I forgot to tell you about my first journey in Henry (his new Ford). I suppose I had not recovered from the jolting up I had. However, it was not so bad, as a trip like that would make one tired even in a Packard.

"Henry did fine, even better than I dared to expect. We covered the distance from here to Greensburg the first day, about 200 miles. About half the time it was raining and 3/4 of the distance I had wet roads...

The next day I was in the mountains and it took from 9 o'clock in the morning until 6 at night to cover the remaining distance of 156 miles. Burning out the brakes the first day kept me from getting a better start the next morning as I spent some time putting on new

Fred's first car, a 1923 Ford Coupe.

ones at a cost of $1.59. Coming back, I left on a Saturday morning and wanted to make it in two days but the weather was so extremely hot, I took three days. Thought it better to take more time and not overheat the motor. Got to Detroit at 3 p.m. on Monday. The expenditures on the car for the trip both ways amounted to $29 or $30 dollars. 62 gals. of gas, 4 qts. of oil, storage three nights $2.00 and brake shoes $1.59. So much for Henry...(Fred was 22 years old at this time).

...I agree with you about women and I will have to get some fatherly advice from you on that subject when we get together. The more I learn about them, the less I know. However, time and experience have cleared up many hazy subjects...

You mentioned in one of your letters that a sweet, womanly girl like my mother to accompany me to a good show would be O.K. I have had some experience along those lines and believe me, those kind are hard to find. However, I haven't given up..."

Fred continued working at Packard and living with the Zahrants. During this period, he had become acquainted with some fellow workers from the Thumb area of Michigan who went up to northern Michigan to hunt deer each year. They invited Fred to join them and he eventually went, against his employer's wishes. When he returned, he didn't have a job but within a few days he was working again, this time in the pattern shop at Chrysler.

Fred and the boat he built, during a fishing trip on the Detroit River.

While still at the Chrysler Corporation in 1925, another opportunity presented itself. His landlord, Clarence Zahrant, had an inventive mind and obtained a patent on a tire cover (spare tires were carried on the outside of the car in those days). His little plant turned out covers for the auto manufacturers. Eventually Zahrant asked Fred if he would be interested in running the place.

He spent the next two years running the Zahrant plant. When Zahrant sold out to an older firm, the Jansen Manufacturing Company, Fred stayed on as plant manager. The Jansen plant also made golf bags and it was here that Fred developed his expertise with leather. By then he was living at the home of his friend Ray Stanard and in their spare time, he and Ray built boats for themselves in the garage.

It took them the best part of two years to finish two beautiful boats, nineteen feet long with six-foot beams. The design called for half cabins, oak keels and mahogany planking. Ray installed a big, two-cylinder Johnson Giant 50-horsepower outboard motor on his boat and Fred used an experimental five-cylinder, 4-cycle radial pancake engine manufactured in Detroit by the Cross Gear & Engine company. Both motors would move the crafts 20 miles per hour. Fred and Ray kept the boats in the Fox River and on weekends ran them up to an area in Lake St. Clair called the Flats.

One day Fred was coming back from a cruise to the Flats and ran into a heavy storm. Because he could not take the high waves head on, he had to tack back and forth. In doing so, he came too close to a rocky point and his propeller hit a submerged boulder, which caused its three bronze blades to

Cutting Room at the Jansen Manufacturing Company in Detroit, about 1927.

wrap around the hub. Fred tossed over the anchor, which took solid hold. Fortunately he was with a companion, the Jansen shipping clerk, who held Fred by his ankles while he went over the transom, head down, to remove the propeller. He used a piece of railroad steel and a five-pound hammer to beat the blades out until they roughly resembled a propeller once more and managed to make it back to port.

That immersion dampened Fred's enthusiasm for boats and when he had an offer to trade his craft, he accepted. A real estate dealer gave him a small one-story house and lot for the boat.

In addition to boats, Fred and Ray had become interested in archery. The spark was kindled after they saw a motion picture at the Adams Theatre in Detroit concerning the Alaskan adventures of Arthur Young, a famous bow-hunter. Since there were very few archery suppliers at that time, the young men ordered raw materials — lemonwood bow staves and birch arrow dowels — from the Stemmler Company on Long Island and made their own equipment. Both were skilled woodworkers and pattern makers but without knowledge of the technical aspects of the weapon. They had trouble matching the arrow's spine to the bow's draw weight, getting the correct length and spiral in fletching arrows and finding good quality arrowheads for hunting. They practiced shooting at bales of straw set up in an alley in back of the Stanard home.

Leonard Osberg, Art Young, Carl Strang, Fred Bear and Ray Stannard on the grounds of what later became the Detroit Archery Club range. Note the early longbow designs. 1929.

Fred's boss, Stanley Jansen, came to him at work one day and said, "With your interest in bows and arrows, why don't you come down to the Rotary meeting with me this noon? We have an archer putting on a demonstration." Fred went with him and met the speaker, who, to his great surprise was the renowned bowhunter he had seen in the film, Arthur Young.

Although not immediately evident, that meeting sealed Fred's future. Art Young had been taught to shoot the bow by Will "Chief" Compton, who had learned the skills of bowhunting during a boyhood spent among the Sioux Indians. These two met and cemented a friendship with Dr. Saxton Pope, who in turn had been taught to hunt with a bow and make archery tackle by Ishi, the last survivor of the Yana Indians of northern California.

Pope, Compton and Young hunted with Ishi until the latter's premature death from tuberculosis then continued to share their common interest. They made their own archery tackle and with it took deer, black and grizzly bears, cougars and elk during hunts throughout the West.

Art Young made two trips to Alaska, where he downed Kodiak bears, Dall sheep and the great Kenai moose, becoming the first white man known to take these big game species with the bow and arrow. Later, Pope and Young went to Africa with the author Stewart Edward White, who wrote *Lions in the*

Fred testing a bow he made while living at the Stannards, 1927.

Art Young and Saxton Pope in the earliest days of modern bowhunting.

Path, a book about their bowhunting exploits. The Fred Bear Museum has on display the two bows used on these hunts and the fine leather longbow case, which Young carried by boat to Africa.

Dr. Pope also wrote of their experiences in *The Adventurous Bowman*, his second book. His first book, *Hunting With the Bow and Arrow*, is considered a classic and was largely responsible for the resurgence of interest in archery in this country. In 1974, Bear Archery reprinted this book in paperback, with a foreword by Fred Bear. Dr. Pope died in 1926 but Art Young's interest in bowhunting continued and he demonstrated his skill and lectured all over the country. Eventually, Young left Detroit for Homewood, Illinois, where he died in 1935.

When Bear and Young first met, they struck up an immediate friendship and Fred, for the first time, became serious about archery. They made tackle in Fred's basement and did some shooting together. Like Fred, Young had been a gun enthusiast. As a matter of fact, he had competed for the Olympic

Fred Bear and Ray Stannard.

Club of San Francisco in both rifle and pistol matches. With these interests in common, the two became fast friends.

To practice archery, they drove to a barren, hilly section of Detroit near Northwestern and Telegraph roads and shot "roving" style, walking along, randomly picking targets — stumps, leaves and small hillocks at various distances. This area later became the range for Detroit's first archery club.

Their hunting heads were provided by Burt Lyons of the Lyons Manufacturing Company, Detroit, from a design by Art Young. Among the things Young taught Fred at this time was the skill of making handmade, double-loop bowstrings from Irish linen.

Fred tried bowhunting for the first time in 1929. He and two friends, Glen Thomas and Bob Todd, drove up to St. Helen, Michigan, in a Model A Ford. This was about as far north as they could go because of limited funds. Snow was falling and it was cold when they set up a tent camp in the shelter of a cedar swamp. The ground was wet and their reluctant campfire was inadequate, but they managed to survive.

It should be noted that the only legal archery hunting for deer at that time was during the gun season. This fact, combined with their crude equipment, was a considerable deterrent to success. They had hoped to live largely on snowshoe rabbits, which inhabit the cedar swamps of that region, but even there they had difficulties. One day while out looking for camp meat, Fred spotted a rabbit and drew down on it. The animal sat perfectly still while Fred

Fred Bear testing one of his first bows, 1927 or 1928.

Fred and "Oscar," a mechanical deer target he made for use by the Detroit Archery Club.

made a neat little ring around it with six arrows, all he had with him, without harming his target. Fortunately, the hunters had brought rifles. It was six years before Fred was successful in getting a deer with a bow.

In 1927, Fred was married to Ann Marie Thomas, the attractive sister of one of his hunting companions. Marie, a nurse by profession, was an outdoor girl who later became proficient with the bow on tournament fields.

They lived in a Detroit apartment at first and later rented a home because Fred thought owning a house would tie him down. He never really thought of Detroit as his home and always looked forward to leaving the city, but as all the jobs in his line of work were there, his plans for living in the woods had to be postponed.

Since these were Depression days, it was necessary to work at odd jobs to supplement one's income. Fred made screens, storm doors and windows for the house the Bears rented from the Belgian Counsel in Detroit. He also made gun stocks and did modest gunsmithing in his small basement workshop — even turning out a bow now and then for a friend.

CHAPTER 5

While running the plant for Stanley Jansen, Fred became acquainted with Jansen's nephew, Charles Piper, who worked there in a sales capacity. Piper had an excellent connection at the Chrysler Corporation and knew many of the buyers. This proved fortuitous when one night in 1933, during the height of the Depression, a fire destroyed the Jansen tire cover plant, leaving a hundred people out of work, including Fred and Charles.

The two friends took stock of their resources and decided that with Piper's connection at Chrysler and Fred's know-how in manufacturing, they might put something together. Pooling a total of $600, they acquired a couple of second-hand sewing machines plus some other equipment and formed a partnership making silk screen advertising banners and flyers for Chrysler. As the Bear Products Company, the small firm rented a commercial garage on Tireman Avenue in Detroit. Fred started building archery equipment in one corner of the business at this time. After a year or two, they were able to move into larger quarters.

By 1939, they had expanded to the point where a third move to larger quarters was imminent. But by now Fred's part-time archery business, which was his real interest, could support him financially, so he and Piper dissolved their partnership, Chuck staying with Bear Products Company and Fred launching out on his own as the Bear Archery Company.

Ye Sylvan Archer, a target archer's magazine, reported in May 1941 that Fred Bear had announced the founding of Bear Archery.

FRED BEAR ANNOUNCES THAT HE HAS ACQUIRED THE
INTERESTS OF THE BEAR PRODUCTS COMPANY, ENGAGED
IN THE ARCHERY AND SPORTING GOODS BUSINESS, AT 2611
PHILADELPHIA AVENUE, DETROIT, MICHIGAN.
MR. BEAR WILL CONTINUE THE BUSINESS AS SOLE OWNER
AT THE ABOVE ADDRESS UNDER THE NAME OF
BEAR ARCHERY COMPANY.

The new plant site was a former Maxwell garage, sixty feet by one hundred feet, on West Philadelphia Avenue. At the front, he ran a partition down the middle using half the space for manufacturing and half for an indoor archery range. He had an office on one side and a retail showroom on the other.

Fred made this lean-to in 1931. The tent is still in use today and has been the focal point of camp scenes in several Bear Archery films.

The small garage on Tireman Avenue in Detroit that was the first Bear Archery plant. Photo taken in 1975.

The second Bear Archery building in Detroit, shown with Fred Bear in 1975.

The third Bear Archery location in Detroit, at Philadelphia and Linwood.

The chief items manufactured at the new company besides bows and listed in its first brochure were leather goods such as shooting gloves, armguards, quivers and bow cases.

The earliest bows made at Bear Archery were lemonwood target models of longbow design. Fred's first real hunting bow was turned out of an $8 Osage orange stave purchased from Fred Kibbe in Coldwater, Michigan. It was somewhat shorter and wider in limb than the six-foot target bows. Bowstrings were handmade of Barbour's Irish linen, obtained from local shoe repair shops.

As time went on, the company's retail outlet improved and Fred found several good salesmen to sell his products to sporting goods dealers. He and Nelson Grumley, an expert woodworker, began now to turn out custom bows. It took them two or three days of hard work to finish a bow, which sold for 60 to 65 dollars. There were ten or twelve other employees, most of whom worked with the leather goods.

The Detroit Archers Club was formed in late 1933 with the express purpose of pooling the members' limited funds to rent quarters for an indoor range where they could shoot during the winter. The club was formally organized at Bear's small plant, which became its headquarters. In fact, Fred Bear was the club's first president and its members were his chief customers.

During the Depression, there were many vacant buildings available and finding a location for an indoor range was not difficult. The Detroit archers began to attract many people to the sport and their organization expanded rapidly. The members put on exhibitions at sport shows and at the annual Trout Festival in West Branch, a sportsman's town a hundred and fifty miles north of Detroit.

The archers next established their outdoor field range near Northwestern and Telegraph Roads. They also got together each fall for group hunts. On one, about 50 members camped outside St. Helen, close to the Ogemaw Game Refuge, in deer season. Only one of the group bagged a deer but it was a start.

The hunters took the deer, a small spikehorn buck, to the nearby Cedar Inn, where the proprietor agreed to roast it. The Inn had a bar, dance floor and small band shell. The banquet was a most successful affair.

One of the members on this hunt had strayed inadvertently into the Ogemaw refuge, where he had been caught by a game warden and severely reprimanded. The club members were determined to get some fun out of this occurrence and secretly contrived a mock trial for the victim. During the height of the party, the truant archer was removed from his seat and brought before the "court." The presiding judge was A. J. Michelson, a Flint attorney and later first president of the National Field Archery Association. While conducting the proceedings, he used a claw hammer to bring the court to order. The prosecuting attorney was a very large policeman brought in from the street.

The charges leveled at the "defendant" were poaching on the preserves of Franklin the Third (at the time, Franklin Roosevelt was running for a third term) and of shooting and eating a deer within the boundaries of the refuge. As the trial continued, hilarity ran rampant. Some bones from the kitchen became Exhibit A. Exhibit B was a shovelful of sand containing one of Fred Bear's size 13 boot tracks, supposedly taken from the refuge (the defendant wore a size 8 boot). Someone had boiled a cedar arrow and wrapped it around a broom handle and this specimen, doused liberally with ketchup, was Exhibit C. When one of the prosecution's witnesses began answering "yes" to a question and then "no" to the same question a minute later, the group broke up and the sketch had to be terminated. This and other events with which club members entertained themselves were remembered with pleasure for years.

There were annual trips to Blaney, in Michigan's Upper Peninsula, a unique resort combining some 30,000 acres of woodlands with more than comfortable accommodations. Most hunters at Blaney relied on rifles to secure game. The contrast between their activities and those of the small group of bowhunters was obvious. One by one, the riflemen hung up fine bucks, while the little band of archers came in day after day with nothing but enthusiasm for a chance to try again the next day.

The bowmen took enough deer, however, to remain encouraged. They hunted every year, sometimes at Blaney and other times near West Branch, Newaygo, or St. Helen. A few record-size bucks harvested in western Michigan's Allegan State Forest during the late 1930's and early 1940's resulted in much good publicity for the growing sport.

It was at Blaney in 1935 that Fred finally got a deer with a bow and arrow. A small and unimpressive spike-horn buck, it nevertheless marked the beginning of what was to become a most remarkable bowhunting career. Just two years earlier, he had shot a record whitetail buck with a rifle. It field dressed at 285 lbs.

In 1935 Fred experienced his first serious illness. A cystic growth in his right kidney caused such severe bleeding that the organ had to be removed.

Nels Grumley, Fred's master bowyer, working on an Osage Orange bow.

Two years later, the trouble recurred in the remaining kidney. Removing the second kidney in those days before transplants would have been fatal, so his doctor prescribed, among other things, an unsweetened grape juice diet that, in about six months, cleared up the condition once and for all.

While on this diet, Fred was invited to hunt bobcats near Oscoda. He took three cases of grape juice with him and upon arriving at camp, put them between storm doors to keep cool.

During the cocktail hour the first evening, a member of the group served some purple drinks that he called "Presbyterians." It was not long before Fred discovered that it was his remedial cache of grape juice the bartender was mixing with gin!

In 1937, Bear and his companions spent Michigan's first statewide deer season for bowhunters at Newaygo. Fred named their camp "Pope Hall" in honor of Saxton Pope, carefully lettering the name on a sign he hung over the door.

Each year, the group grew larger. In addition to Bear, the more successful hunters in those years included Nelson Grumley, Barney Grenier, Bill Loomis, Norman Reid and Larry Mytinger.

During the mid to late 1930's, Fred was becoming an outstanding shot with the bow and won three Michigan State Championships, the Target Championship in 1934 and Field Championships in 1937 and 1939. His skill provided excellent opportunities for him to promote archery and for many years he barnstormed throughout the Midwest in places such as Cleveland, Chicago, Minneapolis and Detroit, giving exhibitions at sport and trade shows. His acts included shooting airborne discs tossed in the air by an assistant, shooting arrows at an inclining board on the floor so they would ricochet and break balloons on a target, bending over backwards to shoot behind him and shooting blunt arrows through heavy boards to demonstrate their power of penetration.

Fred also did a great deal of public relations work promoting bowhunting in meetings with state legislators, conservation officials, outdoor writers and photographers.

He was instrumental in helping promote the first special bowhunting seasons in both Wisconsin (1934) and Michigan (1936). After two years, Michigan Conservation officials realized that archers were not going to do any great damage to the deer herds and opened the entire state to bowhunting.

In 1939, firmly established in archery, Fred and Marie, with their friend Larry Whiffen of Milwaukee, made a lengthy trip to California to attend

Detroit archers in 1935. Fred Bear is in back row center. His father and mother are at the right end of the back row.

an NAA Tournament at the Golden Gate Park in San Francisco. Crossing the Continental Divide en route, they stopped the car for pictures of Fred and Larry shooting arrows in celebration, from either side of a sign designating MacDonald's Pass. And again, driving through the celebrated base of an enormous redwood, they stopped for pictures there.

All three of the travelers participated in the Tournament and met many old time "first" archers of the country, among them Cassius Styles.

By the early 1940's, bowhunting was firmly established, not only in Michigan and Wisconsin, but in Pennsylvania and California as well. An urgent need arose for education in proper bowhunting methods and for selling the sport's merits to state conservation departments. Filling this need made inroads on Fred's time for many years.

It was necessary not only to manufacture archery products, but by his promotional efforts, Fred also had to create a market for them.

He quickly learned that even national newspapers and magazines, while indifferent to tournament scores, were extremely interested in photographs and stories of game obtained with the bow and arrow and might occasionally even use them on the front page or cover. Jack Van Coevering, sportswriter for the Detroit *Free Press*, gave the archers some excellent publicity with news stories and photographs of hunters who had secured game with a bow in those early years. In 1942, he accompanied Fred to Blaney where they made the first film of a Michigan bow hunt. After several days of interesting but fruitless encounters, Fred finally downed a nice buck on Friday, November 13. The resulting film was viewed by audiences for many years. Fred's field notes of this initial film are unique in that they were the first in a long series of such reporting that led to Doubleday's publication in 1976 of his popular book, *Fred Bear's Field Notes*. However, that book began with his first African trip in 1955. Following are his notes from that first Blaney film trip in 1942:

DEER HUNT AT BLANEY
1942

Nov. 11th First Day — Jack Van Coevering and I drove up from Detroit yesterday. The sky threatened snow and we were thankful for the special Bow & Arrow Season which got us across the Straits of Mackinac before the gun season. When there was only one season, we had to plan on an extra day to get across the Straits, waiting in the parking lot with hundreds of cars for the ferries.

Today is Dad's birthday. I should have gotten a deer to celebrate it. It was snowing when we got up this morning and has snowed off and on all day. A strong wind was blowing from the southwest and the temperature was down to 25. The roaring fire at the Lodge felt good when we got in tonight.

We started hunting the northwest section and saw a nice buck on the trail ahead of the car going in, but no shot. When we got to the hunting area, we parked the car and still-hunted a trail for about three miles. We saw a sizeable buck cross over about 15 yards ahead of us but I muffed the shot by fumbling the arrow. Jack was behind in camera position and the air was blue for the next few steps over missing that shot.

We had a long hike back to the car — hungry as wolves. We built a fire and toasted the sandwiches the lodge had packed for us this morning. My hands were so cold I could hardly get my boots and wet socks off to dry over the fire. Thoroughly warmed and dried out, we got in the car after lunch and drove to the other end of the property. While traveling through some small, dense hardwood we saw another buck standing near the trail about twenty yards away. I got out of the car and Jack drove about a quarter of a mile down

Fred Bear takes a few practice shots upon arriving at the site of a Detroit archery tournament.

Fred with his first bow and arrow deer. Blaney Camp in the Upper Peninsula of Michigan, 1935.

This 1933 buck was the largest Fred ever shot with a rifle. The deer weighed 285 lbs. field dressed.

the road while I went after the buck. After following him for about three hundred yards, I got a walking shot broadside. I aimed for the shoulder allowing for one step while the arrow got there, but he jumped the string and the arrow struck a glancing blow somewhere on the rear quarter and he ran off. I found the arrow with a tuft of hair still on it about twenty yards from where the deer stood. I can't understand why I didn't get better penetration — even the tip of the head was still sharp. So much for that. He had a nice rack but not the biggest I ever saw.

We drove on after this and parked the car and still-hunted until dark. We saw two more bucks, one of them chasing a doe. I got a broadside, running shot at him at about 60 yards but was a jump behind. I did not get a shot at the other buck.

Total bucks seen today was five. All had racks. We must have seen twenty does also.

Jack took some pictures of a partridge and some other footage that we need and we called it a day. I'm tired tonight.

Nov. 12th — It was snowing hard when we went out this morning and it kept up until about 11 a.m. There was about three inches on the ground.

We drove to Dr. Christopherson's cabin the first thing this morning. Christopherson is a snowy-bearded, self-styled Norwegian naturalist who has some sort of arrangement here at Blaney where he is living out his retirement in a cozy cabin in the woods. Guests driving the trails at Blaney count it a must to stop at 'Old Doc's' to admire the fine silk Norwegian flag he flies from his flag pole and to watch him feed his pet Canadian Geese, squirrels, birds and fawns he has around his place.

We started hunting in the same area we'd been in yesterday but saw very few does and no bucks at all during the morning. After the storm the deer started moving around again but up until the time we ate lunch between two and three o'clock, toasting our half chickens over a fire, we had seen only one small buck. Jack took pictures of our luncheon scene.

Warmed and refreshed, we hunted along a saddle trail until dark and had an exciting time. Not that we saw many deer — just some does and a fair-sized buck with which I could do no business because of the brush. But just after stirring up a dozen or more partridges, we

Detroit News, 1936: "What is believed to be the first wildcat ever killed with a bow and arrow in Michigan was shot in St. Helens Swamp in Ogema County recently by Fred Bear"

Fred Bear with George Bigly in the Porcupine Mountains of Michigan, the year he shot his record-class buck.

noticed bear tracks on the trail. The tracks spread out for a quarter of a mile and we counted five sets in all. The tracks were very fresh — we estimated they had been made less than a half hour before. One was very large, nearly six inches wide and seven to eight inches long. The tracks were very plain in the melted snow. We saw a lot of stump bears from then on in!

We had two and a half miles to walk by auto trail to our car and it was beginning to get dark. Skirting a swamp about midway back we could make out something in the road about two hundred yards ahead. It was too dark to tell if it was a deer or a man or a bear, but it was traveling the same direction we were and by increasing our speed, we began to gain on it. Jack concluded that it was too low for a deer or a man and I was convinced that it was a bear. We had the wind on the backs of our necks and soon the bear crossed the road and went into the swamp. It was when he turned broadside that we knew it was a bear. A study of his tracks revealed that he was a small bear.

I didn't have time for a shot and we've just now found that it is illegal to kill bear in that section of the property. This is very agreeable to Jack.

Nov. 13th — Friday the 13th might be unlucky for some, but not for me. It was cold as hell and snowing and blowing when we went out this morning. We had decided to go over into the northeast section down in the swamp by Moon Lake and hunt. We plodded around all morning. Deer had made some tracks but we could not locate anything except a couple of does. It was so cold we headed straight for Doc Christopherson's cabin to have an early lunch. The tea kettle was singing at the back of his big kitchen range and we made some tea to wash down our cold sandwiches. Jack took pictures of snow outside the cabin and we saw a spikehorn from one of Doc's windows.

It was still snowing and blowing when we started out after lunch. We had planned to go back to the swamp but changed our minds and headed northwest up the trail to Camp 23.

Fighting the snow and wind all the way we suddenly saw what looked like an enormous buck in a clearing ahead and changed our course; turning left, over a ridge to head him off. Jack followed about twenty feet behind me as we hurried through a thick growth of small

Early group of Michigan bowhunters at their camp near St. Helens. Fred Bear is in the center.

Fred tallying up the day's deer sightings inside "Pope Hall" during Michigan's first state-wide bow season, 1937.

In 1933, when Fred Bear drove to Eaton Rapids for the fall Michigan Archery Association tournament, his reputation and skill as a bowyer preceded him. His small Company was just months old, but he was out to show his fellow competitors that Bear-built bows could really shoot. He rode back to his home in Detroit with the Gold Ribbon, his first of many tournament victories. The same year he helped form the Detroit Archers. In 1934, he won the Michigan Archery Championship.

Fred practicing trick shooting at aerial targets in 1939. He is an instinctive snap-shooter and visualizes the flight of the arrow just milliseconds before release.

Fred poses for a Sports Show publicity photo, 1935.

poplar. Just as we came out in the clearing again he called softly and I turned to see a nice buck coming straight toward me quartering from the rear. He was only about thirty yards away when I started raising my bow for a shot. I was uphill from him and had to wait until he lifted his head and horns to expose his chest for a shot. In a split second he saw me and raised his head. I was not at full draw but I had to shoot now or not at all. He was head on but saw my movements and started to turn. The arrow, a large four-blade, struck the left chest about four ribs forward and just pierced the hide on the opposite side. He ran about one fourth of a mile before he fell.

Van Coevering later told a group of outdoor writers, "During the course of a long career of outdoor writing, I've been privileged to meet some fine woodsmen but none more knowledgeable of the wild and its inhabitants than Fred Bear."

This first Fred Bear bowhunting film set the formula for the highly successful promotion of bowhunting in America for the next 40 years. It was the first of a total of 25 Fred Bear films, most of which are still available today from Bear Archery.

Fred Bear demonstrating trick shooting at a Sportsmen's Show.

Fred Bear and Carl Strang cutting Osage Orange for bows during a National Archery tournament held on the grounds of Franklin & Marshall College in Lancaster, Pennsylvania, 1937.

Fred Bear and Larry Whiffen shooting arrows at the top of the Continental Divide while enroute to the 1939 N.A.A. Tournament in California.

On the left, Larry Whfffen and Marie Bear. Fred Bear on the right, clowning in the Sequoia National Forest, 1939.

Fred Bear (on left) at the 1939 N.A.A. Tournament in Golden Gate Park, San Francisco. Next to him are Cassius Styles and Wayne Thompson.

CHAPTER 6

By the early 1940s, Bear Archery was doing a great deal of private label work in the leather goods end of the business. This included armguards, shooting gloves and quivers. Bear was actually making the items sold by Ben Pearson, Indian Archery and American Archery, among others. The same work crew also silk-screened colored target faces, first on oil cloth and later on less expensive paper. The private label goods accounted for about 50% of Bear's business, 30% went to bow production and the remaining 20% was in arrows.

While the private label merchandise covered much of the United States, it did not carry the Bear Archery name and Fred was anxious to expand his small company's reputation nationwide. One way this could be done was through the national archery magazines. However, his funds were limited in the fledgling company and so he struck upon the idea of getting "free" advertising by virtue of the "first person" bowhunting adventure stories mentioned earlier. In this way he could gain invaluable publicity for the company and sport with no outlay of advertising monies. It was at this moment in his career that things really started coming together and Fred was able to combine his creative genius with the promotional skills that he had been schooled in during the sports shows he worked around the Midwest.

Armed with Jack Van Coevering's old movie camera that he had since purchased, along with a still camera, some notebooks and the stub of a pencil, he strode out into the forest. Before he was done, this 40-year-old young man would create a legendary figure known all over the world and a company that would dominate his sport for scores of years. Among the millions of sportsmen in North America his name became the first one that both rifle hunters and bowhunters mentioned when asked by researchers to name this continent's best known hunter.

Fred got his promotional feet wet with the Blaney hunt with Jack Van Coevering. He then decided to go after bigger game than whitetail deer, realizing that such a strategy would make his stories all the more newsworthy to the national magazines. Following are several stories he wrote for Archery Magazine about those early adventures. These have not been published since the 1940's.

MOOSEHUNTS
by Fred Bear

During the war it was difficult to make hunting trips. If one could manage a couple of weeks away from military service or defense work, there was always the problem of transportation. It would have been easier to walk than persuade a ration board to provide tires and gasoline for anything remotely suggesting recreation or travel beyond the city limits of one's hometown.

The archery business was going very well, however. Raw materials for making bows were not on the rationed lists and men, away in training camps and at home in defense plants, liked the sport of archery as a change from their strenuous routines.

We did our fair share of defense work also in our small factory in Detroit. So close to the center of the greatest automotive industry in the world, converted now to the war effort, we ran a constant flow of jobs suited to our particular set-up. These jobs, together with the growing demand for bows helped us grow and growing called for new and better ways to make archery equipment.

An absorbing problem confronting me in those days was a hunting head for arrows that would be effective on larger game than the soft skinned deer I had been hunting. Canada was not far from Michigan and up there was the lordly moose that I was sure could be success-fully hunted with the bow and arrow. We had developed a stronger broadhead but there had been no opportunity to test it and with the war dragging relentlessly on, no opportunity seemed likely.

After several months of frustration, we decided to go by train. My diary dated October 12, 1942, says we left Detroit at 7:45 a.m. and got into St. Paul at 7:30 that evening. I was with a group of friends all hunting with guns. They tolerated my bow and arrows good naturedly, confident that I'd get nothing if I didn't use a gun. We changed to the Northern Pacific at St. Paul, leaving there at 9:40 p.m. There were no sleepers available so we had to sleep in our seats.

Arriving at International Falls the next morning, our baggage was not with us. We had no choice but to go on without it after making arrangements with a taxi to bring it up the next morning for $12.00, an exorbitant taxi fee in 1942. We got into camp on a beautiful lake just before dark.

This is the whitetail Fred shot in a blinding snowstorm while making his first hunting film at Blaney Park, Michigan, with Jack Van Coevering. Friday the 13th, November, 1942.

Early hunt at Blaney Park. K.K. Knickerbocher is third from the left. A.J. Michelson, first president of the N.F.A.A. in the center (dark coat and glasses). Nels Grumley, Fred's bowmaker, third from right and Fred Bear in front, 1943.

We had two Indian guides on this first trip, "Smoky" Lorne Fadden of Gaudry's Camp, Kenora, Ontario and "Hank" Henry Nordin of Bergland, Ontario. Both were fascinated with my bow and arrow and completely astonished when I shot partridges and spruce hens with it.

There were about 35 hunters in the camp and there was much confusion about guides and boats. Frank Ash, member of the Swan Creek Conservation Station at Allegan, Michigan and I went with one of the guides to look for moose on some islands nearby. We saw tracks and some sign but it was not until five days later that I got my first shot at a moose. Missed, but what a hunk of meat, I wrote in my notes.

It was very hot the first week in camp. I wrote toward the end of the week that "I was damn near carried off by the ravens today. Guess I had better take a bath." By Tuesday of the following week it had cooled off and a strong wind was blowing. By the end of the week, there was snow in the air.

There had been no fresh moose signs for several days and the guides wanted to give up and hunt deer, but we told them we had deer at home and had come up here for moose. I was disappointed not to have a chance to try out my new hunting heads. We persuaded the guides to make another scouting trip, which they did, getting back on Friday and reporting that they had jumped a bull moose and cow.

Saturday, October 24th, the two guides and I started after them. We traveled about five miles through rough country. It was cold and snowing with a strong wind. When we got to the area where Smokey and Hank had seen the moose we separated, Smokey circling one way and Hank and I another. The country was hilly and burned over, making walking difficult. Toward noon Smokey ran into the bull and we heard some shots. He was too far away and the shots were not good ones. The cow showed up through the trees and we found the bull's trail behind her. There was not much blood, but what there was showed up plainly on the fresh snow.

We trailed him for some time and then he appeared suddenly from a little patch of spruce about 15 yards ahead. The bull looked at me, trotted about two lengths and stopped. I gave him two arrows low in the chest behind the front leg. He stood there a few seconds and then fell over, stiff-legged, on his side, breaking both my arrows.

Deer hunting near Boulder Junction, Wisconsin, in 1941. From left: Otto Blaho, John Brikoski and Fred Bear.

Fred Bear and companions on an early hunt at Blaney Park.

That was all. I can't claim him for the bow, but I learned some things about my equipment for moose hunting. A postmortem revealed the following: One arrow through both sides of the chest, the other went in about half-way — cutting off a rib. I did not have any more arrows to make further penetration tests, but the hide on the front of the chest is about 3/8 of an inch thick and I feel certain that one would have to have a hundred pound bow and very much heavier arrows to get into the chest from the front.

He was a beautiful animal and looked most damned big looking at me at fifteen paces in the open. My bow seemed suddenly inadequate and if he had started my way, I think I would have dropped it and headed for the timber. His antlers are about 10" shorter than my strung bow and he stood, at the shoulders, about three inches higher than my head. Making him seven feet to the top of his head and eight feet to the top of his horns.

1943

The next year I tried again for moose. Ken Knickerbocker of Barrington, Illinois, was my hunting partner this time. We made the trip by train as before and hunted with Archie MacDonald at Cliff Lake near Quibell, Ontario. We went up in mid-September — hunting season opened the 15th that year.

We were up at six a.m. the first day and hunted from a sturdy, square-sterned canoe with a five horsepower motor. This enabled us to cover a great deal of territory and scouting the little creeks ,we ran across several cow moose but no bulls. We got some good footage with the camera, however and always hoped that the next day would bring better luck.

After a few days of fruitless hunting I wrote, "We fished for about two hours this afternoon and I caught a ten or twelve pound musky. We took pictures and then turned him loose. Had another, still larger one on the hook but he did cartwheels on top of the water and shook himself loose. We hunted the rest of the day but saw nothing except a snow white seagull sharing a fish with a coal black crow."

There were hundreds of trees going to waste up there. Plenty of poplar twenty inches in diameter and Jack pine eighteen inches across that grew straight up for 25 or 30 feet. There were vast stretches of Norway pine, white ash and black spruce with a scattering of cedar,

Hunting in the St. Helen area of Michigan, 1940. Left to right: Barney Grenier, Nels Grumley, Bill Loomis and Fred Bear.

Fred drying his cold, wet socks over a campfire at Blaney Park, 1942.

tamarack and birch. Small islands in the lake were covered so thickly with black spruce that from a distance they looked like storm clouds. The lake was clean and cold with hilly, rock shores.

By Sunday, we were tenting on Cliff Lake at the Pickeral Lake Portage. We had two tents, one for Vic and Bill, our guides and the other for Knick and me. They were warm and comfortable with down filled sleeping bags and air mattresses. Someone had put kerosene in the gas lantern, however, so Vic poured it out into a Canadian Club bottle, made a wick from his shirttail and I wrote my notes by this light from then on.

We were so confident of finding moose that we'd towed a freight canoe coming in to haul the moose horns, hide and meat back to main camp.

Waiting for the guides to set up camp, Knick and I did some fishing in Pickeral Lake for Jackfish to use as bear bait. The lake was full of Jackfish that took any kind of bait. We caught a dozen or more in an hour running from two to eleven pounds.

We hunted all around this area for several days with no luck. I got some footage of a Pileated woodpecker (called Woodcock here and Jack-of-the-Woods in Michigan). But we were discouraged by this time and went back to the main camp. Just two hours before we got back, a nice bull had walked by camp and a caribou had swum the lake...

A night or so after this, I was writing in a trapper's cabin on the shores of a nameless lake. On the door, outside, was written in pencil, LEAVE THIS CABIN *A LONE* and was signed, "Victor McQueen."

Vic and I had decided to go up there and scout the country. It was an exhausting job getting in with four portages. We both carried the canoe and then went back for the motor and other things on the second trip. It was beautiful country, though and a wonderful day. I took many pictures. Vic had a nice cabin, well built, with two stoves to keep us warm. We had a spruce hen for dinner, which cost me three broadheads. I went to bed tired that night, wondering whether I was built for toting freight over portages.

We hunted the area thoroughly the next day but saw no big game. I did get some fine pictures, however.

On Sunday the 23rd, Knick shot a duck with his bow and saw his first bull. Hopes were high that night. The cows were beginning to

Jim Henderson and Fred Bear on a hunt in western Ontario, 1946. Fred's first bear hangs on the pole.

call. But the weather was still warm and the mosquitoes bad. We had a German war prisoner in camp temporarily on this date.

Until Thursday of the following week we made drives, hunted from canoes and scouted on foot but saw no moose except a cow or two.

At one point when Knick and I were separated from the guides, I shot a nice buck. Vic and Bill were very surprised to find us with a deer since, of course, they had heard no shots. We took pictures and I wrote up my notes of this episode on a canoe paddle laid across my knees for a desk.

The only arrows we shot on the last day were into the wall of the dining cabin as a memento of our hunt there.

Two milestones occurred in Fred's life during 1945 — he and his wife Ann Marie were divorced and went their separate ways (they had no children and the parting was amicable — a case of Fred's love of the field and Ann Marie's preference for the city) and in the fall of that year he felled a record class Canadian Moose with his bow and arrow. Archery Magazine printed his journal concerning this hunt.

MOOSE DIARY
by Fred Bear

Sunday, September 17, 1945 — K.K. Knickerbocker and I left his home near Chicago before daylight this morning. Drove to Duluth and then northwest to arrive in International Falls as darkness fell. Crossed the river and spent an hour clearing customs on the Canadian side. Officials had difficulty finding a classification for an entry of an armful of bows and several cases of arrows but between grins they wished us luck and sent us on our way.

Am writing this from our room in the Rainy Lake Hotel at Fort Frances. Knick and I thought it would be in keeping with the weather to put up here, as we have been driving through rain since early afternoon. Were given special permission by the police to park our car and trailer in front of the hotel rather than the unlighted lot in the rear. One of the pictures they have hanging here in the lobby is of my last year's guide, Victor McQueen, proudly standing over a giant moose.

Fred and his first bow and arrow bear, 1946.

Canada, 1945. A fledgling outdoor photoqrapher and film-maker, Fred loads his still camera. His early movie camera is at his feet.

Monday, the 18th — Rain again today. Arrived at Archie McDonald's place in Quibell before noon, parked the car, sorted baggage, changed to woods clothes and had lunch.

Shortly after lunch we left by truck for Clay Lake, crossed it in a powerboat and made the two and a half mile portage by horse and wagon. At Twilight Lake, we found our hunting canoes with 5-horse outboards awaiting us and came on north through Twilight, Evening and Mystery Lakes. Had a cold rain all the way and were glad to enter the cheery warmth of the main camp here on Cliff Lake and to get a good meal under our belts. It was a pleasure to see Mrs. McDonald and Herman the head guide again and to learn that we would have our last year's guides, Vic and Bill.

We spent this evening talking over plans for our hunt and reminiscing about our hunt here last year. The boys have a complete camping outfit ready and our plans are to leave in the morning for a selected campsite about 50 miles north of here on the Cedar River near the north end of Lake Wabaskang.

Tuesday the 19th — Raining hard this morning and blowing, too. Cliff Lake is too rough to navigate, so we putter about camp. Rain finally stops and the wind goes down somewhat, so we take off. Made the half mile portage to the Cedar Lake Camp and had more bad weather, so decided to stay there and leave early in the morning before the high winds come up.

Knick and Bill went out to fish and hunt while Vic and I went hunting. Saw a doe. On our way back to camp, we paddled quietly up to the summer camp dump. A cute little brown bear was there pawing among the refuse, too small to shoot on the first day out, I decided. He saw us and made off into the bushes. We paddled close to the shore and waited quietly within ten yards of the dump. Apparently he was both curious and hungry, for we soon located his beady little eyes peering at us through some bushes. After a lapse of time, we heard him make his way through the brush, circling to come out to the left of where we were.

Whenever he came to an opening, he would first peek at us through bushes, size up the situation and then in a very dignified but nonchalant manner stroll slowly across without looking in our direction. As soon as he reached cover, he would quickly turn to see how we took it. Three times he did this, crossing the same opening,

Fred with record-class moose taken with his bow in Ontario, 1945.

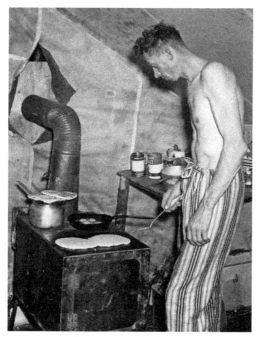

A sleepy-eyed cook makes some pancakes before setting out on the day's hunt. Ontario, 1946.

a space 15 feet wide, not more than 15 yards from our canoe. It was the chance of a lifetime for pictures but it was raining and almost dark. We paddled slowly back to camp and left him to tend to the business of filling his stomach.

Wednesday the 20th — Left Cedar Camp about nine this morning. Plenty of rain and wind again. Went up the "Narrows," through Perrault Lake. Portaged around Perrault Falls and continued on across Wabaskang Lake to our campsite. The spot is known as "The Jump-Over" and has been so named because it is a short portage; one needs only to toss equipment over the rock that extends across the river and acts as a dam where Wabaskang becomes the Cedar River.

Our camp is on a small hill that rises from the rock. From it we can see up and down the river for a half mile. The lake water spills over the rock with a drop of about 10 feet, creating some nice eddies and looks like a good place for fish. We brought casting rods with us and intend to fish at every opportunity.

Thursday the 21st — Great morning for a change. No sun, but anything short of rain is good weather to us now. Up before daylight and got the camp in ship shape — two 8 x 10 wall tents and a fly to cook under. Have a small stove with an undersized pipe in one of the tents — can only have a limited fire in it, too much and she belches back out the draft hole and fills the tent with smoke. If smoke kills human odor, we should be in top shape to stalk moose.

Friday the 22nd — Weather looked threatening this morning, so we hunted the bush near camp. Planned to have lunch here together at noon. Saw a doe and a cross fox. Shot an arrow at the fox but failed to connect. Came back to camp and had lunch, then went downriver with the motor, through the creek and into Wine Lake. Met an Indian in a canoe. Gave him an arrow and a cigarette and tried to strike up a conversation. Mostly about where we could find a bull moose. All we could get out of him was yes and no and a few grins. He had a rifle in his canoe and said he had just shot at a cow but missed.

Saw a total of seven deer today. Caught a few fish. Knick and Bill came in saying they had seen nothing but had caught many fish. These fish will tackle almost any kind of casting lure. We have filed the barbs off the hooks so they can be released with less injury.

Saturday the 23rd — Another wet day. Have had rain every day since we came. Our evening meals at camp are really something. Af-

Fred bags a fine whitetail buck on a hunt in Ontario, 1943.

Fred finds an old trapper's cabin in Ontario. A bear had broken through the roof and raised havoc inside.

ter a week in the bush, it is amazing what one can stow away without ill effects. Bill is chief cook and issues all orders at this period. Vic acts as general utility man, peels potatoes and does general K.P. duty. We use dead standing jackpine for wood. Usually bring a couple of logs with us when we return from hunting, as there are none on the hill or adjacent to camp. Cooking is done over an open fire under the fly. The conversation is varied as we huddle about the fire during meal time. Knick gripes at Bill for not having a moose tied up for him beforehand and Vic wonders how his newborn daughter, whom he has not yet seen, is getting along. The sun goes down about 5:30. Our meal is finished by 8:30 or 9:00 o'clock. We check the hunting clothes to see how they are drying and then turn in.

Sunday the 24th — Well, we have company! Knick went out the little path back of the tent this morning before daylight and met a good-sized black bear facing him at close range. Knick turned the flashlight on and stared him down (he claims). The bear finally made off and Knick concluded that it would be wiser to walk this path during daylight hours. An owl kept up raspy screeches from trees about camp all night.

Did some reconnoitering and find the place is covered with bear trails. The path to our outhouse is a bear trail. Another goes along the river past the rack where the motors are hung. Our tent sits right in the middle of one that leads through a berry patch behind the camp. Trails all over the hill that rises back of camp.

The bear has taken the fish we hung up near the river. This is fine, our license includes the taking of bear and this one would make a good-sized trophy.

Vic and I went to Wine Lake today. As we passed the Indian camp they waved us down. They had killed a young bull moose and wanted to know if we would be interested in buying the head and antlers. Not just exactly in those words: the youngest squaw pointed to it and said "You wanna buy?" The skinned and quartered carcass was lying on the rocks at the water's edge and was being sniffed suspiciously by an assortment of off-breed dogs. The men were very skinny and the women were very plump. They have tents as temporary quarters while they are replacing a cabin that had burned last winter. The old man of the group got quite a kick out of my binoculars and bow and arrows.

Detroit Sport Shaw in 1939, showing interest at the Bear Archery booth. Fred is on the right and his first wife, Marie, is on the far left.

Bear booth, manned by Nels Grumley, at the Grand American Open in Milwaukee, 1939. This was the first archery money shoot. Bear Archery pioneered in the introduction of aluminum arrows.

Vic and I felt full of steam and climbed the highest mountain just to explore the country and see if the hill really was greener on the other side. Found the top to be bald. Just a big oval rock top with some scrub jackpine and blueberry bushes growing out of the cracks. Plenty of old moose, deer and bear sign but nothing fresh. On the way down we ran into a big buck. He ran off and I followed, got a shot at about sixty yards, good elevation but not a good line.

Met Knick and Bill as we were crossing Wine Lake. Knick was leaning back on a good-sized lake trout and grinning from ear to ear. Got my rod into action and we had a good hour's fun with the trout. These fish, taken on casting equipment when they are up in shallow water at this time of year, are the best fighters I know of. Was dark when we got back to camp this evening. Knick and Bill had gone in earlier and surprised the bear in the culinary department helping himself. Knick shot at him as he was making off but claims the bear was going faster than the arrow.

Monday the 25th — Last night, we decided to hunt together for a change and chose the unnamed lake where Vic and I had seen the cows and deer the first day hunting. Day was just breaking as we prepared to shove off. A strange light appeared in the east and Knick predicted that the sun was really going to come out and shine for us. As we went down river Old Sol burst over the tree tops, melted the river mist and brought the frostbitten leaves out in full color. Wonderful day, wonderful world. Strong breeze coming in from the south, not too cold, not too warm. Ducks rising ahead of us, ravens and eagles soaring overhead, whiskey jacks unusually friendly. Small wonder after ten days of rain.

Knick and Bill started out ahead. We paddled past them on the river as they were exploring a bay. Paddled through the creek into "Arrow Lake" (just named it) and were sitting there in the canoe studying the shore line. Just as Knick and Bill came out of the creek behind us, a rack of antlers with a bull moose attached stepped out of the alders into the shallow water across the lake. I put the glass on him and saw that he was walking along the shore, down-wind in our direction.

We crouched low in the canoes and paddled vigorously to the far shore to land in the high reeds a good 300 yards ahead of the bull. I jumped out before the canoe beached, ran into the bush and took a game trail parallel to the water's edge. Went towards the moose as fast as silence would permit until I came to a trail leading to the lake, which led me to the shore about 200 yards from the canoe.

The wind was blowing strong and making noise in the leaves. Although I had reached the water's edge, I could not see along shore because of overhanging bushes and wondered if my plans of ambush had gone wrong as they have many times in the past.

After a few anxious moments, I heard him splashing and grunting and finally caught sight of his majesty through a hole in the bushes. He was 60 or 70 yards away, walking toward me in two feet of water about 25 yards offshore. Just that glimpse was worth the trip up here. The sun shining brightly on a set of antlers too big to even wish for, cast highlights off his glossy black coat as well.

It's tough on the nerves to hear that monster splashing and grunting and all the while coming your way unseen. I was ashamed to find myself wondering if it would not be better just to take his picture and let it go at that. Knick and Bill and Vic were waiting in the canoe downshore. I had a mental picture of them standing on tiptoe to see over the reeds to witness this bit of drama; the moose and I were the actors. I was to be the hero and the bull was to be the victim.

My mind went back to the two weeks we spent last year and the week just past looking for just this thing. I could even recall numerous statements I had made about how I would fell a big moose with the broadheads I was sharpening with a file in camp evenings. I would shear ribs as if they were matchsticks. Nope, I was on the spot. This was it.

Then it happened. The bull walked into my opening. No time for dallying now. The hole was narrow and action fast as I drew back full length and drove a big four-blade head into the center of his rib section. He stiffened and froze for an instant, then turned and made three lunges out into the lake and stopped in about three feet of water. He then decided to make for shore but rolled over in the attempted turn. Just a tip of an antler and a small section of his body were visible above the water. I let out my victory yell and Knick answered from just a short way down the shore. He had left the canoe shortly after I did and had located a spot to intercept the bull in case he got by me. Much handshaking as Vic and Bill came paddling up with anxious puzzled expressions on their faces. They had been unable to see over the reeds and asked which way he went. I pointed to the visible remains and Vic said, "Well, I'll be damned!"

Biggest problem was to get him on shore. We hooked both canoes together and with both motors going towed him across the lake to hard ground. We cut birch trees to use as skids and rolled and tugged until we had him out of the water and went to work with the cameras. Made some tea and had lunch.

The arrow had gone between ribs. Through both lungs and through a rib on the far side and wedged there.

Finally finished with the meat and loaded it into the canoes. Vic and I took most of it so Knick and Bill could hunt on the way back. When we came into camp, we found the bear had paid us another visit. He was making camp life interesting. The bear had eaten a batch of prunes, a loaf of bread, bit through a cocoa can and chewed a can of lard until only bits of tin were left. Have agreed that he is Knick's bear since he was the first to encounter him at close range on the path. I have a clause in there to waive this claim in case he starts chewing on me.

Put a tape on the moose antlers — 48 inch spread. Wide heavy palms and 27 points. Across the ears he measures 31 inches. Six foot two at the shoulders. The boys estimate his weight at 1500 pounds and guess him to be 15 years old.

Tuesday the 26th — Woke up this morning as Knick and Bill were preparing to leave for hunting. Had slept through the breakfast period. Vic and I plan to trim up the meat, pepper it and sew it up in burlap we brought for that purpose and get everything ready so we can leave early tomorrow before the wind comes up on the big lakes. Plan to take it down to the ice house at main camp.

Last night we piled the moose meat on the rock beside the river and covered it with a tarp. This morning we discover that the bear has made off with some of the meat and Vic's tarp, which makes him very unhappy but which we later recover a short way into the bush.

Wednesday the 27th — Waiting now for something to eat. After wards we plan to make the first leg of our trip back to the tent camp and go over to Cedar Lake and spend the night in a fishing camp there. This will give us a better start in the morning and will get us across Wabaskang with a chance of missing the high winds.

Thursday the 28th, 4 p.m. — Here we are storm-bound at the

Fred Bear in his office at 2611 Philadelphia Avenue, Detroit.

deserted Indian Reservation on Lake Wabaskang. Left Cedar Lake camp this morning. Had fair going to Perrault Falls, where we had tea amid snow flurries. Came across the portage and started north again.

The storm forced us on shore here at 1 p.m. Regular gale blowing and the lake is plenty rough. Tried to navigate but turned back. Vic says we could make it with a new canoe but ours is of prewar vintage and might break in two. Vic thinks the wind will ease up at sundown.

Friday the 29th — Pulled in last night at 1:00 a.m. Dragged the canoe up and Vic started to carry the motor over the rock. Called for the flashlight which I brought up and there, not even 15 feet away, was a bear that would go 250 lbs dressed. Stood there facing us.

Sunday, October 1st — Except for some mice trying to make a

nest in my hair, I had a good sleep last night. Last week's frosts have colored the leaves. The scrub maple and hazel are bright red. Birch are a golden yellow. Next comes the poplar in a very light green. Cedars are a darker shade followed by the tamarack, balsam and jackpine, backed up by dark spruce.

Tuesday the 3rd — We had a royal feast at midnight. Moose tenderloin fried in onions and bacon, diced red beets, canned pears, canned blueberries, cake, cookies and some tannic acid that Vic calls tea. (Just spliced to a piece of hazel to make my pencil stub longer.) Vic is a good guide and a hard worker. He talks to himself and sings when he is running the motor. He is an agreeable fellow and was very impressed when I bagged the big moose with my bow. Bill is a prince of a fellow, too and Knick keeps things going about camp. The trees have turned color rapidly in the last few days. Tamarack are a very pale yellow now. Plan to leave here for the outside tomorrow morning. The trip will be rather uneventful I suppose. Unless we run into more bears I will write no more.

****

The fall of 1946 found Fred heading north into Ontario for his fourth trip. This time he was accompanied by Jim Henderson of Detroit. Jim had a moose license while Fred intended to hunt bear. The previous year he had seen several black bears and hoped to get one on this trip. The men hired Johnny Negonapinee, an Ojibway Indian guide at Quibell. Johnny was a small, trim man with piercing black eyes, a sparse mustache and a dark copper complexion that Fred admired and wished he could acquire before each year's hunting season as an aid to camouflage.

They set up camp on Lake Wabaskang again. The guide had been told Bear and Henderson were bowhunters but this had created only mild interest. When the packs were undone and no guns appeared Johnny was skeptical about their tackle. He plucked the bowstrings, however, and carefully examined the arrows, showing signs of respect when he thumbed the keen edged broadheads. His respect was greatly compounded when on the first day of hunting, Jim made a perfect shot on a good-sized bull moose.

Fred got a nice black bear that came near their camp a few days later, drawn in by the tantalizing scents of moose meat and northern pike they had caught for camp fare. This was probably one of the first Canadian black bears to be killed by a modem bowhunter and was the first of a series of fascinating encounters Fred had with this species during his hunting career.

Left to right: Pat Chambers, Larry Whiffen, "Babe" Branaka, Fred Bear and H. King with Fred's mechanical deer target at the 1952 N.F.A.A. Tournament in Minneapolis.

JIM'S FIRST MOOSE
by Fred Bear

Knick Knickerbocker and I had been planning another moose and bear hunt and had arranged to go back to the same place we were last year.

It was a very bleak day for both of us when Knick phoned about a month before the season opened and advised that business conditions would not permit him to get away. I had business problems too but had kept fighting my conscience and telling myself that everything was in top shape. Knick's decision brought me to my senses and I told him to cancel our camp arrangements and I would abandon any thought of going.

For a week, I did not earn my salt. My mind was far away and then Jim Henderson dropped into the shop. Someone asked him if he would like to go moose hunting. He thought it was me, said yes and that is why I am writing these lines, sitting alone in our snug tent while rain patters down at the "Jump-Over" on the north end of Lake Wabaskang at the mouth of the Cedar River in western Ontario.

Jim is an archer of several years, pulls a mean bow and is at home in the woods. We left Detroit last Friday noon by auto, pulling a utility trailer loaded with camp equipment, two motors and a 12-foot skiff.

A short way out of Fort William we rented an 18-foot canoe and lashed it to the top of the car.

Drove into Dryden at noon Sunday. Had not been able to reclaim our camp reservations with Archie MacDonald with whom we hunted last year and I had wired my friend, Doctor Jack Pickup of Dryden, practically demanding that he locate a guide for us.

Had lunch with Jack and his pleasant wife, Mary, and learned that we might be able to obtain an Indian guide near Quibell. Drove up there in the afternoon and met Johnny Negonapinee (pronounced Ne-gon-a-pin-ee). John is an Ojibway, living in tents with a party of about 25 of his people in a poplar grove along the Canadian National Railway near Quibell. Ernie Paradais introduced us and made the arrangements in the Ojibway tongue, as John speaks little English. We were to meet him Monday when the sun was high.

Had a good night's sleep and were on our way next morning. The portage at Perrault Falls was quite a task and Jim wanted to know if photo film became lighter after it was exposed. Johnny went to work, however, and we were soon across. The rest of the trip was rather uneventful. Some rain and wind but we docked at the campsite and had camp established by nightfall.

Next morning we put the camp ship-shape, cut wood, had lunch and then paddled down the river to the lower portage. Saw no game. Jim caught a 36-inch northern pike at the falls here at camp.

Fishing is not as good as it was last year when we could catch a walleye anytime we wanted fish to eat. Neither the weather nor the water is as cold and I doubt if the trout are up to spawn yet. Hung Jim's big pike on a tree. This will tell us whether there are any bear cruising this area.

This is the waterway for points north. Never saw so many hunting parties; one or two a day.

John says he is 65 years old. Got the question across by asking him, "How many winters?" He held up both hands, counted to six on his fingers and then held up one hand.

He is a pleasant, jolly fellow, as were the friends of his that we met. He washes when he gets up in the morning, before each meal and again before he goes to bed. With him he has a medium size pack-sack containing three cotton quilts, a pair of leather boots, a can of Copenhagen and nice shiny hair clippers. These clippers were immediately unpacked and have since been on display on a board beside his bunk. Have not questioned him in this respect. Apparently, they are a prized possession and he is most likely the tribe barber. Perhaps he will cut our hair; better still, we may cut his.

John has good heavy wool underwear, a wool shirt, wool pants, rubber hunting boots in addition to the leather ones and a water-proof lined jacket and wears a black felt hat that has a high crown and a narrow brim. But he has no knife, not even a pocketknife.

John sleeps in his underwear on one of his quilts and covers with the other two, huddled up with his knees pulled up to his chest. He is very active and strong. We have given him to understand that Jim wants a moose and I want a bear. We got the idea across that we had to be close to game and, I believe, convinced him that we might kill a partridge after we had shot some blunts through a cedar board.

Wednesday noon. John took our map, pointed to the northeast end of Lake Wabaskang, said "MOOSE," and grinned. We piled into the canoe and were off. Paddled for about two miles. Jim shot at a duck and while we were looking for the arrow, John said excitedly, "Moose, moose in water!" and started paddling out into the lake and towards a bay we had passed earlier. "Big moose," added John and Jim, who sat in the bow, grabbed a paddle.

I took the binoculars but could see nothing. Jim took them and got the same result. After about five minutes of paddling, I pointed to the motor. John grinned and shook his head to mean yes. He cannot run it, so we changed places and were on our way. At about this time, Jim and I sighted the moose. He was swimming the bay and was almost to shore. I opened the motor wide, still a half mile away as he disappeared in the tall reeds.

As we rounded a cluster of reeds there stood his black hulk among the reeds in about a foot of water. I made a blind stab for the throttle

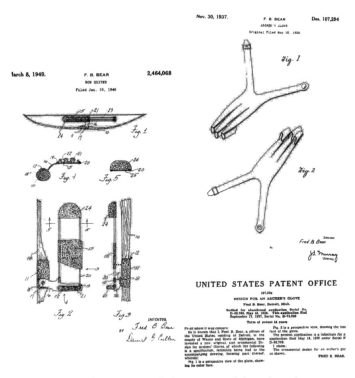

Early Fred Bear patents, the bowquiver and the archery glove.

but grabbed a spark plug instead. Almost upset the canoe getting loose from it, but finally stopped the noise.

The moose was feeding in the water, so we waited until he raised his head and identified him as a good-sized bull.

We were about 200 yards away at this time and John was in the rear, as we slowly closed that gap. Seventy yards, sixty, fifty, forty-five, forty. I felt that we were overtaxing the law of averages and whispered to Jim to shoot at somewhere between 35 and 40 yards. I lost sight of the arrow in the reeds but heard it hit as the bull threw mud getting out of there. He ran along shore then angled out into the lake and stopped broadside at about 60 yards.

We separated and "blind" hunted in hope of finding him on the ground. Soon I heard a call and hurried over to find Johnny standing beside the bull, grinning from ear to ear.

He had fallen 20 yards from where he left the lake. Went down beside a spruce wind-fall.

After proper ceremonies over the fallen monarch, we set about to find the arrow. It had gone between ribs, through the heart and lodged against a rib on the far side. Jim had made a perfect shot on the first moose we saw on our first day of hunting. He was a good sized bull carrying eight points on a nice symmetrical 35-inch spread.

After an hour of filming, we loaded everything in the canoe, headed back for camp and wondered how we could keep that moose in good shape in such warm weather.

The remainder of the day was spent in preparing the meat. This was done by covering all exposed parts with black pepper and sewing it up in clean burlap bags we brought with us for that purpose. John erected a "meat pole," and we hung our parcels up high and dry, protected from the sun by a tarpaulin.

Two pieces of the rib section about a foot square that the arrow had passed through were chopped out and spiked to trees about six feet up. We wanted the "Whiskey Jacks" to pick the bones clean so we could observe the effects of the arrow where it had struck bone.

While doing this, I noted that the fish had been taken — I hoped by the bear. With this encouragement, it seemed proper to pursue the same tactics as before and the moose head was placed near camp and connected by a fine wire to a cluster of empty tin cans secured to a springy stake inside the tent.

About midnight, I was awakened by a rasping noise that sounded like claws sliding down a tree. Fell asleep again and was later brought to my feet by a violent banging of cans that awakened Jim too. We peered into the darkness and saw that the head had been dragged about 20 feet, but the bear was not in sight. After a long wait, his head and shoulders came into view over the ridge. He was silhouetted against the river background, but would not come closer and finally walked off down the river.

We waited about ten minutes and then stepped outside. The bear was on the trail where Knick met him last year; he was walking away.

Next morning was warm and raining. Jim decided he had better get that meat on ice, so he and Johnny loaded the canoe and set out for the 40-mile trip to Cedar Lake, expecting to be back the following afternoon.

I am sitting alone in our tent writing these notes as the rain patters down on our camp.

The rasping sounds I heard last night were the spikes leaving wood as the bear took the rib section we had put up for the Whiskey Jacks. He also made off with another fish and I have hopes of making connection with him tonight.

Being alone offered an excellent opportunity to be quiet and perhaps lure him into camp in daytime and get pictures.

The antlers are chopped from the moose head and wired high in a tree for cleaning by Whiskey Jacks. The head is securely wired and spiked to a tree 35 feet from the tent. Just in case he comes after dark, a fine signal wire is attached to the cans inside the tent and strung on trees down beyond the one where the head is fastened.

Just as I finish this job, an Indian family pass by and I trade a moose tenderloin for some wild rice. They are man and wife, about 65 years old, with a 2-year-old papoose which they explain by pointing to the child and saying, "mama dead." They and their equipment are clean and orderly. Both paddle the canoe, with the youngster tucked away in the bow.

The tent flap is prepared for a shot in the direction of the moose head. Strings are fastened to the flap so that it can be drawn to make a vertical opening about six inches wide and two feet high. I had made a small slit beside the stovepipe to serve as a peek hole and for photography.

The fire has burned out, so I put on all my extra clothing and settle down to be quiet. Cameras are all arranged and set for current light conditions. Whiskey Jacks are doing double duty on the skull and a Downy Woodpecker pecks at a poplar tree here beside camp.

The day, a dreary one, drags slowly by and as the light becomes weaker I keep pace by opening the diaphragms on the cameras. At 4:40 p.m., they are opened up to 1.5. This is as far as I can go and 15 minutes later they are put away in their cases.

When this is finished, I have another peek through the hole and there is the bear coming up our path toward the tent.

He spots the moose head and walks over there but notices the fine wire that leads to the cans. This he does not like. He sniffs it suspiciously and makes a long detour around it and up to the tree. He stands up on his back legs, gets a firm hold on the neck with his teeth and gives one husky yank. The spikes and wire hold, but his teeth pull out of the meat and in regaining his balance, he strikes the signal wire with a paw. This makes a hell of a racket and scatters cans

106

all over the tent. The bear leaves on the run.

As yet, I have not opened the flap. Want him to get real busy at the head and not notice this action.

Fifteen minutes later he comes up over the hill again but will have nothing to do with that head. He walks up to within 10 feet of the tent and looks things over. Our casting rods with baits attached are leaning against the tree below the moose antlers. He sniffs these and then stands up and puts his nose on the antlers that are over six feet up. I have visions of him getting caught in the fishhooks when he drops down on all fours and wonder how a person lands a bear on casting equipment. He spots a piece of meat we have put out for the birds, takes this and goes off into the bush.

Up until now my shooting hole has been open. It is arranged for a shot towards the bait and requires some changes for game on the path or at the tree that contains the antlers. These changes are quickly made and the hole opened. I also have to clear out part of the pantry to be able to crouch behind and shoot over the stove.

Shortly after this the bruin appears broadside at the washstand 10 feet from the tent. I start to draw and he ambles over to the tree. I have to get behind the stove for this angle and just as I do he stretches up for the antlers with his back toward me.

I snap-shoot an arrow into him hoping to enter the lung cavity. When the arrow strikes, I know that I have my bear at last.

Thus ended our two-week Canadian hunt, which had been made most pleasant by fine weather and good hunting. Vowing to return soon, we hurried home to be kings for a while, at least with 500 pounds of meat in our meatless OPA country.

While all these early bowhunting trips were taking place, Fred was also spending long hours experimenting with new products designed to improve the sport. One of his earliest archery tackle innovations came about as a result of a small game hunt. He was after snowshoe rabbits in a very thick, swampy area near Newaygo one snowy winter day. Each time he kicked up a rabbit he found it impossible to shoot because there wasn't enough space to maneuver the long-limbed bow into position.

Returning to the plant, he directed Nels Grumley to make a shorter bow with wider limbs. This Osage orange, (tougher than lemonwood and better able to withstand cold weather) "Bush Bow" was an immediate success with the bowhunting fraternity, proving to be a considerably more convenient woods weapon than the old longbow.

Fred's first patented archery invention was the shooting glove. Prior to its introduction, archers used separate finger stalls that slipped over the ends of the drawing fingers. These were uncomfortable and often flipped off when the bowstring was released. Fred made a skeleton glove composed of a back, three finger stalls and a wrist strap to hold it in place. He filed for a patent on this item in 1936 and it was granted in 1937.

His next important patent was a bow quiver that fastened to the side of the bow with a threaded brass bushing and screw in early models and spring steel arms that slipped over the bow limbs later on. The bow quiver patent, entered in 1946, was one of the very few to go through the patent office with absolutely no references cited. This type of quiver is still used by practically all archers who hunt with a bow.

Bear also invented the modern style armguard used to protect the bow arm from the slap of the bowstring. Another first was a fletching jig that applied feathers to an arrow shaft in a spiral pattern, an aid to flight stability. Shooting rough fish such as carp and suckers with the bow and arrow was a growing off-season sport and Bear devised a simple bowfishing reel that was fastened to the back, or outside, of the bow. Many more innovations were to emerge from his analytical mind as time went on.

In 1943, Fred began studying the problem of bow portability. He experimented with take-down models but did not readily come up with what he considered a satisfactory product. He could not find a way to produce a take-down bow that kept costs within the desired limits. Then other more pressing problems caused him to shelve the idea temporarily but twenty years passed before he found time to perfect the design for his beautiful streamlined take-down bow of today.

Often, inventors turn out original and tricky items only to find there is no market for them. Bear was fortunate in possessing a natural marketing instinct. He seemed able to determine whether there would be a market for something he had in mind. He also had the ability to design products that could be produced economically.

Beautiful and functional hunting bows soon became his company's major product. They were made of Osage orange, yew, or lemonwood and backed with a layer of material such as sinew, silk, or rawhide to provide added strength and prolonged life.

In time, Bear began to recurve the limbs and add "brush nocks" to the tips. These kept vegetation from jamming between the bow and bowstring in heavy cover. His first recurved limbs had static tips that curved away from the shooter and lengthened the bow at full draw, resulting in smoother, faster action. By the 1950's, Bear's 'working recurve' became the standard design for all composite bows.

The first Bear bows were expertly designed and performed well but because they were made one at a time, few were produced and they were expensive. A good bowyer in the early days of Bear Archery Company was a combination of talented mechanic and artist, someone who could take a rough billet of wood, study it and get the most out of it, just as a diamond cutter studies a stone before deciding how best to cut it. It was hard to find good bowyers and as artists they were likely to be prima donnas and thus difficult to handle. In the late 1940's however, the production of bows changed drastically.

During the second World War, Bear was commissioned by General Motors to make wooden models of anti-aircraft guns for use in training. He also turned out models of a 2-cycle internal combustion engine used in instruction classes. By interchanging parts on the models, instructors could show how 4-cycle engines functioned. Bear did this work in his plant while his employees were busy making archery products.

Around this time, an engineer from the Coming Glass Company dropped into the plant with a sample of woven fiber glass developed during the war. When he mentioned that it was elastic, Fred immediately showed interest, thinking it might be useful in bow construction. He took some of the material to a chemist friend, Don Swayze, who was in charge of Chrysler's Cycleweld Division and had invented a resin to bond rubber to metal.

Swayze did some experimenting, coating the fiberglass with resin then curing it in a press. He came up with a material suitable for use on the back or extension side of a bow. It worked extremely well and cut down greatly on bow breakage.

They also tried using it on the face, or compression side of the bow, but when the bow was bent, the cross threads in the woven fiberglass created friction that led to material failure. It was another two or three years before this problem was solved.

A patent covering the use of fiberglass on the extension side of a bow was granted to Bear in 1946. This patent, like many others he received, was allowed to be ignored through the years by other archery manufacturers. Fred's philosophy was that furtherance of the sport should take precedence over profits.

Bear Archery's first important advertising came out in the war year of 1943, when the company bought the entire back page of *Ye Sylvan Archer* and dedicated the space simply to "Appreciation for Our Servicemen." BEAR AR-

CHERY COMPANY, DETROIT, MICHIGAN

And, as early as September 1, 1946, the Detroit *Free Press* carried a double page spread on the first National Field Trial Tournament to be staged in the United States. The tournament was held in Allegan, Michigan and drew more than 500 bow and arrow enthusiasts in competition. Fred Bear was the power behind the scene that made this affair so successful. His natural aptitude for publicity caught the eye of editors and this unprecedented spread of copy and pictures was due to his efforts. The pages were dominated by a scene showing a slim young Bear adjusting the machinery that propelled his moving, life-size deer target. Crowds were ten deep around him, rapt with interest in this ingenious contrivance on which to test their hunting skill.

Harry Bear had initially been disappointed when his son began to favor the bow and arrow over firearms. However, Fred finally aroused his father's interest in archery and Harry proved as adept with the bow as he was with the rifle. At the age of 68, three years after he started using the bow, the senior Bear shot his first deer with it and in 1946 won the National Archery Association's Mail Matches.

That year, Fred determined that his business, which had literally outgrown its quarters, should be moved to another area. He wanted to get away from the retail business, realizing that it was not compatible with manufacturing in a small company. He preferred to limit his efforts to manufacturing and shipping to dealer outlets. He also wanted to be closer to his raw materials, chiefly northern maple and to be in a community that offered ready access to the wilderness.

His choice was the town of Grayling, Michigan, 200 miles north of Detroit. Grayling, a one-time lumbering and sawmill town, was struggling to survive the loss of its eight lumber mills and related chemical industry. Its location on the famous AuSable River in the midst of large tracts of second growth timber had long attracted tourists, hunters and fishermen. It seemed to be an ideal place, not only to manufacture archery equipment, but also to enjoy the out-of-doors as well.

Relocating the plant to Grayling involved more than just finding a piece of land and paying for it. Grayling did not have an industry or a chamber of commerce at that time. Many of its 2,000 citizens were vehemently against a big city stranger upsetting their peaceful surroundings and tightly knit society with a manufacturing plant.

Fortunately, Fred found an ally in the local real estate magnate, John Bruun. In the early part of the century, Bruun had run away from his home in Denmark at the age of 16. After a stint in the Russian Czarist Army, he immigrated to the United States and settled in Grayling. Because he was one of the few skilled bookkeepers around at that time, he became a clerk for the Salling-Hanson Lumber Company and later the executor of its estate. Most of the land in and around the community was either a part of those holdings or personally owned by Bruun, so anyone wishing to purchase land had to go through him.

John also ran the community bank but not by the Michigan banking laws — nor did he pay too much attention to credit ratings. John's decision in lending money was based on his personal opinion of the applicant.

An illustration of his unusual approach was seen in his dealings with a pulpwood cutter who came into the bank one Saturday. (Bruun kept the bank open on Saturdays because most of his customers worked the rest of the week.) The woodcutter had $50 in the bank and wanted to withdraw it. John noted that the man, who was notorious for his consumption of alcohol, was already under the influence and asked him to step into his office. After a few pleasantries, John explained to his client that it cost a great deal of money to run a bank to pay for heat, lights, rent and telephones — and concluded by saying he was sorry but there wasn't any of his visitor's money left at this time. The woodcutter admitted the logic of this explanation and departed. He got his money later, of course, the banker had merely saved it from being dissipated during a lost weekend.

Fred had met John Bruun a couple of years earlier on one of his fishing trips north and had visited with him every time he was in the vicinity thereafter. Bruun thought Bear's plan for a small, quiet and clean archery plant employing local people might not be bad for the town and Fred arranged to look over some property with him one weekend. What took place then is best told in Fred's own words:

"Since John was busy at the bank all day Saturday, I spent the day trout fishing in the AuSable. I slept late on Sunday morning, thinking the talk with Bruun would take but a couple of hours, after which I could get a good start and beat the traffic back to Detroit. John was about 60 years old at that time and lived in a handsomely furnished bachelor apartment above the bank. It was here we had agreed to meet at 10:30 a.m.

When I arrived, John was drinking Scotch to sort of ease the pain of the Scotch consumed the night before. Well, I usually don't drink much. I don't have the body chemistry to take care of it. A couple of drinks and I've had enough.

This was a special occasion, however, so I forgot all about my capacity and tried to match my host's mood. It got to be around 2 o'clock in the afternoon when John said:

"Maybe we should go across the street and have a sandwich."

I said, "Fine." So we went to the hotel and had a couple of sandwiches.

Bruun kept a pair of spirited horses in a stable back of the bank and after we had finished lunch he said, 'Would you like to go for a horseback ride?'

As I had grown up on a farm and spent some time in the cavalry, I thought this was a great idea. We saddled the horses and started off cross-country, through the woods and brush. We wound up at a lake, where a friend of John's, Waldo Hildebrand of Lansing, had a cottage and were invited in for a sociable drink. We tied our horses to some trees on his lawn. After several hours, while the impatient horses trampled Hildy's lawn, we started back to town. It was past midnight. John stuck his heels in his mare's flanks and took off through the jackpines and scrub oaks. All I could do was lay over my horse's neck to keep the limbs and gravel out of my eyes and follow him.

I do not know how we got to town but my cavalry training saved me from disaster. I came through the trip scratched and light-headed but otherwise unscathed.

John was a meticulous man — the saddles, bridles and blankets had to be hung up, each on exactly its own peg. The horses were sweaty and had to be rubbed down. I tried to do my share but all I wanted to do was go across the street, get a room in the hotel and go to bed. And I thought that was what I was going to do as we walked back out to the street. It was then two o'clock in the morning.

I must have looked better than I felt. John, obviously impressed by my staying power said, "Well, shall we look at that property?"

One doesn't usually look at property at night, but I'd gone this far and was determined to stick with him. We got in his car and drove out to the proposed plant site. John stopped the car.

"How does this look to you?" he said.

All I could see were the tops of trees against the sky but I knew they were growing on high ground. We had discussed earlier this six acres along the highway with the AuSable River bordering the far side. At that point, I would have bought anything I wanted so desperately to get to bed. So I said, "It looks all right to me."

"What's it worth to you?" John asked.

"What do you want for it?" I sparred.

"Well," he said, '"How about $1,500?"

"That sounds all right to me," I replied, to which John concluded:

"Okay, you can have it for $1,200."

I woke up the next day about noon and reviewed our transaction. Disheartened, I realized he'd been drinking and I'd been drinking and I'd have to come up the next weekend and go through the whole thing again. However, two days later I got a letter of confirmation from John, the terms exactly those we had made on the highway at two o'clock in the morning!

My friendship with John Bruun remained as firm and reliable as our initial business deal until the day he died. Grayling never produced another man like him."

John became very fond of Fred's grandchildren a few years later when they came to Grayling to live with the Bears for a while. On one occasion he produced a precisely creased, expensive linen handkerchief from his pocket and gave it to Hannah to wrap around her doll and another time took three year-old Chris for a Sunday morning spin down Main Street in his shiny black cutter and dashing, spirited horse. New York-reared Chris, who had never had this experience, asked John with great solemnity:

"Mr. Brunn, where do you put the gasoline in the horse to make him go?"

Frank Scott, the present day curator of The Fred Bear Museum in Gainesville, is shown behind the counter of this 1941 Bear Archery Sport Show booth.

Fred camping out at Bear's Bend on the Manistee River west of Grayling. Fred went there often during World War II to hunt and fish.

John Bruun, banker and landowner in the small town of Grayling, became a friend and ally in Fred's efforts to locate there.

NTY
ied at
LING

3AN'S
ROUND
LAND

Avalanche

IURSDAY, MAY 1, 1947.　　　　　　　　EIGHT PAGES — PRICE 5 CENTS.

Some Production Under Way

Bear Archery Company Now Occupying Grayling Plant

* * *

The Bear Archery Company, formerly of Detroit, is now installed in their new, modern factory building on West Lake Street, within the limits of the City of Grayling, and production h a s been started in some departments.

The company is a Michigan corporation that began the construction of archery equipment in 1927. They have been located in Detroit —but over eight years ago plans were made for moving of the plant to Grayling. The war made the move impossible, but last year a permit was granted to the company by the Civilian Production Administration for construction of the new plant. Company officers stated that letters obtained from local men and groups were deciding factors in the issuing of the permit.

The new building is 170 feet long by 50 feet wide, encompassing a total of 8,500 square feet of floor space. It is of cement block and brick construction and has an all-steel flat roof that is insulated with fiberglass. It is heated by an oil-fired hot air Jackson and Church furnace with a humidifying control. All the windows in the plant are double glazed.

The factory building was constructed by Melvin Marshall and wired by Calvin Church, while Hurl Deckrow handled the plumbing work. All three are Grayling residents. The building is estimated by company officials to have cost $40,000. The first work on it was started in May, 1946.

Fred Bear, formerly of Detroit and now of Grayling, is president of the new local company. K. K. Knickerbocker of Chicago is the company's vice-president, while Charles D. Piper of Grayling, formerly of Detroit, is secretary-treasurer of the . firm. Nelson Grumley, formerly of Detroit, is head of the bow department.

The concern makes only high-quality archery equipment and has a nation-wide reputation for the superiority of its merchandise. Its production is exclusively for field shooting and hunting.

Bow and arrow hunting is growing in popularity by leaps and bounds, as witnessed by the bow and arrow hunting bill recently passed by the Michigan House. The bill is now in the hands of the Senate, and would open Montcalm, Ionia, Alpena, Benzie, Iosco, Leelanau, Newaygo, Gogebic, Roscommon, Montmorency, Oscoda and Crawford counties from October 1 until November 5 for the hunting of either buck or doe with bow and arrow. The vote in the House was 82 to 1 in favor of the bill.

Mr. Bear and the company have been active in promoting the sport and he and Mr. Grumley are well known for their hunting exploits with these weapons. Mr. Bear has both a moose and a bear to his credit in hunting with bow and arrow.

The company normally employs about 20 or 30 men and women when in full production. Work has been started in several departments, but may increase slowly in others due to a new tooling program.

The company expressed their thanks to the citizens of Grayling for their co-operation in many ways in getting the building ready for occupancy, and for the many expressions of welcome. Future plans of the company call for a field archery practice course near the plant very soon.

A page from the Grayling weekly newspaper, The Crawfard County Avalanche, announcing the new Bear Archery plant, 1947.

CHAPTER 7

After the Grayling land was secured, Fred incorporated his self-owned business. Charles Piper sold the Bear Products Company and put the money into Bear Archery. Ken Knickerbocker, Fred's friend and hunting companion, also decided to invest. The new organization had a total of $40,000 to move the Detroit operation to Grayling, set up a new plant and get into production. Bear was President, Knickerbocker Vice-President and Piper, both Secretary and Treasurer.

Operations had continued in Detroit while the Grayling plant was being built. The lapse between the shutdown in Detroit and the start of production in the new plant in April 1947 was no more than a month. Eight or nine employees moved up from Detroit and the rest of the thirty-five people on the Grayling payroll were hired locally.

Bear had his first customers while moving into the new plant during a spring snowstorm. The inconvenience caused by retail customers was tolerated because extra money was essential to keep the business running.

In the fall of 1946, Fred had gone to Blaney again with a party of hunters and unexpectedly met Henrietta Thomas who a year later, became his second wife.

Henrietta was a widow who had been working at Blaney as social director for the summer season, coming from a similar situation at a resort hotel in Florida.

Her late husband had been keenly interested in the new sport of hunting with a bow and arrow and liked to build his own equipment. Just before his terminal illness, at their home in Oshkosh, Wisconsin, he had been experimenting with catgut backings for bows. He glued guitar strings together and bonded them to the back of his bow. He needed help with this and wrote a letter to Archery Magazine about his project.

In Dover, Massachusetts, W. B. Wescott, a physicist dedicated to the mushrooming sport of archery read the Thomas' letter and immediately responded by mail. His letter arrived too late, however, and Henrietta replied telling him her husband had died and that she knew very little about his archery pursuits. Nevertheless, Wescott was determined. He wrote again, asking her to see if this catgut-backed bow was still among her husband's effects. The letter was written with such style and persuasion that to ignore it was impossible and Mrs. Thomas prevailed upon a friend to help her look for the correct bow.

Fred and Henrietta Bear at the conclusion of their marriage ceremony.

(Wescott had enclosed a check for forty dollars in payment.) A bow was sent but it proved not to be the one Wescott wanted to see, so the check was returned and the matter forgotten.

Now, three years later, Henrietta noticed the name of W. B. Wescott on the hotel register at Blaney and introduced herself to him. He remembered his correspondence with her and in turn introduced his friend, Fred Bear, his host for the hunt. Incidentally, it was for Fred Bear that he was trying to track down the merits, if any, in the idea of catgut backing for bows.

During the day Fred was out from dawn until dark with his guests hunting deer in the vast forested region surrounding Blaney. At night, however, the group showered and refreshed, trooped in to dinner. No one noticed that Bear made it a point to pass by the table of the social director each evening, surreptitiously dropping an offering from his day in the woods at her plate, a crimson maple leaf, a sprig of hard-to-find white flowers he called Pearly Everlasting, or an oversized acorn still in its green sheath.

After bidding his friends good night and assuring Wescott (who had long since caught on) that he would be up in a minute, he and the social director would spend a couple of hours playing Gin Rummy in a small alcove off the lobby.

This went on for two weeks. There was more talk than Gin Rummy and by the end of the season, they both knew their relationship was more than friendship. Fred, who thought 'Henrietta' was far too cumbersome a name for one so small (she was a petite, blue-eyed Norwegian), changed her name to "Hank." They talked of their lives, Fred's divorce and her former marriage; of their plans for the future — surprised to find they had so many interests in common. Hank told Fred about her two grandchildren who might be part of her responsibility one day since her daughter, Julia and son-in-law, Eli Waldron, a popular writer of that time, were talking of divorce. Fred wanted to meet Julia, so they called her one evening at her home in Wisconsin and he introduced himself to her. They seemed immediately compatible.

They talked also of Henrietta's foster son, Michael Steger (the son of her deceased younger sister), whom the Thomas' had taken to raise. Michael was a junior at West Point and Fred invited him to spend a week of his vacation with him the summer before the Bears were married. Fred taught Mike to fly fish and outfitted him with archery tackle. Mike reported to his foster mother at the conclusion of this visit that if her plans to marry Fred Bear did not materialize, he would be extremely disappointed.

Time ran out. Henrietta left for her job in Florida. Fred returned to his manufacturing business in Detroit. Both felt they might never meet again. But, upon arriving in the South, Henrietta found a letter waiting — the first of daily letters exchanged during the winter. Fred made a trip to Florida in February and by spring it was settled. They were married the following September at the close of Henrietta's summer job at Wequetonsing Resort in Harbor Springs, Michigan.

Henrietta's employer, L.G. Davis and his wife, Mayme, wanted the wedding at their attractive home next to the hotel. About twenty guests, still on hand in those waning days of the season, attended; among them the Eigelhardts of Swans Down Cake Flour fame. The Eigelhardts, with their chauffeur, George, drove up from the south every summer to spend the season at the exclusive Wequetonsing Hotel. On a high hill overlooking Little Traverse Bay and the town of Harbor Springs, George was annually ordered to stop the car while Mr. Eigelhardt stepped out and respectfully doffed his hat to the magnificent scenery below. Following this ritual, they resumed their journey to the hotel.

Fred had been obliged to spend far more than he could afford at this time keeping pace with the setting for this wedding. He doubtless would have preferred that the ceremony take place in the log "Chapel In The Pines" near

Grayling but typically could adapt easily to whatever circumstances he found himself in.

Along with the plant site in Grayling, Fred had purchased 40 acres of beautiful woodlands some seven miles from Grayling, on the banks of the Manistee River. He had camped there often during the War and now lived there all summer in a small tent high on a bank overlooking a bend of the river and "Bear's Bend" consequently became Fred's and Henrietta's first home. The surroundings were completely unspoiled, with legions of wildlife as neighbors and a view unsurpassed at any season.

Returning from their honeymoon on a wet, rainy night, Fred was horrified to find his tent cabin (where Henrietta had suggested they spend a few weeks) in much the same shape he had left it — a loaf of moldy bread on the table, unwashed dishes from his hasty breakfast and sandy wader socks drying on a line overhead. He had arranged with his secretary-treasurer's wife, Winnie Piper, to come in and tidy up before they returned but Winnie had forgotten the date and appeared a day late with a broom and a bottle of wine with which she meant to greet them — everything ship-shape according to Fred's instructions. This state of affairs was far more disappointing to Fred than it was to his new wife.

Bear's Bend was situated more than a half mile from the road, in a latticework of dappled sunlight and shade cast by a few gnarled white pines. These survivors of the logger's axe lined the high riverbank, giving way to a background of wildflowers and blueberries. Underfoot, the earth was soft with lichens and moss, showing here and there the sharp imprints of deer that came to drink at the river. Idyllic surroundings in which the Bears began a new life together.

From thickets of pin cherry and dogwood, the song of the white-throated sparrow could be heard. Flickers and nuthatches together with chipmunks and red squirrels accepted the cabin dwellers and soon came close for their daily offerings of food.

When twilight hovered over the river and swallows skimmed low over circles of quicksilver widening on the water, (signaling a hatch of insects), Fred would slip into his waders and ease into the glassy currents of the Manistee, casting above the rising brook and brown trout with his tiny artificial fly.

With the onset of winter, the Bears moved to a rented house on Lake Margrethe near Grayling, but they returned to Bear's Bend in the summer of 1948.

In later years when the family no longer spent much time at Bear's Bend,

Fred put up a durable metal sign fastened high on a tree, inviting fishermen to use the spot for access to the river. The sign cautioned them about fire and asked that the place be left without the trace of their presence, which was honored in all instances through the years. Fred took pleasure in sharing the property with sportsman who came up from the hot cities below seeking a place to camp and fish.

YOU MAY PARK OR CAMP HERE
FROM THE YELLOW STUMP UPSTREAM TO
THE DEAD TREE THAT LEANS OVER THE RIVER.
PLEASE KEEP THE AREA CLEAN.
TAKE YOUR REFUSE WITH YOU.
DO NOT BURY IT. BEARS DIG IT UP.
DEAD WOOD MAY BE USED.
BUT BE CAREFUL WITH FIRE.
FRED BEAR

While pondering the possibility of living in a northern Michigan town the size of Grayling, Henrietta had asked Fred if there was an Episcopal church in the vicinity and Fred, a man with complete confidence in his ability to accomplish things, replied, "No but I'll build you one."

True to his word, he chaired the building committee for an Episcopal church in Grayling, taking time from his busy schedule to consult with the Bishop and architects in Detroit.

The handsome little church stands in a pine woods on the outskirts of town. Henrietta's proposal for naming the parish, "St. Francis" (honoring that Saint's love for wild creatures) was enthusiastically accepted and duly recorded in diocesan archives.

In 1950, the cabin took on an additional room. Julia and Eli Waldron were divorced and Christopher, 3, and Hannah, 2, came to live with the Bears for a time. Fred, who had no children in his first marriage, took them to his heart. They called him "Papa Bear," of course. When he sat at home with a drawing board designing machines and archery tackle, a child on either side of his chair, combing his hair with doll-sized brushes and combs, he insisted they did not disturb him, instead, he maintained their presence inspired him to think better.

The children became very close to the Bears during the two or more years they lived with them. After Julia's job brought her closer to Grayling, she was

*Fred's sister, Elizabeth Bear, ready to leave for her job as
director of a nursing home near Carlisle, 1947.*

able to have them with her again but vacations, weekends, holidays and birthdays found them all back together in Grayling with "Papa Bear" and "Baba"
(their name for Henrietta).

Fred and Hank's first Christmas together was spent in Carlisle, Pennsylvania, with the senior Bears. Her journal kept an account of this visit:

"I thought the Cumberland Valley of Pennsylvania, where Fred
was born, was one of the loveliest spots I'd ever seen. Dark blue
mountains surrounded a widespread depression in the earth in which
tall stone houses and overshot barns stood like a page from history.
One could see Carlisle down in the valley where Fred's parents lived,
a sturdy little town dating from Revolutionary times.

We spent our first Christmas there driving out from Michigan in
crisp December weather. The highway went through gentle, rolling
mountains, all new to me from the flat middlewest where I was born.
Every mile was filled with beauty and I loved everything, including
my new husband's family. 'Mom' was a serene, slender woman with
white hair and blue eyes that flashed a spark of humor when you least
expected it. Dad was tall, boney and full of fun. He resembled his

son with the exception of his eyes, which were black.

Elizabeth, Fred's sister, lived at home with her parents. She had never married and worked as head nurse at a facility nearby, which cared for the indigent of the county. Her work in revitalizing this County Home, endowing it with love and excellent care, to say nothing of the fine new modern building that materialized during her tenure, was so outstanding that her reputation was known all over the valley.

Our few days in Pennsylvania were filled with pleasure. Elizabeth invited us to her hospital where every window was decorated for Christmas and at the end of the long, sunny hall a fragrant balsam with handmade ornaments harbored a pile of gifts beneath its branches. Elizabeth introduced us to the patients, her kind blue eyes smiling behind thick lenses.

Dad took us for rides along the narrow blacktop roads that undulated and turned through the countryside. Here was where Fred went to school. There were the old picnic grounds at Mt. Holly Springs. We stopped at the Bear family cemetery where the weatherbeaten gravestones fascinated me with family lore. A large white house a few miles from town, still showing traces of former beauty, was where "the Aunts" had lived and Fred worked as a boy in their truck gardens. We drove across the Conodoquinit Creek to Walnut Bottom and on to Elliottson and past the church. These were the roads along which Fred pedaled his bicycle to high school every day racing along between the hedgerows of honeysuckle. Pedaling that machine up and down these rolling roads might well have been responsible for the fact that he could scale mountains so easily in later years.

Dad took us to market one day. I was familiar with the rich dairy farms of Wisconsin, their towering silos bursting with fodder. But I was totally unprepared for the sight of this bounty flowing through the building as if from a giant horn of plenty.

The Market Place was a spacious, high-ceilinged building in Carlisle's tree-shaded town square. I stood spellbound with the beauty before me — a sea of vegetables, flowers and fruit. Carrots, parsley and Hubbard squash, 'pokes' of shelled walnut, popcorn and the famous Pennsylvania dried corn. Baskets of eggs and wheels of cheese were arranged beside rolls of sweet butter stamped with the imprint of a leaf by the red-cheeked farmers' wives in their little net caps. We

At Bear's Bend. Papa Bear is making pancakes for Christopher and Hannah. 1950.

passed trays of coffee cake and cinnamon buns reminiscent of the ones that had tortured Fred years ago on market day. Dad filled the basket on his arm and Fred added ponhaus, Lebanon bologna and dried corn to take home.

One evening, I was shown the family photos including those of Aunt Lib and Aunt Sarah, the Mennonite aunts I had heard so much about. No one else in the family was of the Mennonite faith, but the influence of those two women is evident to this day. Not only in remembrance of their gentle lives but by the fine antique furniture inherited from their home.

Fred had acquired some of these handsome pieces and transported them five hundred miles to Detroit, where there was never any room in his apartment-dwelling life to accommodate them. He carried them with him again when he moved north to Grayling and in the early days of our marriage, I was electrified to discover a nine-drawer, solid walnut highboy in a corner of the factory in which he was storing nocks and points for arrows!"

The first years at the new factory were difficult. Although the move to Grayling did not cause a drop in business, expenses were much greater than anticipated. Capital expenditures and a substantial interest rate ate into profits and many times Bear Archery was without operating capital. Often employees were told they could not be paid for a week or two. Their faith in Fred Bear held fast, however, and not one of them ever failed to show up for work.

Ernie Van Patten's story is a prime example of the loyalty engendered by Fred's fairness and consideration. Ernie came to work for Bear in 1948, when he was 55 years old. He had been a steam engineer for the Salling-Hanson Lumber Company of Grayling and was an excellent mechanic. He became the Bear Archery custodian, his main job was to keep the place clean and the machinery oiled and operating.

Ernie was a bachelor, taciturn and fiercely independent. The only person he would listen to or take orders from was Fred Bear. He didn't believe in coffee breaks and worked constantly, sweeping the floors when there was nothing else that needed his attention. During the period the company was having difficult times making ends meet, he did not cash any of his payroll checks for a period of three months.

Another facet of Ernie's individuality was evidenced one day. He had purchased a bank draft at the Grayling State Bank. Sometime later when Ernie happened to be in the bank, he was asked, "Ernie, are you still holding that bank draft?"

Ernie replied, "Yes, what's the matter with it? Isn't it any good?"

The official explained that of course it was good but since the draft was non-interest bearing there was no advantage in holding it for any length of time. To this Ernie replied tersely, as he turned abruptly to leave, "Young man, you mind your business and I'll mind mine."

In the same vein, when the Bear insurance agent approached Ernie on the subject of life insurance, Ernie replied, "I'm taking care of my future and you take care of yours."

After 15 years with the company, Van Patten retired at the age of 70. A short time after his retirement, the Detroit Bank & Trust sent him a check for $1,300 from the Bear Archery retirement fund. Ernie mailed the check back to Fred with a short note: "You paid me well when I worked for you. Please put this in the company treasury."

Fred tried on three occasions to return the check but Ernie would not accept it. The situation finally was resolved after almost seven years, when the bank told Fred that if the check was not cashed soon it would revert to the state government.

"Ah ha!" Fred thought, "Now I've got him!" When he passed the news on to Ernie, the latter said,

"Give me the check," and he promptly cashed it rather than let any agency of the government, which he thoroughly distrusted, get its hands on it.

While still struggling to keep abreast of sagging profits in 1948 and 1949, a friend and hunting companion, Ross Siragusa, president of Admiral Corporation, came to Fred with a proposition. His company needed TV and record cabinets for a sales program and he thought Bear Archery could tool up and make them.

The order came in and Fred soon had a production line set up using small trucks fitted with rollerskate wheels to move the cabinets along the route. The order was filled and while the result amounted to little more than trading dollars, it helped with current bills. Indeed, if it had not been for this help from Siragusa, Fred might very well have had to abandon his dream for Bear Archery.

During this anxious time, Fred was also working long hours trying to develop a practical system for using fiberglass backing on the compression side of his bows.

Things almost came to a halt in 1949. With the company about $8,000 in arrears on federal tax payments, the Internal Revenue Service sent a representative from its Alpena office, accompanied by the state police, to padlock the doors of the Grayling plant and put them out of business.

When the group arrived, Fred was back in the factory working on a new bonding process. Charles Piper came back to deliver the news, "It looks like we've had it," he said, "What should we do?"

"Well," replied Fred, "I'm going to keep on working at what I am doing and you are going back to the office and get us out of this predicament. That is your job."

Piper went back to the office, wrote the I.R.S. representative a check for $500, signed an agreement for monthly payments until the debt was cleared and the plant was saved from closure that day.

Bear Archery Company did not have $500 in the bank when the check was written but hoped to have it by the time the check cleared. In the past, the company had depended on a clerk at the bank to call when Bear's balance was insufficient to cover a large check. Somehow the company always had managed to scrape up the needed amount. When it got the I.R.S. check, however, the bank did not call the plant. Instead, it sent the check back marked "insufficient funds."

What saved Fred this time was a personal loan from a friend, Franklin Hills, who lived downriver from the Bears. Hills, an affluent paraplegic who could hunt and fish better than most men with sound legs and who, with his wife were bridge partners of the Bears, had everything to lose and nothing to gain in this transaction. But, upon hearing the circumstances, he merely said, "Mildred, bring me the checkbook"; cementing an already warm friendship that lasted thirty-five years until Franklin died in 1981.

In 1949, a bonding process that made possible the combining of new bow materials finally was developed. For a bow to function efficiently it has to recover completely from the stresses of elongation on the back side and the material on the face of the bow must continually resist and recover from compression. While this elementary fact was known, it was often neglected in bow design because of the difficulty in joining materials with the required physical properties.

In this stage, fiberglass was used on the back of the bow, hard northern maple laminates formed the center or core and a thin, hard aluminum alloy strip formed the face. The aluminum facing was pinned to the core wood at first but this proved unsatisfactory, so a separate operation was developed whereby the aluminum was first bonded to a very thin veneer and then to the core laminations.

Beginning in 1949, a written registration and warranty accompanied every Bear bow produced.

But catastrophe struck again in July of 1950. The new aluminum-faced bows appeared for the first time on the shooting line at the National Field Archery Association Tournament in California and many of them failed. Fred stopped production immediately until the trouble was found and then re-placed every bow with a new one, a catastrophic blow to the finances of the young Bear Archery Company. Letters poured in from all parts of the country, however, lauding Fred for his integrity in standing by his warranty.

At this same time, soon after Thanksgiving in 1950, *The New Yorker* carried a piece expounding the popularity of a new trend toward archery and men-tioned Fred Bear as the foremost exponent of the sport. *Colliers Magazine* ran an interesting story also, citing Fred's prominence in the sport and of course, the outdoor magazines showed more and more interest, including the *Ford Times* and the *Detroit Motor News*.

Fiberglass fabric embedded in plastic resins rapidly became the standard material for bow backings. Because of the abrasive action of cross threads in the glass fabric, however, it was not suitable for use on the compression sur-

Fred working with high-speed photographic equipment in Bear Archery's testing laboratory.

Bear Archery pioneered in the use of continuous filament fiberglass for bow backing and facing.

face. Bear and his crew worked on this problem for more than two years and by 1951 they had solved it by eliminating all cross threads in the fiberglass. A rack holding multiple spools of fiberglass yarn fed some 250,000 parallel strands of the filament through a tank of plastic resins into metal channels.

The resulting unidirectional strips were then oven-cured, after which they could be bonded to the wood core laminations of a bow.

The higher proportion of glass thus obtained and the straightness of the fibers made possible for the first time the production of bows with fibers of glass on the compression side as well as on the back. For the art of bowmaking, this material approached perfection, recovering completely and instantly from both extension and compression stresses without fatigue.

This product of Bear technology and its use in bow construction was fully patented in 1951, the year the first Bear bows using it appeared. Of all the archery manufacturing innovations that Fred Bear developed, it was perhaps the most important. It changed bowmaking from a one-at-a-time operation to a manufacturing process in which dimensions were controlled by micrometers.

Fred also converted a hydraulic system formerly used to operate a machine-gun turret in a World War II bomber to the travel control of an intricate

Fred selecting a fly for the evening's hatch on the Manistee Bear's Bend.

Henrietta Bear outside the cabin at Bear's Bend, soon after their marriage.

contour sanding machine. The contour sander took a bow fresh from the bonding press and shaped both sides in one pass, a job that formerly had to be done by hand. A high-speed router then shaped the recurve limb ends. Tillering the bow for correct limb balance and hand sanding for finish was still an individual job process and remains so to the present day.

All of the techniques, machines, jigs and fixtures devised to accomplish the various tasks were products of Fred's inventive mind and all were designed, tested and built in his plant.

Fred did not take an active part in production but spent his time designing, constructing and testing prototypes and the equipment to produce them. He often spent 14 to 16 hours a day in his office and adjoining workroom. His research and development laboratory expanded over the years to include high-speed filming equipment, an oscilloscope, mechanical shooting machines, chronographs and many other devices for evaluating materials, some of which he designed and built himself.

Many articles also came from Fred's pen in the early days. He was always teaching, sharing experiences and "showing them how". Here is a short piece he wrote about whitetail deer.

ABOUT DEER

Sometime I hope to meet "Wild Bill" Childs to find out just how wild he is — and how lucky. In the meantime his recent article prompts me to write about the emphasis he lays on LUCK in hunting — even though he eventually boils it down to around 10% which is about right in my opinion.

One of Webster's definitions of the word luck is "good fortune as the result of chance." Which means that the more chances one has, the better luck will come to him.

Not forgetting the hunter who steps out of his car and downs a fine deer in ten minutes, the law of averages is still in effect. *The more chances one create for himself, the more likely he is to be lucky.* One of the reasons that some hunters are more successful than others in arranging meetings with game, chance meetings if you wish, is that they conduct themselves in such a way as to encourage their chances. For instance, if you are hunting quietly through the woods and are stopping occasionally as you should be, you do not make these stops only at places where the stumps are most inviting. You make them near deer trails or at locations where deer sign are in evidence. And you don't sprawl out on the ground with your tackle out of reach or situate yourself upwind from where the deer might come.

Neither do you go crashing over a ridge without carefully looking things over on the other side. And when you see a deer, you assume that there are more and look for them, making no move until you are sure that you have seen them all.

More hours in the woods and being still more than you are in motion will increase your "luck." Do more hunting on rainy and blustering days. Remember, too, that we are a race of palefaces and keep in mind that the Indians' war paint was camouflage in the highest sense and that you can increase your chances by following this example.

Luck could well be a factor in bringing an eight-point buck along the runway you are watching, instead of an undersized doe. But the buck's I.Q. could be the factor too. If "Wild Bill" hadn't gotten me started off on luck my purpose would simply to have bared both flanks in exposing the "mighty buck".

Of course I admit that an antlerless trophy has a certain bald look about it and I certainly admire a great rack of horns as well as the next, but don't be too sure that the reason the buck is too hard to bag is because his I.Q. is so high. If you analyze the deer family and place credit where it belongs, you might come to the conclusion that the old mossback is not really so smart after all. More accurately, he is actually shy, timid and retiring.

Many times I have seen the "inferior doe" lead the "wise buck" out of harm's way and the six-month-old fawn display a better show of reasoning than the so-called monarch of the forest. The doe is the "Seeing Eye" of the deer herd and the shy old buck will not venture out of deep cover until he has had the "all is clear" tail signal from her.

All bucks, however, cannot be classified as shy. The young fellows with their first or possibly second winters behind them are the most brazen of the lot. They are the teenage group who are full of vim and vigor, with places to go and worlds to conquer and they are the ones who make fatal mistakes at hunting time. As they grow older they seem to sense that the headgear they wear is very much sought after and gradually acquire the disposition of a recluse readily accept the doe's apparent willingness to pull their chestnuts out of the fire.

It is hard to understand why the doe assumes this status of guardian so faithfully. Only twice in my life have I been able to separate a doe from a buck. On the first occasion, the doe came back after she had seen me and took the buck away with her. The second time concerns the spike-horn in the accompanying picture. In typical yearling style, he refused to heed the alarm that sent his companion doe and fawn off at a full gallop. The three of them were feeding in a grassy opening in the woods late one evening last fall and it was difficult stalking through the dry oak leaves to get near them. The doe and fawn took fright and were off but I got close enough for a twenty-five yard shot at the buck. The mistake he made was in obeying his adolescent curiosity to stop in the edge of the woods for a look to see what the fuss was about. He went down at sixty yards. I have seen full-grown bucks get frantic when pressed or cornered and dash about doing things entirely devoid of reasoning. And, in contrast, a surrounded doe once got down on her belly and crawled under a pile of drifted tumbleweed to hide. The doe has had to assume the responsibility of bringing up her family and has learned through necessity the trick of self-preservation. For a lesson in nature's sign language, there is no finer example than the communication that flows from the white tail of a doe who is leading her fawns out of a swamp in the late afternoon or evening.

Give due respect to the buck for his ability to keep out of trouble, of course, but timing is the most important element in promoting the chance of placing him within bow range and then it all depends upon your ability to concentrate on that tiny spot behind the front leg where the arrow should hit. This is the hardest part of the assignment, but if you can do this, you have made your mark. Just because you have been able to do this once, however, or even several times, don't assume that it becomes a habit. It is just as difficult for the seasoned hunter to do this as it is for the beginner and as soon as you recognize this fact you will begin to register regularly and could possibly even stave off starvation with your bow and a handful of arrows.

A happy Fred Bear on a 1951 western hunting and fishing trip. Whenever he could, Fred combined his two favorite sports, bowhunting and flyfishing.

CHAPTER 8

In 1951, Fred finally was able to take a break from the pressure of a long workday schedule and embark on a western hunting trip, the first since his two Ontario moose and black bear expeditions in 1945 and 1946. He had finished his second bowhunting film, "Moose Diary" in 1946 and hoped to film a western adventure for use in his sales promotion work. For the next three or four years, he hunted on ranches in Wyoming where antelope and mule deer were plentiful — the Maycock Ranch in Gillette and the Murphy Ranch near Lander were the favorite spots.

Ken Knickerbocker made these trips with him. One year they hunted the Hoback Canyon country south of Jackson Hole, Wyoming, with guide Lon Imeson. They saw a great many elk and had a few chances at them but were not successful. They also tried for antelope on the plains near Lander but without success. There were at this time only four bowhunters in the entire state of Wyoming, according to the Fish and Game Department. It was an exciting time for Fred, however. He had never before hunted in such rugged, beautiful terrain and was determined to try again for these majestic animals the next year.

September 1952 found Fred once more in Wyoming, tenting on the Murphy Ranch some 70 miles from Lander. His companions on this trip were Dr. Judd Grindell from Wisconsin, Nubby Pate and Bob Morley from California, Ken Knickerbocker from Illinois and Ed Henkel, Charlie Kroll and Duke Underhill from Michigan.

The men hunted along an intermittent stream from blinds camouflaged with sagebrush. The blinds were located within bowshot of water holes frequented by game. Fred and three more of the party each bagged one of the speedy antelope.

From the Lander hunt they proceeded to the Hoback country again for a pack-string hunt with Lon Imeson. It was an unusually dry and warm fall in the mountains, which made hunting difficult. Near the end of the hunt, only one elk had been taken, a 5-point bull, by Kroll. But on the very last day Fred succeeded in getting a tremendous herd bull with an impressive 6 x 6 rack of antlers. It was his finest trophy to date.

Following is Fred's account of this hunt:

Fred and Charles Piper at the Bear Archery Company drawing board. Grayling, 1950.

*Fred's parents, Harry and Florence Bear, serving their 50th wedding
anniversary cake in Carlisle.*

WYOMING ELK HUNT
by Fred Bear

Up Hoback Canyon in the Jackson Hole country of Wyoming, there is a grassy knoll some 9,000 feet high on the north side of a mountain. I once spent an entire day on that spot. I think I could still find the place blindfolded, although it's been almost two years since I last saw it.

Lon Imeson of Jackson Hole, who has been guiding in that area for many years, was ending his second season with me. He was determined now to have me bag an elk.

At three o'clock in the afternoon on the last day of our hunt, we were lolling in the sun on this grassy mound just over the top of the mountain. Six or seven bull elk had been bugling below us since daylight that morning.

While waiting for them to move up closer, we spent the day catnapping, telling stories and occasionally sounding our elk bugles — always getting an immediate answer.

Towards the middle of the afternoon, Lon's patience had reached its limit. He sized up the situation this way: the big bull we were after was farthest down the mountain and he had the cows safely corralled within his territory. The younger bulls, who seemed closest to us, were hanging around the outskirts waiting for a chance to move in on his harem.

We could plainly hear the big fellow far below us. His bugling had more volume than that of the younger bulls and was easily distinguished from theirs by the way he ended up with a series of guttural grunts — haw, haw, haw — like the braying of a donkey.

There had been no rain for the past two months and the country was bone dry. Stalking was about as quiet as an early morning milk wagon on cobblestones. There wasn't a chance of sneaking down to the herd and getting an arrow at the big bull. Instead, we tried to wait until they moved up the mountain to feed on the south side where some grass still grew in spite of the drought.

It was just after three o'clock when we noticed a change. The elk were on the move, coming up the mountain at our right. Our strategy had been planned. We moved into the timber, climbing a steep ravine en route and saw a nice young bull drinking at a trickle of stream about 250 yards away.

The herd was working up just beyond this ravine and when we reached the top, Lon said that this looked like the place to wait. We gave them another toot on the bugle and were answered promptly as before. The big one, whose bugling was so distinctive, was still the farthest down.

Time dragged by. Every sound from our bugle brought an answer from the big bull, as far down as ever. It seemed unlikely that he would get up to us before dark and our nerves could hold out no longer. It was finally decided that Lon would make a big circle down the mountain, get below the elk and hope to put them up to me.

For the past seven days, we had been trying everything we knew that would put us within bow range of a bull elk. We had almost succeeded on three or four occasions but were defeated each time by the wind.

In flat country when the wind is blowing from the north it comes from the north. But in these mountains, cut up with ridges and canyons, it can blow from the north and also from the south at about the same time. For the time being, however, the wind was right, coming up the mountain and off across the ravine we had just crossed.

Lon left and I looked around for a place that offered the best cover and shooting possibilities. It suddenly occurred to me that the elk could come up through there anywhere within a distance of 200 yards. If I got myself snarled up in a blowdown or in a spot where it was too noisy to move, I would simply be out of luck.

Just below me was an open strip covered with fairly fresh-looking grass. There was very little cover, but I decided to risk this and settled down beside an old log and blew my elk call.

They were coming now. No doubt about it. The answer I got was positive. The bull couldn't be more than 200 yards below me. I could hear a great horning of bushes and crackling of limbs as his bugling came closer and closer.

There was a moment of doubt concerning the wisdom of having moved down here out of cover. Elk are big. In the rutting season they do things in a big way. The year before, in the same area, I had sneaked to within sixteen steps of a bugling bull. It was too brushy for a shot but I can still feel my spine vibrating from that challenging bellow.

The log beside me seemed to shrink to the size of a twig. Even down on all fours, my back stuck up above it. My bow was under my hand with an arrow ready on the string.

My legs began to cramp just as I caught something out of the corner of my eye. Over to the right, a cow elk was feeding, apparently unaware of my presence. Just past her were two more cows and a couple of half-grown calves coming in for some of this choice grass.

The bull was not yet in sight. I was afraid the herd would see or wind me and this last day would end like all the others.

There was no way of getting out of sight without flattening out on the ground and I couldn't shoot in that position. I tried to hold as still as possible, desperately hoping the bull would catch up with the cows that were moving in toward me. Twenty-five yards now, noses sniffing my way, ears pivoting front and back. Nice, fat sleek creatures nibbling dainties from the forest floor. They seemed to pay no attention to the crescendo of bugling about them.

Off to my left and down the hill about sixty yards something else moved...and there he was. A great beast of light tan, blending into dark brown. His neck and head were black and he carried antlers the size of pine trees. Master of the harem and a right to be. This was the one we had waited for.

Lon had analyzed the problem well. He was the head bull. Those heavy shoulders and massive antlers had won him the right in combat. He was in a frenzy now, grunting and bugling and ripping up a cluster of scrub maple with his horns. It was impressive and behind my little log I was impressed!

He was in the timber, too brushy to get an arrow through.

Several cows were within 20 yards and by now almost downwind. The cows were at my right and the bull to my left. Worst of all, Lon was somewhere down below. Since I had moved from where he thought I would be, he might come in sight anytime and put the herd to flight.

Suddenly the bull, having conquered the maples, walked straight up the mountain angling in my direction. This *couldn't* last. He would see me or the wind would shift. Something was bound to go wrong. But he still came on. He walked out of the brush to within twenty yards and stopped, turning his head away from me.

There had been no time to look at the cows for at least a full min-

Fred's father shows his many trophies won by his skill with both gun and bow. Christmas, 1947.

ute and I had the feeling that every one of them was looking straight at me. I couldn't risk moving my head to check. Past experience with elk had taught me that they can vanish as quickly and completely as a white tail deer. At the cows' first sign of alarm the bull is the first to leave. He would be two or three jumps away before I could draw my bow. It was shoot from this position now, on hands and knees, or not at all.

Working my knees forward under my body, I slowly raised the bow horizontally, about a foot off the ground. The arrow lobbed into his midsection and I fully expected all hell to break loose around me. The cows were behind me now and the bull in front.

The arrow struck through the back ribs, went through and lodged in a rib on the far side. The bull made a quick turn and walked back to where he had torn up the maples. He stood there, his head hanging low. It was clearly a fatal hit and he would drop on the spot in a very short time.

The cows didn't flick an ear. They continued to feed without looking up, even when I raised on one elbow to watch the bull through my glasses.

But, suddenly they were gone and the bull went with them, spooked by Lon, who came over the mountain just in time to hear the crashing of hooves and see the last of them disappear down the mountain.

Upon hearing the news his face broke into a "well-done" grin, a sight I had coveted these two years of hunting with him, almost as much as I'd coveted the fine trophy I knew was now lying not too far over the hill. Lon was more than a guide. He liked the spirit of bowhunting and went far beyond his job to inspire success.

We walked to the edge of the brush and picked up the back end of my arrow. It would soon be dark and we took up the trail without delay. We tracked my elk to where he'd slid down the mountain, the great antlers caught around a tree, which kept him from going farther...a day to remember.

Fred's wife and often another hunter's wife, shared these western jaunts. The women stayed in the town closest to camp, generally 60 or 70 miles away. Hank had no interest in camping. (Fred has been heard to say of these trips that his wife stopped off at the last hot water faucet.) With or without a companion, she stayed in comfortable lodgings meeting interesting people, reading and writing and enjoying the West.

Between hunts there was usually time for the Bears to spend time together. On this particular trip, after the triumph of the elk hunt, they drove leisurely from the Jackson Hole country to various spots in the Southwest, including Bryce and Zion Canyons. That year Arizona had announced its first fall bowhunting season in the Kaibab National Forest on the north rim of the Grand Canyon. The Kaibab was famous for producing large-antlered mule deer and Fred had included it in the trip. They headquartered in the rustic but comfortable Jacobs Lake Lodge with other bowhunting parties who had gathered from many states for the occasion.

Bear had made a film of the elk hunt and now spent so much time filming the magnificent Kaibab, its spectacular deer and the successful stalks of other bowhunters that he had little time to do any serious hunting on his own. The scenery was breathtaking and the weather clear and mild. The evenings when the group gathered in front of the lodge's fireplace rounded out a most fascinating trip. One of the highlights of this trip was seeing the beautiful Kaibab squirrels for the first time. A splendid all-black creature with long ear tufts and a dazzling white tail. This squirrel is found only on the north rim of the

Fred took this magnificent elk in the Hoback River country of Wyoming, 1953.

Charlie Kroll congratulates Fred on his arrival in camp with his trophy elk.

Grand Canyon.

After the Kaibab hunt, the Bears left for home. It had been a relaxing and satisfying two months, far from the cares of business and Fred returned to Grayling with renewed vigor and a great deal of film footage with which to promote the growing sport of bowhunting.

By the end of 1952, the Bears had a new home built in the woods on the banks of the AuSable River. The plant was nearby but completely out of sight. Fred gave the architect's plans to a crew of five old-world Scandinavians on a time and material contract. John Cedarburg, a tall, well-built Swede, was the boss.

On the crew's first day at work Fred walked back through the woods to see what was going on. He found all the workers sitting on a pile of lumber drinking coffee. John jumped up from his seat, embarrassed to be caught not working. But in dead earnest and in his deliberate Swedish accent, he said: "Ten o'clock we have ten minutes for coffee. But nobody smokes."

He proved to be entirely sincere. One could set his watch by their schedule. Exactly eight o'clock to start the day, exactly ten o'clock for coffee, exactly four o'clock to pull off neat bib overalls for the trip home. Their workmanship was flawless. That Bear residence will, no doubt, be standing when many of the other homes in the little town are gone.

By the end of 1952 there were sixty employees at the "Archery" (as it was called by the natives in Grayling) which now shared a national sales force with the Bancroft Tennis Racket Company.

1953 saw completion of the first addition to the Bear plant, a special wing with controlled atmospheric conditions for the production of fiberglass for bows. Bear's fiberglass process was fully protected by United States patents, but as with other Bear innovations in those days the patents were never enforced and no royalties were sought from competing firms.

In midyear, the Bear's daughter, Julia Waldron, was married to Charlie Kroll, who had come back with Fred from the western hunt of the previous year to work in the plant. This also brought the grandchildren, Christopher and Hannah, back to Grayling. While the Bears had always been in close touch with the children, having them in the same town again was better for everyone. The family had winter vacations in Florida, trips to Detroit for the Nutcracker Ballet and archery tournaments far and wide. Chris was only ten when he accompanied his grandparents on his first trip west. In her teens, Hannah left home for school in Lake Forest, Illinois, but Chris stayed in Grayling for his high school years. He was a star on the basketball team and

Knick and Fred ready to ride into the Wyoming mountains in search of elk, 1951.

Fred with antelope taken on the Murphy Ranch near Lander, Wyoming, 1952.

graduated fourth in his class.

Because of the distance between their homes, the Bears did not see as much of their Steger foster family as they would have liked. Mike's career in the Air Force took him from post to post around the country. The only time they were consistently close was the year Mike moved his family to Grayling while he served a year in Vietnam. Chris and Hannah were both away at school at that time and to have the five little Steger children in town was a period of great enjoyment. The three oldest girls were enrolled in school in Grayling and made life-long friends there as a consequence. There was a time of adjustment, of course, as on one of the first days, Shannon, age 7, came home in tears because "the kids at school wouldn't believe that Papa Bear was her grandfather."

During Michael's year as an advisor to flight officers in Vietnam, he had a close brush with death. In a letter to Fred dated November 1965, he gave an account of the incident.

"Friday afternoon I was leading a mission of three planes. Everything had checked normally and the take-off was good. About 200 feet in the air the engine started running rough and losing power. With these planes, one can often limp back to base on reduced power, but this time there wasn't enough.

I kept losing altitude as I was turning. I was over water here shortly after passing the end of the runway. There were several ships in the harbor and I had to dodge them in order to jettison my bombs.

I kept trying to nurse the engine but with no results. Things went pretty fast. I did remember to call the tower...I told them I had a very rough running engine and didn't think I could make it back. I remembered a lot of other things but sure forgot a lot of them. Just last week I'd been discussing ditching procedures with a Navy pilot attached to A.F.A.T. He said the most important thing in ditching was to keep the wings level when hitting the water to prevent a cartwheel. If the plane cartwheels that is the end. Another procedure is to pull down full flaps and 100 knots to touchdown. I did this and also remembered to open the canopy just before touchdown.

I almost got back to land. The plane finally touched down about 100 meters from shore. I had expected it would float and that I would have time to unstrap and step out on the wing and dive for a swim. What happened was that before the spray from touchdown had sub-

144

*Bob Morley, camp cook from California, outside the Wyoming hunting cabin with Fred.
The camp was on the William Maycox Ranch near Gillette, 1954*

sided, the cockpit was underwater and me with it. I barely had time to take a deep breath. Fortunately, the canopy stayed open. I undid the seatbelt and started to get out but the parachute hindered me so I unsnapped the chest strap. At this point things were not going well and the thought went through my mind that this may be the end. Anyway, I tried swimming to the surface (I could see light above) but made no headway at all — with my jump boots and all the survival equipment we carry, I had little buoyancy.

Finally, I pulled the handle that activates the Mae West. It inflated at once and I immediately floated to the top. It was good to take a deep breath again...I turned in the water and saw the plane pointing straight down with just the tail showing. It slid from sight as I watched. Several boats in the harbor started towards me and I tried to relax while waiting for them.

The water is about 30 feet deep where the plane sank. We are trying to salvage it — everyone is interested to learn exactly what happened to the engine.

When I got to shore a large crowd had gathered and Major Ninh was there with a jeep. He took me to the hospital for examining and questioning.

The bad thing about this is that we lost a plane and we just don't have any to spare. I flew yesterday again for an hour, just to make sure that I could, I guess."

Mike was recognized for his coolness during this unexpected accident with the following Flying Decoration:

"From 66nd Wing tp VNAF Hdq/Commander in Chief.

VNAF Hdq/Personnel Staff

Notice: 524 Fighter Sqd (to make a proclamation of merit)

62nd Wing American Advisor Officer Major Steger

Message 23 Nov. '65

During combat Mission No. 2513 on 12 November '65, the engine of Major Steger's aircraft failed immediately after take-off from runway 12 of the Nha Trang Air Base.

Major Steger, flight leader, remained calm. As if it were a routine happening he turned to avoid ships on the sea before jettisoning his bombs and made a safe ditching.

He distinguished himself by this outstanding airmanship, which prevented damage to ships and people."

Fred was not only a master bowyer and fine woodsman, but his genius also extended to writing and cinematography. In the early years, he did virtually all of his own film work.

Fred stood on the threshold of becoming a legend when this photo was taken in Wyoming in 1953. During the next 20 years he was to hunt exotic game around the world, in promotion of his sport.

Fred often tells this story to friends, saying in his inimitable way "that his foster son was decorated by the Vietnamese for missing the target."

In the early '50's, Fred worked with Jack Van Coevering, Wildlife Editor of the *Detroit Free Press*, to produce a softcover booklet entitled, "Fun with the Bow and Arrow." It was an excellent public relations publication and thousands were sold over the next few years.

The Bear Plant now had one hundred employees. One of them, having occasion to write to Mr. Bear who was away on a hunting trip said: "This is the first time I ever worked for a man who the employees were not glad to see leave the office and sorry to see return." In 1955, $1.5 million sales made possible the formation of a profit-sharing plan among the employees. Other than that, all profits were plowed back into the company as operating capital, with no dividends paid to the stockholders.

The company had become large enough to support its own sales force, so the arrangement with Bancroft was terminated and Bear's first sales manager, Robert Schulze, was hired. Another addition to the plant was constructed in this year.

Fred returned to Wyoming with various companions for hunts in 1953, 1954 and 1955. He did not get an antelope in 1953 but made up for it the following year with a pronghorn and a large mule deer. Fred later was a member of the first archery team to participate in the unique annual One Shot Antelope Hunt out of Lander. The others on the team were Larry Whiffen, Milwaukee and Howard Hill and Harold Hill of California.

One year, hunting from the Maycock Ranch in Gillette, Wyoming, Fred wrote the following to the office:

> Bear Gulch, Wyo. 1952
> Sunday, September 25 — 9 a.m.
>
> Howdy: We are isolated from the rest of the world. Rain has been falling for 36 hours and still coming down. Mixed with snow now. This country is a quagmire. Can't even move with the jeep. Can't hunt afoot. Just sit here and cuss things in general.
>
> Judd Grindell left two days ago. He and Doc Beall each got a spike horn. I got an eight pointer and that is the total bag.
>
> Krohler and party came in two days ago and have been rained in since. Weather forecast is not good. We are hoping for the best.
>
> Have straightened many bows since I left home. I find that I can bring them back in shape by moving the string groove over and by

Julia and Charlie Kroll's wedding day — July 3, 1953, with Julia's children, Hannah and Christopher.

making it *bigger* and *wider* with a nock file. I mean, the single groove over the outside of the recurve. Not the nock grooves. These grooves must be made *very* wide at the point where the extra serving occurs on the string at the juncture of the loop.

Del Kroehler had an old Kodiak with a walnut riser that was in terrible shape. Both ends were bad. I worked on it and the bow is in fine shape now.

Mel should look into this. The string groove should be longer and bigger with plenty of width at the heavy string serving near the loop.

I hope that Hess has come through with the new (hunting) heads and that you can get some out for testing this fall.

Not much other news here. Sounds like you are really busy — 300 bows a day...

Fred

In the meantime, Henrietta lived in one of the ranch bunkhouses — working on a book and enjoying the company of the Maycocks.

"I live in a bunkhouse," she wrote to Julia, "It is clean and that is about all that can be said for it except for the blessed privacy…The bed is a lopsided affair that rolls you violently to the wall the minute you lie down on it. In order to prevent freezing at night I have to keep a fire going, stoking the stove with smelly, sooty coal mined right here on the ranch. The reason I endure this hardship is that the companionship and food at the ranch house is delightful…This is the only place I could find to be alone so I can write.

The ranch women, Audrey, Mamie, Dovey and I rode horseback down to Fred's camp one day where we had been invited for lunch. Knickerbocker and Fred greeted us with smiles and since all four of us had on red jackets, they took our pictures."

Responding to the many inquiries coming in from hunters taking antelope with a bow and arrow, Fred prepared the following for one of the sports magazines about 1954.

HUNTING THE ANTELOPE
by Fred Bear

The antelope, or pronghorn as he is sometimes called, originally outnumbered the buffalo. It has been estimated that at one time there were more than thirty-five million of these beautiful creatures roaming the plains of the western United States.

As in the case of the buffalo, misuse by man of another of our natural resources resulted in the depletion of the herd to such an extent that twenty-five years ago only about thirty-five thousand of these animals were known to exist within the boundaries of the United States. Since that time, however, careful game management has brought about an increase in the size of the herd until now more than a quarter of a million antelope browse on the sage that covers much of the grazing lands of western cattle.

Once again, antelope hunting is beginning to come into its own as a sport. Hunters from all over the country flock to the popular territories and enjoy excellent hunting during the month of September.

Fred working at home on a new Bear Archery innovation.

Until very recently, few archers seized upon the opportunity to hunt the antelope with bow and arrow. Articles that have appeared from time to time in our outdoor magazines have been concerned with hunting this game with a high-powered rifle and telescope. Almost invariably such articles have gone into detail telling how the animal was shot at a distance ranging from 200 – 700 yards. This report is not encouraging to those who like to do their hunting with a bow and arrow as the shooting distance so far exceeds the extreme range of the bow.

Antelope can be successfully taken with the bow. It is one of the most fascinating types of hunting, but the methods used are entirely different from the accepted methods of gun hunting where the hunters often ride around in jeeps or automobiles to obtain their long-range shooting.

During the first few days of the season when these hunters are cruising around the flat plains they have a tendency to chase the game into the hilly, rocky sections of the country where they can be stalked most successfully. Hunting them in this type of country is not different from hunting any other kind of animal. You simply steal around among the rocks and hills to locate your quarry and then place yourself in a position in the path ahead of them if they are moving along or feeding. If they are bedded down, try to make a stalk by using a rock or hill or brush or some natural object of concealment. Binoculars or field glasses are almost a must for this kind of hunting, as the antelope are very hard to see even when they are out on the open plain lying down amongst the short sagebrush. They blend in with the natural surrounding and can easily be overlooked. Also, if you are bent on bagging a buck you can determine the sex of the animal more readily by the use of glasses.

Both male and female antelope have horns. The doe rarely has horns as high as the ears whereas the horns of a mature buck are well above his ears. These horns are ebony black in most cases; they are hooked on the tips and have a single, rather short prong pointing forward. The bucks are distinguished also by a black spot on the throat just under the ears. Both sexes of antelope have white rump patches which show up dazzling white when they are alarmed. They also have a musk sac that emits an odor so that other antelope can get warning signals by both sight and scent.

Contrary to popular opinion, antelope can also be successfully hunted with a bow from a blind at a water hole or a runway near a water hole. This antelope country is quite barren except for sagebrush that grows on an average of 12–18 inches high and the problem of making a blind is one that requires serious attention.

First of all, your hunting gear should include a mattock, which is a pick having a rather broad hoe-like blade on one side. You will also need a shovel.

The site for a blind should be along a runway or near a waterhole or both. Dig a hole about two or three feet in diameter and about fifteen or eighteen inches deep in which to put your legs while you sit on the rim. Then drive some stakes, which also must be brought with you, in a circular pattern six to eight feet in diameter around this excavation.

With the mattock grub out some sagebrush and build a sort of barricade by piling it up between the stakes. When one row is completed, run a string around the circle of stakes through the sage. Con-

Fred is shown examining the tip of his bow, damaged when it was accidentally stepped on by his horse. He repaired it expertly, hundreds of miles from the proper tools and materials. His embarrassed horse looks on.

A western bowhunting camp in 1952. Left to right: Fred Bear; Tom Burke, Nubbie Pate, unidentified cook, Charlie Kroll, Ed Henkel, Duke Underhill and Bob Morely.

Here Fred relaxes at home, prophetically close to the globe by his chair that he used to plan his travels. It was toward the end of the 1950's and he was soon to begin his worldwide bowhunting travels in earnest.

Fred's father, Harry Bear and two young archery friends during an N.F.A.A. Tournament in East Tawas, Michigan.

tinue in this way with rows of sagebrush and string until the wall is about the height of the top of your head when you are sitting down but will allow you to stand up and shoot in any direction.

The reason for the stakes and twine is that the wind blows over the plains most of the time and will blow your blind all over the prairie unless the sage is anchored with string.

One of the most annoying difficulties of antelope hunting from a blind, or by stalking too, lies in the fact that the cattle that inhabit the ranges use the same runways and waterholes that the antelope use. While these whitefaces are sleepy-looking animals they are not to be regarded lightly. We found them to have a sense of sight, hearing and scent that seemed superior to the antelope. They come ambling down the trails to the waterholes and though you sit very quietly with the wind and other conditions in your favor, they sometimes stop immediately in front of the blind, turn their heads slowly and point you. We found that antelope watch the actions of the cattle and if they find them content and serene, all is well. But if the cattle show the slightest alarm or watchfulness the antelope are reluctant to come in.

In one instance, two of us had blinds on opposite sides of a waterhole about a hundred yards apart. We had been watching the area for some time when several cattle came down. They proceeded to line up in stoical formation and point us like bird dogs holding down partridges, although as far as we knew we had been absolutely motionless. This kept up for an unendurable period until my partner's patience snapped and he jumped up, letting out a war whoop that scattered cattle and the fringe of cautious antelope all over the plains. He later shot an antelope from this blind, however, at a distance of about fifty feet.

Most antelope ranges are hunted rather heavily during the opening days of the season and again on the first weekend. During these periods it is well for the bow hunter to stick to the stalking methods as the gun will interfere many times with blind hunting and, too, the hunting activity on the plains pushes the game back into the hilly and rocky areas. It is not meant to imply that stalking in these rough areas cannot be done successfully at any time, because a certain number of antelope live in this rougher part of the country, especially the larger old bucks.

It is often said that the antelope is a curious animal. I did not find it so unless having an animal look you over at four or five hundred yards can be classed as curiosity. I found them to be very little different from deer in respect to intelligence and wariness. They have a bark or snort that sounds something like a crow but more rasping. The sound can be mistaken for the call of a crow and one is inclined to look up on the rocks or the scraggly trees that grow in the hilly parts of the country when he should be looking down below him on the plains. The gnarled trees, by the way, that grow up in the tops of the hills are very interesting specimens. They have a difficult struggle to keep alive and develop in spite of the elements. The wind blows almost constantly and the trunks are twisted and deformed. One sees skeletons of trees that have died many, many years ago. The bark is gone and their naked trunks and limbs seem to have been burned by fire but actually it is the everlasting sun and wind beating on them and the cold and biting blizzards of winter that give them this stark appearance.

These hills are also the home of the cottontail rabbit and mule deer, although in the area where we hunted we saw no deer. We found traces of them, however, in the form of shed antlers. Coyotes, badgers, prairie dogs, gophers and jackrabbits live here too. There are sage hens in large flocks that are quite impressive, some of them as large as young turkeys. The flocks often number seventy-five or a hundred at times. The jackrabbits, which are almost white and of enormous size, live in dry washes in lower ground where sage has grown to greater heights.

Antelope hunting is fascinating for many reasons. Game is in sight almost all of the time, whether you are stalking or hunting from a blind. This in itself adds greatly to the interest of the sport. Another encouraging factor is the weather. The temperature is warm during the day. In the middle of the day and early afternoon it is hot, sometimes going to a hundred. The nights might be cool or very cold, even below freezing.

One's tent has to be staked down solidly. For this you will need good hardwood or steel pegs. The earth is hard. Tent poles must be brought with you. The only firewood except for discarded bits that may be picked up around an old corral or from the remains of a cabin, are the roots and dried sterns of sagebrush, which are satisfactory for cooking fires.

Normally it is possible to drive a car right up to the campsite, which should be near a waterhole. The water in these holes is suitable for bathing but drinking and cooking water must be taken with you and is obtainable from the nearest ranch. Several five-gallon cans should be taken along for this purpose.

An antelope hunt is not a costly one. No guides are required and most ranchers will welcome you since they receive a revenue for each antelope killed on their property by way of a coupon attached to your permit. It is interesting to note that of the estimated 36,000 antelope that were taken in the United States in 1950, 22,000 were from Wyoming. Ninety-five out of every hundred hunters were successful.

To obtain a Wyoming permit, write to the Wyoming Game & Fish Commission, Information Section, Box 1589, Cheyenne, Wyoming, 82002 and ask for their antelope hunting map and for an antelope permit application form. You will discover upon examining the map that the state of Wyoming is divided into a number of hunting areas. You need to select the area you wish to hunt and apply for that area. While the season generally runs from mid-August to mid-September, the deadline for permit application is normally March 15th. The necessary fees must be submitted with your application and the approved licenses are mailed out by the first of July. Some areas presently allow the taking of more than one antelope per season. Incidentally, our hunting was done in the Fremont Natrona area, about halfway between Lander and Rawlins.

Once you have your permit it is simply a question of getting your group and camping equipment together and driving to the area in Wyoming that your permit calls for. Drive along the highways and make inquiries at the numerous ranches scattered about concerning the hunting on their lands. You will find them quite cooperative for the most part. I might add that it is better to settle on a hunting area that has waterholes spotted around rather than one with a stream running through it. As obviously, with a stream flowing through a large section, game can water at just about any place, whereas if they are dependent upon waterholes at infrequent intervals, they are almost compelled to use these places for drinking. Antelope have no particular time to water. They come all day long, as many during the hottest part of the day as in the morning or evening.

The best hunting clothing is medium weight wool. Even in the hottest part of the day wool feels good, in the cool of early morning and late evening it is really necessary. Canvas top gym shoes are preferable to heavier hunting boots even though you occasionally brush against a sharp cactus and wish you had more protection. The light-weight, rubbersoled gym shoe is a great help in climbing over the rough and rocky terrain, as well as when walking on the flats.

While the days are extremely warm, the humidity is practically zero and game will keep for several days if stored in the shade during the day and hung out in the air at night. Locker plants with facilities for storing and shipping the meat are available in towns of medium size.

If you are one of the army of north-central deer hunters you will get a kick out of this hot weather, open plains hunting. Take plenty of bedding along to keep you warm at night but don't try to coax antelope up by waving a white flag. They won't come.

EDITOR'S NOTE: We suggest you write the Wyoming Game & Fish Commission, at the address noted above for the very latest in season dates, hunting areas and fees.

"Radar," Fred's tracker, interpreter and guide during his first trip to French Equatorial Africa in 1955, helps display a large iguana.

CHAPTER 9

Early in 1955, Al Vander Kogel of Abercrombie & Fitch in New York asked Fred to join the first organized bow and arrow safari to Africa. Deciding it was time to expand his hunting horizons and realizing the tremendous advertising and promotional benefits of such a trip, Fred accepted and in March left New York via Air France in company with Vander Kogel, Ken Lockridge, John Smith, Zoli Vidor and Frank Travins of New York, Cliff Wiseman of New Jersey and Joe Woodard and Steilson Ferris of Michigan. Also in the group were photographers Don Redinger, Pittsburgh and Robert Halmi, New York. They were assigned to make a film of the hunt for Bear Archery. (Halmi is now a successful New York television producer.)

After brief stops in Paris, Tunis and Fort Lamy, the party was met by Professional Hunter Jean Gerin at Fort Archambault. Gerin spoke only French, in which none of the hunters were conversant but they managed to get along through one of the assistant guides who spoke a smattering of English.

The safari, complete with a retinue of native trackers and skinners, a cook, a mechanic, a laundry man and so on, traveled in motor trucks. They were in the Chad District of French Equatorial Africa, almost in the center of the African continent and about 300 miles north of the equator. It was a wild section of the country where many tribal conflicts had occurred and where cannibalism had not been outlawed until 1947.

Following a day of travel through the bush, including two river crossings, the group made camp near the native village of Golongosso.

From the start a great variety of game was encountered but Fred soon realized that approaching to a respectable bow range of animals would be difficult. It was no trouble to get within one hundred yards or so — good rifle range — in the flat, semi-open terrain but to cut that distance in half was a real problem. Bear's intention on this trip was to test the bow and arrow only on smaller African game.

Many stalks on various antelope species ended in frustration. One of the main exasperations for Fred was the lack of direct communication. To plan a stalk, he spoke English to the assistant guide, the guide spoke French to Gerin, Gerin spoke the native tongue of Sango to the trackers, who used sign language to Fred and the plans usually went awry.

Lunches and evening dinners were an unexpected delight for the Americans, excellent five-course meals complete with five changes of china, sil-

A native leopard trap is examined.

Natives carry Fred's Damalisque back to camp. French Equatorial Africa, 1955.

The beautifully marked in-velvet antlers of Fred's British Columbia moose are admired by Fred and Wes Loback, his host for the hunt.

verware and various wines. Fred could not avoid comparing the situation to some of the hunts he had been on in the States where the guide carried an old frying pan tied to his saddle, a chunk of bacon and a loaf of dry bread in his saddlebags. As the paying guest hauled in water and firewood, the guide cooked the bacon, handing over the frying pan to be scoured when he was through. In French Africa, if the hunter so much as picked up a pitcher to pour another glass of water, the outfitter's raised eyebrows intimating that gentlemen leave such things to the native help.

Among the most interesting aspects of the trip was the opportunity to visit and become acquainted with the customs of various native tribes, including the Pygmies of the Belgian Congo and the plate-lipped women of Chad.

The game bag was not spectacular. Fred came back with two reedbuck, one oribi, a large iguana and a fine topi or damalisque.

But the country fascinated him. Bowhunting in Africa for the first time was not too different from first hunting trips to any country or territory. The initial trip is more or less experimental, a chance for one to learn about the terrain and animal habits, amassing the experience that would stand him in good stead on succeeding trips. Bear was determined to return.

Further details of this, plus two more African safaris and a dozen of Bear's other major hunts in various parts of the world between 1955 and 1967, are to be found in a book he authored a few years later entitled, *"Fred Bear's Field Notes"* Doubleday, 1976. (Available in paperback from Bear Archery.)

In the fall of 1955, Fred and his wife left Michigan for another western trip. They drove to Seattle through spectacular country with stops at Glacier National Park and Mount Hood, etc. At the latter, they had to step over a huge St. Bernard dog in order to get into the lodge. The beautiful animal was "tired" and he had found a spot of warm sunshine in the doorway and meant to stay there. They also remembered for years the dinner that night of fresh salmon, garden peas, red raspberries and cream.

At Glacier one day, a tourist asked Fred (who was photographing eagles) how much his telephoto lens cost and Fred replied genially, "Oh, don't ask me that on such a nice day." Fred's growing inventory of camera equipment soon equaled that of a professional and says a great deal about the dedication he brought to the job of doing the very best he could to help promote his sport of bowhunting.

Arriving in Seattle, they met Wes Loback, who had invited Fred to share a hunt in British Columbia. Henrietta, who had planned to stay in the Washington-Oregon area during the hunt was persuaded to join the party in British Columbia instead. The Lobacks lived in Seattle but had a summer home in Tweedsmuir Provincial Park, B.C., east of Bella Coola. Their lodge was located on the shores of Ootsa Lake. Fred and his photographer, Don Redinger, flew up with Wes in his Cessna.

The hunting camp was a 20-minute flight from the Loback lodge. Despite generally bad weather (Fred's diary mentions sleeping at camp in four layers of clothing and two sleeping bags), the hunting proved good. During their 13-day stay, Fred, besides completing a film of the hunt, bagged a large

This Yukon Grizzly was the first big game animal taken by Fred with his new broadhead design, the Fred Bear Razorhead.

Larry Ostrander operating the Razorhead machine; another of Fred's inventions. The Razorhead hunting point became the most popular style of all time.

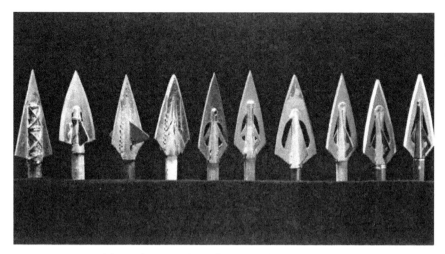

Progression of design changes in the Fred Bear Razorhead. Latest model at the right.

moose with antlers in the velvet and an Osborne or mountain caribou. The moose was an unusually handsome trophy, its chocolate brown antler velvet patterned with white swirls.

Fred's wife did not like flying in small planes. She wanted desperately to go but the thought of flying up in the little Cessna terrified her. Driving by car through that wild and mountainous country seemed equally alarming. Fred laughed off her fears as always and said to Wes, "If settling this country had been left to my wife, we'd all be clustered around Plymouth Rock!"

However, someone had to get supplies and gear up to the wilderness and Henrietta finally set off on a two-day journey in an overloaded station wagon with the Bear's long time friend, Glenn St. Charles and the hunting camp cook.

"I sat like a hen in a crate surrounded and packed in solidly by other crates for the journey," she wrote in her journal. "The camp cook was a reckless driver, speeding around curves and teetering on the outermost limits of the narrow road. There was no traffic and we seemed to be the only human beings on earth foolhardy enough to attempt this dangerous expedition. My imagination flew out of bounds over what would be left of us after plunging down those beautiful but terrible cliffs.

"I was finally moved to tell Glenn that I was dying of fright and

Fred presents Arthur Godfrey with a bow and arrows at Grousehaven.

Fred instructing friends in archery at Grousehaven in the early 1950's. Left to right:
General Curtis LeMay, Arthur Godfrey, Bill Boyer, Basil Hughes and Fred Bear.

could he influence the driver to slow down. He tried but the message fell on deaf ears and we careened ahead as before. The scenery was unbelievably beautiful, however, and since there was no turning back, his driving had to be endured."

On the second day, the terrifying twisted canyons of the Fraser River were gone, but the ride now became a veritable trail-blazing experience. A new road was being cut through the wilderness. Giant trees lay along the shady trail, the great circle of their exposed roots resembled the up-flipped skirts of cancan dancers. The sand was so deep and fine that it seeped into every crevice of the station wagon, covering the contents and passengers in a thick layer. "Even our eyelashes were heavy with a coating of gray dust," she noted.

They were met at the Lodge, a completely modern dwelling cozy with stone fireplaces and bearskin rugs on the floors, by the hunters.

When Bear was not field-testing his products in the mid-fifties, he was doing continuous research on archery equipment, sending home suggestions and orders from the hunting camps. One such communication concerned a faulty bow tip:

"…make the bow as is. Cut the grooves even wider and then bond a piece of fiberglass (impregnated but not cured) about an inch wide across the ends of the belly glass — pushed down into the grooves with a rubber male form and cure. I don't know whether the bow will stand the curing heat or not. If not, use a piece of glass cloth impregnated with epoxy.

That is all I have to say about this problem. I don't want another twenty-seven thousand write-off like we had in August on the Magnum. Bill, this is your problem."

An outstanding example of Fred's product research was the Bear Razorhead, first marketed in 1956. Fred had realized for some time the need for a more effective head for hunting arrows. He had come up with the basic design in 1953 and tested it for three years on hunting trips. The final test, in which Fred brought down his 50th big game trophy, a Yukon grizzly, with a Razorhead-tipped arrow, satisfied him that it was ready for production.

The main blade of the Razorhead was of a special steel alloy hard enough to hold an edge, yet soft enough to sharpen with a file. It featured a slotted ferrule that accepted replaceable auxiliary blades. These were of thin, razor blade stock, sharply honed and designed to increase appreciably the cutting pattern without reducing penetration. Further advantages lay in the fact that the auxiliary cutting edges eliminated pinch on the arrow shaft, yet were limber enough to fold or break when they struck heavy bone, again aiding penetration.

The biggest problem posed by this new broadhead model was producing enough to meet demand. To do so, Fred designed a complicated machine with some 14 stations and hired a shop in Prescott, Michigan, to make it. Long after the promised delivery date, the machine had not been assembled. But the Razorhead already had been announced and a great many heads had to be brazed and finished by hand to meet the demand. For a time, Bear took a substantial loss. Finally, he canceled the job contract and had a broadhead machine using an in-line process built in his own plant. A second broadhead machine using a rotary process was constructed later.

Perhaps the most significant and far-reaching "advertising" for Bear came about through the 1952 radio and television broadcasts of the extremely popular "Arthur Godfrey Show." Godfrey's style of carrying on homey talks laced throughout with his pitches for the sponsors and performers was on everyone's list.

Fred first met Godfrey at 'Grousehaven', a private 3,000-acre prime hunting area near Rose City, Michigan, that was owned by Harold R. "Bill" Boyer of Grosse Pointe, Michigan. Boyer hosted a group of celebrities who were interested in hunting every fall at this untamed tract of land in northern Michigan. In the early fifties, Fred had become a member of the group that included, besides Godfrey, such friends from Boyer's war years (he had been head of General Motors' Cleveland Tank Division and architect of its Air Transport Division) as General Curtis LeMay, Commander of the Strategic Air Command and later Chief of Staff, U.S. Air Force; Harley Earl, head stylist and designer at General Motors for 35 years; Four-star General Hank Everest, head of T.A.C., World War II and Dick Boutelle and Larry Bell, heads of Fairchild Aircraft and Bell Aircraft, respectively, plus whoever was president of General Motors at the time.

Fred, of course, introduced archery to the group and the most enthusiastic response came from Godfrey. He soon began talking about Fred Bear and the sport of archery on his radio and television shows. Letters of inquiry concerning archery poured in as a result. Fred was twice featured on Godfrey's television shows — one out of the New York studio and the other staged

The Bear Archery group during a recent hunt at Grousehaven: left to right, Art Botzenmayer, Director of Purchasing; Bob Owens, Personnel Director; Fred Bear; Dick Schmelz, R & D Department; Gene Goldacker, Customer Service and Bill Granlund, Bear Archery President.

at Godfrey's farm in Virginia. The setting for the latter was on the sloping lawns of the farm. Attendants were responsible for keeping peacocks, ducks and barking dogs at a safe distance; not a leaf fell unbidden from the trees. Everything clicked into exact time-slots, all of which belied the easygoing, one-on-one tone of the broadcast.

At Fred's daughter's home in Grayling during this broadcast, when the familiar voice of Fred Bear came on the air, "Crazylegs," the Krolls' little Dachshund, suddenly jumped from his seat between the children and ran excitedly around the room searching for Papa Bear. With no success, he crawled under the television stand and refused to come out for several hours. The following account of these broadcasts came from the Crawford County Avalanche, the weekly newspaper in Fred's hometown of Grayling, Michigan:

A few of Fred's hunting trophies and archery innovations were on display for some time in the Bear Archery reception room, but it finally became so crowded (note displays on ceiling) that plans for a separate museum building were begun.

Thursday, July 10, 1958
FRED BEAR TO DUEL ARTHUR GODFREY

To those who follow Arthur Godfrey's TV and radio programs, his show scheduled for 10 a.m. next Friday, July 11, should be particularly interesting. The program, direct from Godfrey's farm in Paconian Springs, Virginia will have archery as its central theme. Grayling's Fred Bear will be there and in addition several other interesting guests connected with the sport of archery will be present. Mrs. Carole Meinhart of Pittsburgh, PA and O.K. Smathers, of Brevard, No. Car., last year's world archery champions, will be in action. Also appearing will be Tim Cantwell, a 16-year-old high school junior from Kirkwood, Mo., who recently shot his way to a berth on the 1958 team to represent the United States at the world championship in Brussels, Belgium. There will undoubtedly be a discussion of this shoot, as well as of the forthcoming National Field Archery championships and the big money shoot in Grayling July 28 through 31. Highlight of the program is expected to be a highly informal shooting match between Bear and Godfrey. Tune in on the Godfrey Show this Friday at 10 a.m.

Godfrey's New York television offices were elegant and efficient. Outside the doors, amateur performers sat nervously waiting their turns in the Talent Scout Competition. Here again, everything fell into place. Godfrey, moving swiftly on crutches (he carried on these activities despite surgery for serious hip problems), was everywhere at once. Every member of the orchestra got sharp attention from Godfrey. He changed the score of some of the musical numbers three or four times prior to the performance.

Fred's rehearsal was just the opposite. Easy, friendly and enthusiastic talk about archery, lasting fourteen minutes. It hardly seemed worthwhile at the time but fan mail pouring in from all over the United States proved otherwise. A wire from the Brancroft Tennis people said: "Wonderful, marvelous, what a show. Especially the segment of the man with the bow!"

This exposure from Godfrey went on for many years, including a trip to Africa in 1964 (see Chapter XI) when he was a member of Fred's hunting party and took several trophies with his bow. It was during this safari that Godfrey's famous radio tapes were picked up periodically from the African camp and flown across the Atlantic for broadcasting in the United States. The publicity and recognition Fred and bowhunting received from these broadcasts would be hard to evaluate in dollars.

Of interest are Fred's notes concerning his planning session for the African trip with Godfrey in New York.

FRED BEAR'S REPORT ON ACTIVITIES IN NEW YORK FEB. 18 & 19

18th: Met in Arthur Godfrey's office 10 a.m. Office in CBS Building. Two-room suite. Large and comfortable. Present: Bear, Halmi, Godfrey and his producer. Talked about Mozambique hunt, radio, television, airplanes and related subjects. Godfrey wants to see tiger and bear films. Agree to meet again next morning for this purpose.

19th: Back in Godfrey's office. Present: Bear, Halmi, Godfrey. Doug

The old Russian trappers' cabin built in 1927. Fred has just walked back to camp with part of his caribou. Scrub willows had taken root in the sod-covered roof, 1958.

Interior of the Little Delta trappers' cabin. Keith Clemmons serves a meal to Mike and Bud Gray, Jack Albright and Fred Bear, 1958.

Kennedy, managing editor *TRUE*, Pete Barrett, outdoor editor, Godfrey's producer, his script writer and his lawyer. Godfrey switched his radio on and we heard his first blast-off of our safari taped the night before. Ran both films. Documentary they say and can't use but they bring birth to Godfrey's suggestion that we make a TV film in Africa, for which he suggests the title, "FUN IN THE BUSH." Much discussion. Discussion about details of the hunt, which at the present boils down to this:

Alitalia supplies two first-class round trip fares for Halmi and me. *TRUE* magazine will send Pete Barrett on the hunt and will pay Godfrey's expenses. *TRUE* will do a story, with cover pix of Godfrey hunting in Africa. *TRUE* will do a story on me with cover pix of hunting in Africa and will also do a story on the tiger hunt. During the last five years, *TRUE* has been doing a series of stories on "HUNTS WITH FAMOUS PEOPLE." Ten of these have already been run. The Godfrey and Bear stories will complete the series to become the contents of a book to be published by *TRUE*. Stories already finished are hunts with Joe Foss, Gov. Quinn of Hawaii, Roy Rogers, Kirk Douglas, the Shah of Iran, the Maharajah of Bundi, King Hussein of Jordan, King Paul of Greece, Prince Bernard of Holland and Tito of Yugoslavia.

The Apache camp trailer people are sending one of their units for our use on safari. They are also contributing to the cost of the hunt.

At 11:30 a.m., Godfrey, Halmi, script writer, producer and lawyer are in a huddle about the TV film. Kennedy, Barrett, Alitalia people and myself are discussing other details. Meeting breaks up at noon. Halmi will work with Godfrey's staff about TV film. Barrett goes to lunch with Alitalia people. Halmi and I go to lunch with Kennedy and complete our discussion. Kennedy may take Justice Douglas to Goldfish Lake this fall to include in the series for their book. Kennedy much impressed with our films. Says he has a contact with ABC's "WIDE WORLD OF SPORTS" and will contact them. I left the films with Halmi. He will follow through on this. (Fred later made many hunting appearances on ABC's "AMERICAN SPORTS-

The morning after Fred fashioned this moose call from birch bark off the trappers' cabin roof, it was used to call in Bill Wright's record moose.

Bill Wright of San Francisco with a moose from the Little Delta that was the bowhunting world record at one time, 1959.

MAN" television series.)

In addition to the above-mentioned proposals, Halmi and I will produce at least one, perhaps two films of the hunt, which will be the property of Bear Archery Company. Still pictures will be the joint property of Halmi and me.

FRED BEAR 2-21-'64

Godfrey, although he appeared in business matters to be deadly serious and relentless, was capable of warm friendship as well. One day he called the Bear residence in Grayling to speak to Fred. Both the Bears' were asleep, suffering from sore throats and colds. Godfrey, upon hearing Henrietta's hoarse and groggy response, quickly signed off, saying he would call again. However, he immediately contacted Lillian Hill, Fred's secretary of many years, to ask if people at the plant knew the Bears were sick and if they needed anything. That Christmas he sent a beautiful Della Robbia wreath for their front door.

Many outdoorsmen, asked to recall their most memorable wilderness experience, will tell of a hunt full of danger and hardship or the taking of a record-class trophy. Although Fred had more than his share of both, he has often said that his favorite memories have to do with a combination of fine companions, a comfortable camp in a relatively untouched region and interesting encounters with wildlife — in that order.

The hunts that most stood out in his mind took place in 1958 and 1959 in the Little Delta region of south-central Alaska. In 1957, while on a bowhunting trip in Alaska's Brooks Range, Glenn St. Charles and Dick Bolding of Seattle and Keith Clemmons of Fairbanks became acquainted with a bush pilot who suggested that they look over an area in the Alaska Range, south of Fairbanks.

On a reconnaissance flight with pilot Marc Stella, St. Charles had discovered a sizeable stream running through a beautiful valley rich with moose and caribou, with white Dall sheep speckling the bordering mountain slopes. According to the map, this was the Little Delta River Valley. From the air, Glenn spotted an abandoned trapper's cabin that he believed was ideally located for a hunting camp.

Ten miles down river, where Portage Creek emptied into the Little Delta River, they found a bush airstrip that was still serviceable. Flying back upriver and looking around the cabin, they came upon a gravel bar that could be converted to a short airstrip for a Super Cub through considerable energy expended with the proper tools.

Bud Gray, one of Fred's hunting companions, stalked to within a few yards of this fine Dall ram.

Fred with a Barren Ground caribou taken in the valley of the Little Delta.

The next day, the entire group flew to Portage Creek and from there back-packed up the Little Delta Valley to the trapper's cabin. It was in remarkably good condition, considering it obviously had not been used in many years. Meanwhile, the pilot air-dropped supplies, including shovels, saws and axes, for hacking out the new landing strip.

Between hunting forays, the men wrestled with boulders, cut alder and willow and rearranged earth and gravel until a suitable but short and hopefully adequate airstrip finally emerged.

Plans were made for hunts there the following year and Fred and a few others were invited along. In flying to the area from Fairbanks the party's baggage was marked "drop" or "no drop." The men were flown in one at a time with their "no drop" gear. "Drop" bundles, containing such unbreakable items as sleeping bags and bush clothing came in later in a larger plane and were kicked out to fall in a clearing near the cabin.

The flight from Fairbanks to the camp was exciting and beautiful. Skimming low over tundra and through mountains, the passengers saw an abundance of game. The flight took 30 to 40 minutes, depending on the wind and to add to the thrill there always seemed to be doubts upon landing as to whether there would be enough runway left to brake to a stop.

The cabin demanded respect. It had been built by two Russian fur trappers and prospectors in 1927 with the finest of backwoods workmanship. Fred met one the builders later in Fairbanks and was told about the construction. The Russians had entered the country with a dog team and a long freighter sled that was still at the cabin, although it had not been used since 1936. Saws, axes, a hand plane and wolf and beaver traps had been left behind. The cabin, 20 by 24 feet, was made of good-sized spruce logs that had been flattened on the inside with an adze. A window in each side of the cabin had birch bars to keep out curious bears.

At the front was a covered porch ten feet deep. The roof was constructed of poles whipsawed in half with the flat surface down. On the upper side, the spaces between these poles had been filled with moss. The whole roof was then shingled with squares of birchbark and covered with several inches of earth, in which large scrub willows had taken root through the years. Stout floorboards had been sledded in and the place had a wood-burning cook-stove, handmade tables, chairs and a bunk bed.

Only the door was missing. Grizzly bears had torn it off and left the inside of the cabin a shambles. Down a trail that led to a small spring creek were dog kennels in decay. Off to one side of the trail a cache resembling a small cabin stood high on two peeled spruce poles. Trees along the trail had been scarred by grizzly teeth and claws and tufts of brown hair were caught in the bark.

The cabin was in a marvelously peaceful setting. Sitting quietly at its rustic table, bathed in sunlight from the open door, Fred felt at ease with his surroundings.

The hunters arrived on August 17, 1958 and hunting season opened on the 20th so there was time to settle in and become acquainted with the territory. Game could be seen from the camp at almost any time. Caribou and moose browsed in the diamond willow thickets of the valley floor and across the lichen-carpeted hillsides. Farther up, contrasting sharply with the surrounding dark rock masses, Dall sheep looked down on the scene with steadfast gazes, their keen amber eyes missing nothing that moved. The weather was beautiful; crisp but not yet frosty, much like early September in the Midwest.

Glenn St. Charles and Keith Clemmons established a tent camp about three miles down the valley, providing easier access to a band of mountain sheep directly across and a few thousand feet above the Little Delta River. Fred spent the first few days there with Glenn and Dick Bolding. Several practice stalks for photographs helped tune up legs and lungs. Fred was making a film and Dick was the photographer.

Their hunting was never hurried. On the contrary, they all seemed content to ease along in keeping with the timeless feeling of the region, trying for bow-range encounters, but never pushing themselves. Not that the hunting was easy. Wild animals that have been hunted for thousands of years have sharp senses and the effective range of the bow and arrow is comparatively short.

The third day of the hunt found Fred and Dick headed for the top of the mountain. To get there, they had to ford a glacial stream with hip boots. In the morning, water in these streams is low and wading across is not too difficult. By evening, however, the water is often considerably higher — a result of the day's glacial melt and hip boots are sometimes not high enough.

They spent three hours observing and photographing a small band of Dall sheep. Early in the afternoon they sighted a good ram about a third of a mile away. It was in fine position for a stalk and Fred was able to work within 25 yards before being detected while Dick obtained some good footage of the action with his movie camera. Fred's arrow proved effective. The ram traveled but a short way before collapsing and rolled down a shale slide. It was not of record size but had a nice, full curl showing 11 annual growth rings.

There is no better meat than that of mountain sheep, consequently Fred

Fred with his Dall ram taken on the mountain slopes above the Little Delta.

Fred's specialty as a camp cook is roasting mountain sheep ribs. Here he is doing the honors during the 1958 hunt.

and Dick were warmly welcomed by the group in camp. Several had shot at caribou, but none had made a hit. Two of the hunters had run into a grizzly in a blueberry patch and took pictures from 15 yards before withdrawing (grizzlies were not legal game until September in that area).

Fred prepared a savory treat for the party by roasting the ribs of his mountain sheep over an open fire. It is worthwhile knowing how he did this and the process was described in his own words a few years later in "The Big Sky" (The Fred Bear Sports Club Publication) as follows:

"I have roasted in hunting camps the rib side of many species of game from deer through moose and have established a grading, in terms of tastiness, with mountain sheep heading the list, followed by mountain goat, then moose, caribou and deer."

"Roasting ribs outdoors is my only culinary achievement. It is not difficult and whatever reputation I enjoy in this field is not deserved. It is a fact however, that on a lazy day in a hunting camp on the Little Delta River in Alaska in 1958, I was cleaning up about camp and had piled up and burned some brush."

"Two hunting companions in a spike camp up on the opposite mountain hunting sheep saw the smoke, thought I was roasting ribs and hiked down for the feast. Here is how it's done:

"Cut two green forked stakes and two poles about four feet long. Make four 'S' hooks from coat hangers or bailing wire. Break the ribs with a hatchet or axe every 4 or 5 inches. Fasten two S hooks top and bottom."

"In the meantime, you have started a fire after clearing away the leaves and other inflammables. If hardwood is available it will take some time to burn to a bed of hot coals, at which time you drive the forked stakes and hang the meat to roast. A good bed of hardwood coals should be sufficient to roast the ribs. If your fuel is coniferous, the coals will not burn as long and wood must be added from time to time."

"If you have aluminum foil, shape a rectangular pan to catch the drippings for basting, although this is not a must."

"Lift the pole from which the ribs are hung and turn from time to time. Turn them upside down occasionally also. To do this, the other pole is made fast to the bottom S hooks. Lift the ribs by the top pole and with the other hand, grasp the bottom pole. Turn them 180 degrees and place back on the forked stakes. These turnings, both front to back and top to bottom, assure a uniformity of cooking and reverse the flow of juices to prevent drying out."

"It will be ready to eat in about two hours, when the meat turns brown or when you no longer can stand the heavenly aroma."

Jack Albright was the next successful bowman, taking a bull caribou near camp. A few days later, Fred shot a bull that made the mistake of stopping for a last look at 45 yards.

The next evening, hunters Bud Gray, Benton Harbor, Michigan and Bob Arvine came into base camp with a beautiful Dall ram. After a lengthy and difficult stalk, Bud had shot the ram from a distance of four yards. The head was a fine one with full curl and wide-flaring horns. A quarter of a century later it still ranks in the top half of the Pope & Young record book listings.

Glenn had also downed what he referred to as an "eatin'-size" caribou, so the party had plenty of the finest meat on earth in camp. The final trophy of the hunt was a huge caribou taken by Keith Clemmons.

At the end of the stay, the hunters were determined that bears would not destroy the cabin door again, so before departing they spiked crosscut saw blades across it with the teeth facing out. The following spring, bush pilot Dick McIntyre checked the cabin and discovered to his amazement that a bear or bears had bypassed the door and broken in by tearing an entry through the roof then had torn up the door from the inside to get out.

Bud Gray later wrote of his association with Fred on the Little Delta: "A long stay in a remote hunting camp is a true test of a hunter's tolerance, good nature and plain consideration of his companions. Fred Bear has got to be the world's best hunter. I could stay with him on shooting at random targets, but on the clutch shots in the split-second action of the hunt, there was no contest. His lob shot over a rock ridge to kill a Stone sheep on our British Columbia hunt is a stunning example of his instinctive skill."

Crawford County Avalanche Thursday, January 29, 1959
BOWHUNTERS OFFER CARIBOU DINNER, MOVIES

Through the generosity of Fred Bear, those people lucky enough to obtain tickets will have the pleasure of eating the young caribou that Fred shot on his recent trip to Alaska.

The Grayling Bowhunters, with the very able assistance of Carrol Wert, are serving a Caribou Dinner, Thursday night, January 29, at Wert's Lone Pine Inn. The proceeds will go to the club. The price of this gourmand's delight is only two dollars and tickets may be obtained from Nels Olson at the shoe store or Bob Smock, or any of the club directors.

An added attraction will be pictures of bow hunting, including the film of Negley's $10,000.00 elephant kill. *The movies will be shown at the indoor range following the dinner, which will be served from 4:30 to 7:00 p.m.

*William Negley of Houston, Texas won a bet of $10,000.00 that he could take an elephant with bow & arrow. The prize money was given to the library in Houston. Negley used equipment made at the Bear Plant in Grayling.

When the group assembled for a second Little Delta hunt in August 1959, everything was in order. McIntryre had put on a new door, but had left it open so the bears could move in and out at will and there was little damage inside.

The year before, there had been considerable backpacking to do. This time, someone in the group brought a "Merry Packer," a sort of elongated wheelbarrow powered by a small gas engine. It had handles at both ends and rolled on a low-pressure tire. A backpacker's dream, the machine could handle 500 pounds easily and would go almost anywhere, through muskeg, over rocks and up steep slopes.

Fred leads the way across a neat bit of engineering accomplished by the Little Delta hunters. His companion is Bob Kelly.

The weather was not so pleasant this year — the hunters experienced considerable rain and toward the end of the trip had several inches of snow. The river rose above wading depth, a situation that had to be overcome by the hunters who built a suspension bridge over the water.

A short distance from camp, spruce trees leaned precariously out over the water. These were joined by two spruce poles dropped into the water on the opposite bank. The poles, supported by guy wires anchored to a tree, were then fashioned with ladder rungs. Handrails completed this ingenious piece of wilderness engineering and served the party well for the remainder of the hunt. Bob Kelly, Jack Albright and Bob Arvine did the actual construction.

Despite stormy weather, the bowmen had considerable success. In two weeks, they bagged six caribou and two bull moose, one of which taken by Bill Wright of San Francisco, occupied first place for its species in the Pope & Young records for 14 years. It was brought into range with a birch bark moose call made by Fred Bear.

After leaving the Little Delta camp, Fred, Glenn St. Charles, Dick Bolding and Russ Wright flew to Cordova, Alaska, where they joined skipper Ed Bilder back aboard his 58 foot commercial fishing boat, the *Valiant Maid*, for a brown bear hunt along the shores and islands of Prince William Sound. In spite of the weather, the hunt proved enjoyable and intriguing, with opportunities to observe first-hand the activities of a great variety of wildlife, from whales and sea otters to mountain goats and black and brown bears. Although Fred stalked and downed a medium-size brown bear, he wanted to try for one of the giants of that species and before leaving laid plans with Ed for another expedition the following year.

EDITOR'S NOTE: Twenty-five years after the photograph of the Little Delta bridge was taken and the raging spring floods of Alaska's glacial streams had carried the bridge to oblivion, Fred was in Waukesha, Wisconsin talking to a gathering of archers when Terry Koper wrote this article about the photograph for the Milwaukee Sentinel.

Fred and his Stone sheep. It stood as the world record for bowhunters for many years and was often described by him as his favorite trophy. British Columbia, 1957.

Bear picture hits target
Terry Koper -*Outdoor Writer*

The instant my eye settles on the men stepping up the primitive bridge, my feet start following in their footsteps.

It happens every time. We must be in Alaska. We must be. It's just that kind of a picture.

Fred Bear's form is easily identified as he crosses the river. Who else would be wearing *that hat* and carrying a bow?

There's another man behind him. He is carrying a bow and his back is bent a little under the strain of a pack.

He must be me. It's just that kind of a picture. Whenever I see it I'm off on another adventure.

"That picture was taken in Alaska, back in 1959," Bear said.

Fred and I were talking. I wish it had been around a campfire in Alaska, but we were sitting on folding chairs, in a maintenance room at the Waukesha County Expo Center. In the main halls, hundreds of bowhunters were browsing through the bows and clothes and gadgets, waiting for Fred's presentation.

"We built that bridge to get across the Little Delta River," Bear said. "It took us about two days to build it, but it worked pretty well for the whole hunt."

The picture captures Bear breaking trail on another of the adventurous trips that have made his name synonymous with back-country big game bowhunting. Behind Bear was Bob Kelly, who'd been hired to cook and carry and was later employed at Bear Archery.

Fred has forgotten who took the picture. For years even, the picture was forgotten, until Dick Lattimer, the company promotion manager, found it in a file. When his eyes settled on the men crossing the river, his feet automatically followed behind the hunters.

"This picture is the essence of bowhunting," Lattimer said.

So in the early 1970's, Lattimer began using the picture in company catalogs. Later, it found its way into magazine ads and in 1974 was used as the cover for a reprint of Saxton Pope's book, "Hunting With the Bow and Arrow."

I know I'm not really in this picture, but it doesn't matter. Each time I see it, I feel the live spruce boughs bending and bouncing with our weight.

It is August in Alaska. It gets cold at night, but during the day the sun is hot enough to melt the glacier. It sends the icy water roaring down the river,

Fred introduces National Guardsmen to archery at nearby Camp Grayling.
Note his rattlesnake skin backed bow. Early 1960s.

making it impossible to cross in hip boots, as the hunters had done the year before.

Somehow I suspected all this before, but now I know for sure because Fred Bear told me. And even though he told me the spring flood washed the bridge away 25 years ago, it doesn't matter.

Thousands of bowhunters still use it. The bridge crosses the gap between the reality of the hunts they have at hand and the fantasy of the ones they'll only make in their minds.

FRED BEAR'S FAVORITE TROPHY

Tuesday, September 10 — Charles Quock, my Indian guide and I rode a long way up Connor Creek to the west branch. Lost some time trying for a moose on the way. Got there at noon and stopped by a creek to eat lunch. Located a lone ram bedded down high on the shale. Put the scope on him. "A full curl," said Charles.

We made a stalk. The ram had been facing away from us but as our heads showed over the ridge, he was looking at us at 50 yards. He got up and started away over the shale.

I shot an arrow at about 60 yards but it didn't reach him. He disappeared around the mountain while we kept hot on his trail. The ram climbed a rocky peak and stood looking at us from the top. We continued along the side, planning to circle over and find him again on the other side.

After crossing the shale we were on a grassy, steep rolling hillside. Charles ahead and me panting along in back of him. Looking back, I was surprised to see three rams in a depression we had passed. One was lying down and two were feeding. We kept on going because the lone ram we had seen first was the biggest.

Just before reaching the top and behind as usual, I saw the big fellow crossing the draw beyond. I signaled to Charles. He came back and we watched him go over the next ridge. We continued after him and routed a flock of seven rams on the other side. No time for them, however.

Circling back, we peeked over a ridge beside a glacier. Our ram was about 150 yards below and just going over the next knoll. When he was out of sight, we ran and slid down the fine shale just in time to see him disappear over the next ridge. We ran again and there he was, about 35 to 40 yards away. Just his head showing, looking at us. He knew we were after him.

I do not like a head-on shot. Just a few inches off the mark will only wound and the hole through the ribcage into the chest cavity is no larger than a baseball. In addition, to shoot an arrow at full draw to clear the ridge would hit him in the head.

The only way was a short draw to lob it over the ridge and drop it into the brisket. If I had been alone, I would not have taken the shot. But Charles barked,"Shoot, quick!" I felt that I was on the spot and to hesitate would have been to lose face with my guide.

The arrow went in a perfect line, but I had a feeling that after it cleared the ridge it had dropped too low. The head disappeared and Charles ran over while I tried to regain my breath. When he got there, he turned to me with a wide grin.

We found him jammed against a rock halfway down the shale slide. He had run about 60 yards and died on his feet, then rolled down the mountain until he hit the rock.

He was a beautiful animal. Horns not broomed, a 41½-inch curl and a 27-inch spread. He would dress out at well over 250 pounds. There was a big hole right in the middle of his brisket. I was very lucky to get such a large ram on the second day of hunting and

Joe Fries and Ann Corby, winners in the first Bear Archery Money Shoot held in Grayling, Michigan, in 1958. Clayton Shenk is manning the background scoreboard.

would have been quite happy with a smaller one. A 42-inch ram is the biggest head that has been taken out of this area.

We had left our hats on the other side of the mountain weighted down with rocks to keep the wind from blowing them away. Charles said he would get them and told me to roll the ram the rest of the way down. I did so reluctantly and he came to rest on a bench far below.

It was now 4:30 and raining. We were four hours from camp. We propped the ram up for pictures and then went down to the horses and back to camp. I was bushed."

Now, 30 years later, Fred's Stone ram was just recently replaced as the World's Record for a bowhunter. The successful hunter was Dr. Brad Thurston of Indianapolis, Indiana.

In 1958, the huge National Guard camp just outside Grayling was picked as the site of the 13th-annual championship of the National Field Archery Association (NFAA). Twenty-eight target field courses were laid out by the host club, the Grayling Bowhunters. More than 1,400 archers participated in the largest archery gathering on record since the sport's modern rebirth. Participants lived in roomy army tents and ate in the camp mess halls. It was an ideal set-up for handling a turnout of that size.

That tournament was also noteworthy because it marked the first large Money Shoot in archery. Bear Archery put up a purse of $5,000 for this special event, which followed the championships. Contestants were limited to the top eight men and the top eight women in the foregoing tournament. A special course — much like a golf course — was set up to allow a large crowd of spectators to follow the action without interfering with the shooters. This proved to be a very popular event, heralding an interest in special competitions among top archers that continues today.

Another significant event at that year's National was the first awards program of the new Pope & Young Club. This organization had begun several years earlier as a Hunting Activities Committee under the NFAA. Due in large measure to the dedication of Glenn St. Charles of Seattle, Washington, the club had decided to move toward becoming a separate entity early in 1958.

At the Grayling awards program, the top trophy of each species of big game entered in the initial listings was recorded as a world bowhunting record for North American big game. Forty-one trophies were entered, with 14 listed as World Records. Among these were Fred's fine British Columbia Stone sheep, his Ontario moose, Osborne caribou, Yellowstone elk and brown bear.

From those beginnings in the 1950's, the Pope & Young Club has become recognized throughout the world as a unique organization of conservationist bowhunters endorsing the rules and principles of fair chase and sanctioning qualitative or selective hunting. They are the archer's equivalent of the famous Boone & Crockett Club from whom they were modeled, recording for posterity the finest trophies of North American big game taken with the bow and arrow.

The 1958 National Field Archery Tournament was such a success that the meet was awarded to Grayling again in 1960. This was the first time in the NFAA's history that the tournament had been held twice at the same location. It was also the last of the single large Nationals. Archery had grown so rapidly that the expense and range preparation involved in hosting the tour-

Fred Bear and Chuck Piper of Bear Archery and Tyler Davis of the Bancroft Racket Company pose with their combined Sales Team members during a 1956 workshop in the Grayling plant.

W.B. Wescott, physicist, co-inventor of the Technicolor process, collector of rare books and archery artifacts and friend of Fred Bear.

nament were too much for a local club, even one with the facilities available in Grayling. After 1960, sectional tourneys were held in various areas of the country to determine a limited number of final contestants for the National Championship.

An interesting sidelight at the 1960 tournament was a National Varmint Calling Championship sponsored by Bear and open to all except professional callers. Judging was done by calling experts and handsome trophies were awarded for the winners.

Fred Bear and Doug Easton of aluminum arrow-making fame sponsored another money shoot with a cash purse of $10,000 after the NFAA Championship and the event again proved highly successful.

Also during tournament week, the Pope & Young Club held its second awards banquet to recognize a dozen new world records. At this point, the club was still under the sponsorship of the NFAA, but six months later, in January of 1961, it became independent. The club was incorporated in 1963 and in 1966 its by-laws were approved, paving the way for an initial election of officers. Glenn St. Charles was its first president, Charlie Kroll its first executive secretary and Fred Bear served on the Board of Directors.

As the growing business entered the 1960's, all seemed to be progressing well. The Bear Plant began using a newly developed Epoxy adhesive in bow construction, replacing Urac which had formerly been used. They made enough fiberglass backing and facing by 1959 to supply several other archery manufacturers. The Grayling Film Service library now had 13 promotional films.

In 1952, a fire in the Grayling plant had destroyed or severely damaged Fred's hunting trophies, but he had rebuilt the collection and placed it in a large reception room of the factory. In addition to Bear's personal items, the display included most of the late William Burton Wescott's collection of archery artifacts.

Wescott of Dover, Massachusetts, a long-time friend and bowhunting companion of Fred Bear, was a past vice president of the NFAA and a recipient of the Thompson Medal of Honor for outstanding service to the sport. A noted chemist, physicist and patent attorney, Wescott was responsible in part for the development of the Technicolor motion picture process and held many other patents in a variety of scientific fields. He spent a good share of his life collecting rare bows, arrows and archery artifacts, as well as uncommon and ancient books on archery, from all corners of the world. This collection came to Fred Bear after Wescott's death in 1952, in accordance with the terms of his will.

Through the years of friendship with W.B. Wescott, Fred turned often to tap his expertise on difficult problems of physics. At the time of Wescott's death, Fred was asked by Archery Magazine to do a piece on his association with the famous archer:

"Words were never so hard to write as these I am called upon to set down relative to the passing of our good friend, William Burton Wescott a few weeks ago.

W.B., as most of us knew him, was past Vice President of NFAA, honorary member of the NAA and a holder of the Thompson Medal of Honor for outstanding service to the sport. The NFAA Medal Awards committee had voted him the Compton Medal of Honor and had he lived he would have been awarded this medal at this year's National Tournament. It will now be awarded posthumously.

We shall miss W.B. in archery circles. Because he was a man of marked modesty, few people realized his influence and valuable contribution to the sport of archery. In preparing this article, I discovered upon inquiring for dates and statistics that I certainly did not know all of the sidelights of his rich life, although we had been closely associated for the past few years. Modesty is a quality of character that commands admiration and respect. But it is also the medium that veils the full blooming of the flower until such a time when one is seeking facts pertinent to a dear friend's life. Archery was Burton Wescott's hobby, which by some means or other he seemed to develop way beyond the average enthusiast's efforts.

He was born on October 7, 1883, in Dorchester, Massachusetts, the son of a physician and one of the first woman architects to practice in this country. The great newspapers of the east, in reporting his death, said that he was educated in Belgium, Canada and England. But the Wescott that I met at the first National Field Archery meet at Allegan, Michigan, in 1946 came to be known to the archery world simply as W.B., the quiet, genial friend whose modest exterior gave no hint of the knowledge and experience with which he was endowed.

Up until last year when his failing health prevented it, he spent a week or more with me each fall hunting in the north woods of Michigan. He had a blind built in a certain spot that seemed to fill him with the joy of living and love of nature. He sometimes spoke of it in his letters — a secluded nest on a low hill overlooking a valley thick with maple and birch — beautiful in the red and gold of fall colors. I choose to think of him, even now, sitting there watching the sun go down."

CHAPTER 10

Early in May 1960, Fred and Bob Munger, who served as Fred's cameraman for the hunt, arrived in Cordova, Alaska. They found Bilderback and his first mate, Harley King ready to go and the *Valiant Maid* was soon headed north to Kodiak Island.

They hunted the large island for three days without luck, then decided to go over to the Alaskan Peninsula which entailed crossing the Shelikof Straits, one of the most treacherous stretches of water in the world. In spite of high winds and turbulent seas, they negotiated the rough crossing and anchored in a sheltered cove about noon.

Taking the small skiff ashore, they almost immediately spotted two bears just below snowline on a mountain that shouldered up behind the beach. One of them looked very large. The men watched them for an hour through binoculars until the bears apparently became sleepy in the warm spring sunshine and lay down. The hunters then climbed the steep slope toward them, through a dense tangle of alders. Melting snow made footing unreliable and it took two and a half hours to make the climb. When they got within a hundred yards of their quarry, however, the bears detected them and moved off.

They never saw them again. One set of tracks in wet snow measured 14 inches and Ed believed it might have been the biggest brownie he had ever encountered. Losing a chance at it was a bitter disappointment to Fred.

Disillusioned, they moved on to Puale Bay to try new territory, losing two days due to bad weather. Another bear showed up in binoculars here, but disappeared over a mountain before they could get into position for a stalk.

As soon as the two day gale subsided, they moved on again. This time to Wide Bay, opposite the extreme southwest end of Kodiak Island. No sooner had they reached the beach when they spotted a huge bear feeding along the shore about a mile away. A heavy wind was blowing down from the mountains and the hunters realized it would be dark long before they could get to the bear.

"No use to try," said Ed, "If we let him alone, we might see him tomorrow."

"The wind raged all night and through the next forenoon, making it futile to go ashore. When it dropped at noon, however, they landed and spent a hard afternoon hiking and climbing in hipboots, again, without success.

They got back to the boat at suppertime, tired and discouraged, ate a light snack and went ashore once more. They had barely beached their skiff when

Fred's world-record bear mount has been displayed at many Consumer Sport Shows and at scores of Sporting Goods outlets. Many old-time Bear employees wear gold bolo tie replicas of this huge trophy, to honor both the Bear and Fred.

*Fred and his "Big Brownie" which held the bowhunting world record for some 25 years.
Shot at a distance of 20 yards in Alaska, 1960.*

the big bear of the previous evening walked out of the alders some distance away. A brief discussion determined it was too late in the day for pictures but too late in the hunt to take chances on missing a shot again. Bob and Harley chose a high observation point where they could watch the show while Ed and Fred started for the bear.

A jumble of driftwood bordered the high-water mark. From it, tall grass ran back 100 yards to the edge of the hills. A quarter of a mile on their side of the bear, an alder thicket replaced the belt of grass. The bear was about 20 yards out from this thicket, on open beach. The wind was blowing in from the sea and the low evening sun was at the men's backs. Everything was finally in their favor and they walked confidently toward the bear, following a band of firm, wet sand left uncovered by the receding tide.

Here again was a bowhunter's dream: a bear undisturbed, wind and sun exactly right, wave noise drowning out any sound the hunters might make, with alders to provide cover right up to ideal bow range. They had to hur-

One of the thrilling moments in Fred's hunting career occurred when he faced this huge Kodiak bear at 20 feet, 1962.

The big bear went less than 100 yards and lived less than 10 seconds after Fred's arrow found its mark.

ry, nonetheless, because of rapidly approaching darkness. Luckily they had changed their hip boots for leather footgear before coming ashore. Ed paced ahead, carrying his .375 rifle. In addition to his bow, Fred carried a Smith & Wesson .44 Magnum revolver in a shoulder holster, a standard precaution for him when after dangerous game.

The bear went on feeding, completely unaware of the intruders. Near the alders, the real stalk began. The men eased over behind a pile of driftwood and entered the alder thickets on a well-used bear trail.

When they again stepped into the open, the brownie was just 50 yards off. He was facing away from them, pawing over a heap of kelp. The bear now looked impressively large, but Fred didn't waste time. He had learned long before that hunting with a bow calls for careful but prompt analysis of critical situations and leaves little time for admiring trophies until they are well secured.

As they paused, Ed said, "What do you want to do?"

"Get closer," Fred replied.

"Go ahead," Ed urged.

Actually, Fred didn't really want to get any closer to the huge animal. But that's what he was there for and in bowhunting, 25 yards are more than twice as good as 50. He had no choice and he knew it.

He slid the .44 Magnum out of its holster and stuck it under his belt, where it would be handy. Then he crawled ahead, partly hidden by the rim of drift wood, until he was between the alders and the bear. When he stopped, they were just 20 yards apart.

Fred realized now that he was facing a much larger than average brown. He was so close he could see the wind ruffle the bear's pelt across its burly neck and make out the long claws. The bear, still not suspecting the hunter's presence, turned broadside. Fred loosed his arrow and saw it bury to the feathers in the animal's side.

The bear gave a growling roar, spinning in a circle, biting at the end of the arrow. After three or four turns, he started toward the archer. Fred had another arrow nocked and shot head-on, but the arrow lodged against heavy bone in a foreleg, doing no damage.

Coming right at Fred at top speed, the huge bear was an awesome sight. The bear was simply following a trail back to the cover of the alders. But the bowman, crouched close beside the trail, did not know this and reached for the .44 revolver when Ed's voice suddenly boomed out behind him.

The Kodiak bear dwarfs Fred's six foot height.

"Don't shoot! He's a big one!" Fred realized instantly what Ed meant. A bowman can't ethically claim as a trophy any animal that shows a bullet hole.

What happened next was unexpected. On hearing Ed's voice, the bear veered to the side and ran headlong into the alders. His claw marks on the trail later showed that when he turned, he was within five paces of where Fred crouched.

The instant the big brown was out of sight, Ed took off through the brush and up the side of the mountain for a better view. When Fred caught up, Ed was holding his binoculars on a dark spot down in the thickets. The men studied it a moment and could make out one of the bear's front legs. They hurried down and found him stretched on his back. He had run 200 yards and lived less than a minute after the Razorhead hit.

It was a minute Bear would remember for the rest of his life, a minute in which he had killed the biggest brown bear ever taken with the bow. The pelt squared 10 feet 2 inches and the skull scored 28, a World Record that stood in Pope & Young records for over 25 years and is included in those of Boone & Crockett. Fred later stated that he could shut his eyes and recall the entire scene: the black volcanic sand of the beach, the sea reddened by the westering sun and the bear standing blocky and huge over the brown kelp washed up by the surf. It certainly was one of the high points of his hunting career.

A national press account of the hunt read:

KODIAK BEAR

On May 10, 1960, Fred Bear of Bear Archery Company in Grayling, Michigan killed the largest Alaskan brown bear ever taken with a bow and arrow. The trophy was bagged in Wide Bay on the Alaskan Peninsula, opposite the southwestern end of Kodiak Island. The shot was made at 20 yards. The Razorhead arrow, released from a 65 lb. Kodiak model bow, cut off a rib and penetrated the liver. The bear ran no more than 200 yards and lived less than one minute after the arrow struck it.

The bear's pelt squared 10 feet, live weight was estimated to be over 1,000 pounds and the skull measured 28 inches. This bear, until recently, held the world's record spot in the Pope & Young big game records. Fred's guide was Ed Bilderback of Cordova, Alaska. The impressive upright mount of the huge bear stands eight feet nine inches tall.

World Renown Hunter

FRED BEAR
IN PERSON
AT
GRAYLING HIGH SCHOOL

A
C
T
I
O
N

F
I
L
M
S

See Him Shoot a Grizzly Bear At 20 Yards
A Kodiak Bear At 20 Feet
— Hear His Stories Of Many Hunts —
HUMOROUS — BREATHTAKING

FRIDAY, NOV. 18
SATURDAY, NOV. 19 # 8 P.M.

ADMISSION $1.00

St. Francis Men's Club

In 1960, a new transparent Bearglas termed "Crystalight" came into use for backing and facing on the top bow models. It displayed the grain patterns of the underlying wood core. However, Crystalight was not popular, it performed well, but archers generally preferred the solid-colored glass, possibly because it looked stronger.

By the time Crystalight appeared, Bear had developed the industry's most modern research and testing laboratory for bow design and performance. Checking the quality of production-run bows became standard procedure. An ultra-high-speed camera capable of taking 4,000 frames per second was used to study limb action, arrow flight and release techniques. A shooting machine and oscilloscope measured arrow velocity within 0.5 percent.

But another disaster was just around the corner. Within a year, despite such equipment and methods and with little warning, Fred came home from a speaking engagement in Fort Knox, Kentucky (an invitation from his Grousehaven friend, General Curtis LeMay) to find his company in trouble.

Humidity is very low in northern Michigan and during the winter is often practically nonexistent. In the manufacturing process within the plant, this dryness caused no problem, but after the finished bows were shipped to dealers in areas of higher humidity, such as Florida and the southeast, the wood took on moisture and expanded even through the finish. The unidirectional glass strips used in the bows had little strength laterally and consequently cracked under the pressure of the swelling core. This did not affect the performance of the bow, but customers naturally shied away from a product with visible flaws.

To protect the reputation of his company, Fred advised his dealers to recall all cracked bows from their customers — which amounted to almost one third of the bows produced in 1961 — and return them for replacement. (Bear Archery was also selling its unidirectional glass strips to other bow manufacturers who had no problem with cracking, since they were located in reasonably humid areas.) Although the company grossed about $2 million that year, it lost $180,000. The bank which had supported Bear Archery until then became justifiably concerned and bowed out.

Fred had to borrow money from a Detroit finance company at 13% interest to keep the business going. It was a hard, slow recovery, but his decision proved wise, especially from the standpoint of dealer and customer respect and loyalty.

In two years, the loan was paid off and the bank resumed relations with Bear, carrying a full-page ad in the *Detroit Free Press*.

In addition to the bow production problem, 1961 also saw a serious management problem arise within the Bear organization. Fred realized he had too many employees. Against the opinion of his secretary-treasurer, he replaced the existing plant manager with Robert Tupley. Tupley, a young physicist, was a friend of Bear's foster son, Michael Steger and Fred had met him on several occasions. The new manager proved to be extremely capable and things improved rapidly. Tupley set up an efficient cost-accounting system and established a workable seniority employment program. Fred admired his industry and successful methods, but after a few years, Tupley announced that he wanted to be president of Bear Archery or he would move on to new fields. It was an ultimatum. He was a brilliant young man, years ahead of his time. In 1961, not many company presidents were his age. "Besides," Bear said wryly at the time, "Bear Archery already has a president! But I believe I made a mistake in not accepting his proposal," he concluded.

At the age of 67, Fred's father, Harry Bear, won the National Olympic Bowmen's League mail tournament in competition with hundreds of archers representing 50 organizations coast to coast. He was a member of the Carlisle Archery Club and Fred was justifiably proud of him.

During their years apart, Fred and his father had always kept in touch by telephone and correspondence. In one of his letters Fred said:

> "Dear Pop:
> Hank has told you all the news...I'm busy as hell getting things in shape for going to British Columbia this fall...Have a new line of bows for next year. Each year we find a way to make them better...I don't know where it will stop.
> Nights are getting cold and mornings feel like fall. This is the best time of the year. Reminds me of the times we used to go to the mountains squirrel hunting..."

After the world record bear had fallen to his son's arrow, Harry Bear wrote:

> "Dear Fred:
> Congratulations on your big bear! Could you get a picture here in time for our annual HARRY BEAR day at the Fish and Game Farm...I am not in top shape yet since the heart attack. Can't get my strength back. Just a little walking knocks me out."

Fred replied:

"Dear Dad:

Am sending a picture for the HARRY BEAR SHOOT. The Brownie was really a dandy…

Am having my field notes typed and will send you a copy…

Everything fine here — Hannah blossoming into quite a young lady and Chris playing a hot game of H.S. football…Hope you are feeling better.

Fred"

Two months later, when Elizabeth sent word that Fred's father was dying, the Bears drove all night from Grayling, arriving a few hours before the end. Harry had told them on a previous visit that he was ready to go and hoped he would slip away in his sleep before long.

Pennsylvania was in bloom that week in May and they buried Harry Bear in the old cemetery beside his beloved wife and daughter, Aileen, not far from the grave of Revolutionary folk heroine, Molly Pitcher.

Greatly saddened by this event, Fred nevertheless found consolation in the knowledge that his father had lived a long and productive life with good health almost to the last.

The year 1961, when Bear Archery had its most serious industrial problems, was in fact the turning point in the fortunes of the company. The rest of the 1960's ushered in new developments, innovations and growth.

In 1961 the Fox line of bows in different colors (Red Fox, Yellow Fox, Black Fox and so on) was inaugurated. Fox bows, designed primarily for youngsters, had draw weights of 10 to 35 pounds. They had built-in recurves and were pressed in a single bonding operation. The Fox bows were not toys, however. They performed much better than the older self-wood bows. In addition, they were practically indestructible. The Fox bows were a great help to families who wanted to get involved in archery but had limited budgets. The popularity of this type of bow continues today under different names.

Other important manufacturing innovations in Bear's products came in 1961 and 1962. Bear began using richly grained tropical woods, such as bubinga, zebrawood, Bengal and Brazilian rosewood for the handle risers of the wood/glass laminated bow models. These woods, plus advanced engineering and designing, resulted in some of the most beautiful recurve bows ever produced.

This period also saw the beginning of Bear fiberglass arrows. Machinery was set up to utilize a woven fiberglass cloth rather than the unidirectional glass used in bows. The material was cut to size, impregnated with resins, rolled on steel mandrels and sealed with a layer of clear cellophane. It was then baked to set the resins after which the mandrels were withdrawn and the shafts sanded and finished.

While aluminum alloy was at that time in use for target arrows, it had not yet become popular in the bowhunting field. Fiberglass arrows were much tougher than cedar and, of course, heavier in actual weight for any given spine designation, a desired factor for hunting arrows. They were more expensive than wood arrows but their toughness compensated for this.

The first of Bear Archery's great tournament bows, the Tamerlane, was produced in the '60's. Its graceful lines and beautifully grained wood were combined with new principles of balance, stability and forward weight distribution. This was the first Bear bow to retail for more than $100. Three years later, a Bear Tamerlane was awarded permanent display space in the Museum of Modem Art in New York for its excellence and beauty of design.

Another important product innovation of the same period was the use of spring steel wire brackets that allowed bow quivers to be instantly attached to or detached from the limbs of a hunting bow.

Fred's top tournament bows were now equipped with a built-in bow sight and adjustable arrow plate, another item in the long list of firsts for Bear Archery.

Fred kept in touch with his home and the business while afield — often sending back observations concerning the equipment he was testing. He wrote to Tapley from Point Barrow, Alaska in 1962:

"...the inserts in my glass blunts are coming off (arrows). I don't think they are cleaning the insides of the tubes properly."

1962 also marked the year that Fred faced another huge Kodiak Bear, this time at a distance of only 20 feet. To add to the drama of the moment, Fred had chafed off three strands of his bowstring on a barnacle as he had climbed out of the boat enroute to intercept the bear. He did not know if they would hold for the one shot as he and Ed Bilderback crouched behind a giant rock on the Alaskan beach.

The entire scene was recorded on film and is a classic in hunting archives. It is part of the "Kodiak Country" videotape offered by Bear Archery. The amazing thing about the footage is that it was shot by an inexperienced cameraman that Fred had trained in the use of the movie and still camera combination in the skiff heading toward the bear.

The bear is on display in the Fred Bear Museum in Gainesville. The skin measured 9 feet square and tipped the scales at 810 pounds. In his Field Notes book Fred said of this encounter: "A bear at 20 feet looks big when one is down on his knees looking up. Again, it was proved that an arrow in the right spot will do the job quickly and humanely, regardless of the size of the animal. It's a great privilege to match wits with a noble animal such as this that nature has so ably equipped to take care of itself."

That same year, he appeared on the nationally televised show, "To Tell the Truth," successfully stumping the panelists. The name of Fred Bear was included in the 1960–61 edition of *Who's Who In America*.

In April of 1960 the Crawford County Avalanche ran the following in its weekly newspaper:

Skipper Ed Bilderback welcomes Fred aboard the "Valiant Maid."

Motor News Magazine Features Fred Bear

Fred Bear, probably Grayling's most widely known citizen, is the subject of a two page article in the April issue of Motor News, official magazine of the Automobile Club of Michigan.

The illustrated story, entitled "Michigan's Northwoods Executive," is authored by Motor News' associate editor Len Barnes.

"Of all Michigan's many successful captains of industry," writes Barnes, "perhaps none enjoys life as much as Bear, who runs the world's largest archery equipment factory in the northwoods town of Grayling."

Barnes describes in detail Bear's rise to the top of the field as an archer and manufacturer.

"In Fred's office is the largest collection of game trophies bagged with bow and arrow by one man in history...but Fred's largest trophy of all, which he "bagged" with the first mass-produced glass and wood bows and arrows made, is the Bear Archery Company, which employs almost 10 percent of Grayling's population"

CHAPTER 11

A most unusual opportunity came to Fred in 1963. His photographer, Robert Halmi, had done some work for the Maharajah of Bundi in India and it was through Halmi that His Highness heard of the renowned bowhunter, Fred Bear. An invitation to be his guest at the palace for a tiger hunt followed.

Throughout history, the Bengal tiger of India has been one of the world's top hunting trophies. Tigers have a well-deserved reputation as one of the two or three most ferocious carnivores and the Asian natives realize only too well their tendency to become man-eaters when they get old or when other game becomes scarce. Today, due largely to the press of human expansion and resulting loss of habitat, hunting tigers for sport is prohibited. In the 1960's, however, they were still quite numerous and considered fair game.

So it was with a great deal of anticipation that Bear accepted the invitation to visit the Maharajah, an experienced sportsman himself, who would be Fred's host during an unprecedented attempt to secure a tiger with the bow and arrow.

Fred and Halmi set out for India in late April. Enroute they stopped off at Istanbul, Turkey to visit the ancient Ok Meydan ("place of the arrow") on a hill overlooking the Sea of Marmara. There, inscribed marble pillars, some of them 50 feet tall, mark the distance of arrows shot from Turkish flight bows during the time of the Ottoman emperors in the eighteenth century. To celebrate the visit and in honor of those ancient bowyers, Fred unlimbered his hunting bow and lofted an arrow at the Ok Meydan, where perhaps thousands of shafts had been launched centuries before.

Arriving in Delhi, India, Bear and Halmi took an eight hour train ride to Kotah where they stayed overnight, continuing the next day to the town of Bundi in the northwestern state of Rajasthan. Here they were met by the Maharajah's aide, David Singh and driven to the palace at Phoolsagar (Flower Lake). The palace, built in 1947, completely surrounded a large pool lush with lotus flowers and bright with many-hued birds.

During this time a letter came to Fred's wife, written on *Phoolsagar Palace* stationery.

Wednesday 8

Hi, Honey — Glad to get your letter, first one since I was in Istanbul. You had me worried. It was a good letter about Chris being

207

admitted to Oberlin, the ducks on the river, etc.

I like Bundi very much. Because of the heat all attire is most informal, including bare feet. But I hate the formality in general and slow pace. Tradition governs much of the activities.

Bundi has a male secretary and four Aide de camps — any or all, with cars, are available to us at any time.

"His Highness" wants to kill a moose. We are talking about setting up a trip. Hope I can arrange to have him visit us in Grayling. He would bring his son.

This heat melts me. I have the time but not the inclination to write other than my notes. Average three showers a day.

Food is excellent. Some dinners are Indian food eaten with the fingers. Some are American. All meat is game.

Following an Indian meal, two 'boys' come with silver basins and silver pitchers plus soap and a towel!

I've never seen so much silver — every day more pieces appear. I drink beer from silver mugs that weigh about a pound each — presentation pieces with inscriptions from Queen Mary, Prince of Wales, Lord Mountbatten, etc.

Halmi was commissioned by Life to offer Bundi $500.00 to photograph the harem, but Bundi says "No." There are no young women in the harem now — just very old ladies living out their lives in the old palace. Indian potentates no longer have harems, he told us.

It is now 11 a.m. Bob and I just finished breakfast here in my room. Bundi usually shows up about noon and we sit and talk and drink on the air-conditioned patio. Tiger news, if any, is known by 1 p.m. and after that, the day is planned.

Tonight we are having roast saddle of wild boar I am told. To be served on an enormous silver platter.

I got a shot at a boar two days ago but missed.

So goes life at the palace. My agenda is very uncertain. Bundi is most cooperative and has the patience or tolerance necessary for the limitations of the bow.

I hope this letter reaches you without too much delay and that I will have a tiger by that time.

Love, Fred

At Phoolsagar, one did as Indian princes do: wait at the luxurious and comparatively cool palace until word is received from natives of a tiger seen menacing their livestock.

As soon as the tiger's whereabouts were known, very careful preparations for baiting the big cat got underway. First, a spot for the bait had to be selected, one that could be seen from a distant hill where beaters would watch the tiger's movements through binoculars. Second, water must be provided so the tiger would not have to leave the area to quench its thirst. The water is carried by natives and poured into a large stone bowl set near the spot. Machans or elevated shooting platforms had to be erected. Up to this point there was nothing for the hunter to do but wait.

During Fred's stay several tigers were sighted, but it was not until two days before he was due to leave that a solid opportunity became apparent. Receiving word that a large tiger and two smaller ones were feeding on the bait about 10 miles away, Bear, Bundi, Halmi and Singh set off in the Maharajah's Rolls Royce jeep, the bright orange and red flag of his princedom flying from the hood.

They parked the hunting car in thick brush and made their way as quietly as possible to the shooting platforms. Fred was alone in the first machan, nine or ten feet up on the stub of a thorn tree. A steep cliff rose about a hundred yards from his position. Thirty yards to his right Halmi, with his cameras and Bundi were ready in the second machan. On his left a third machan supported David Singh.

Suddenly out of the quiet they heard the beaters, a band of 50 or 60 natives forming a semicircle strung out on the mountain and along the sides of the steep canyon walls. Some of them had muskets and some tin pans. All had sticks and stones, which they threw or rolled down the steep walls to accompany their yells, whistles and gunshots. The racket increased until the whole countryside rang with the din.

After several minutes of frozen concentration, Fred detected a slight movement to his right. He caught his breath as he turned and saw a large tiger stealing along the edge of the cliff, about 70 yards away. It was a very long bowshot, but he believed it might be the only chance he would get. He loosed an arrow that looked good but struck the flinty hillside just beyond the cat. A second arrow, released as the tiger whirled around, hit true and brought on a blood-chilling roar. The tiger headed straight into the brush and just as it disappeared, Bundi's gun went off. He had told Fred that he would never allow a tiger to escape if he could prevent it and the bowman thought, "Oh no, there goes my trophy!"

Fred launches a flight arrow on the Ok Meidan, ancient shooting fields of Turkish bowmen.

He looked over toward His Highness for the first time and greatly relieved, saw that he was shooting at one of the other tigers. No one else had seen the cat Fred shot.

The roaring from the thicket stopped abruptly. Soon after, Bundi's head tracker went in and found the tiger dead. Some of the natives carried the beast out on a pole, the big carcass swinging as if in a hammock. When the group came to an open space, photos were taken and the handsome three hundred pound feline was driven back to Phoolsagar in a truck, where a great victory celebration took place. Bear's triumphant proving of his bow resulted in a long-lasting friendship with his host.

Crawford County Avalanche
May 16, 1963
Fred Bear Bags Tiger

A cablegram received by Mrs. Fred Bear from her husband in India on Monday revealed that the noted hunter had bagged the Indian tiger he went to stalk. His wire stated: "Fine tiger shot at 70 yards. Greatest hunt ever. Fine pictures. Home in 10 days."

In letters sent back home, Fred Bear tells of stopping off in Turkey to make up a film story on ancient artifacts stored in museums there. *LIFE* photographer, Robert Halmi, is working with Mr. Bear and the two men were allowed to take some of the jewel-encrusted quivers and similar items outdoors to photograph them in good light.

After a week in Turkey, Mr. Bear and Mr. Halmi went on to India, where they are at present engaged on the tiger hunt which was the prime object of the trip. They are guests of the Maharajah of Bundi near New Delhi but out of touch with communications other than by messenger until the hunt is completed.

1963 had seen national tragedy mixed with the personal triumph of the tiger hunt. An account of the day President John F. Kennedy was assassinated came to light in the pages of Henrietta's journal. She and Fred were staying at the Gotham in New York and scheduled to leave for home in a few days. Their visit was cut short, however, when the death of the young President stopped all activity in the city.

"...We are on our way home today with heavy hearts after the terrible news of the President's death yesterday.

I was shopping at Bonwit Teller's near our hotel when I came upon a group of women clustered around a jewelry counter talking frantically in subdued voices...I shamelessly edged closer and heard them say the President had been shot. I did not believe this, of course and I am not sure they believed it. The clerks stood open-mouthed with eyes bugged out of their sockets. I said to myself — someone has taken a shot at the President, but, of course, missed. But when I reached the French snack bar and joined a line of frozen-faced customers perched on stools but not eating, the inquisitive little waitress kept looking at me trying to determine if I had yet heard the news. After I gave her my order and prepared to eat, she gave a terrible sigh and

The Indian "beaters" and Rosie the elephant join Fred and the Maharajah of Bundi in admiration of his great Bengal tiger.

muttered, "How awful!"

"What is awful?" I asked. At this, the line of women on their stools all began talking at once. One said that both the governor of Texas and the President were dead. Another said she'd stood by someone with a transistor radio in his pocket and heard that they were both critical. "Who could have done it?" they kept asking each other.

Still hoping this was just a rumor or that the President was only slightly injured, I started for the shoe department. When I found the area empty and the male clerks knotted together, whispering, I felt great apprehension. "He died a little while ago," I heard one of them say.

I made my way out of the empty store — customers had vanished. Walking back to the hotel, I saw that the shops along the route were closing. It was eerie and unbelievable.

Back in our room I found Fred lying on the bed looking at television. He'd returned from his meeting at ABC through quiet, shutter-drawn streets upon hearing the news. We could find no words to express our feelings and sat mute before the television screen as reports began to pour in. Lincoln had been shot in our grandmothers' lives, Cleveland was assassinated at the beginning of the century but in our time there had been no murdering of presidents.

We had planned to see Tom Jones that night, but could think of nothing but staying inside. In any event, it was soon announced that all Broadway plays were canceled.

At eight o'clock we ordered dinner in our room. The waiter was grey with sorrow and had nothing to say. Finally he blurted out in anguish. "To think something like this could happen in our country."

We called home and later Fred went out to get a paper. "The streets are deserted," he reported on his return. Television continued to inform the world of the catastrophic events that had taken place on this day.

Former President Eisenhower, in New York for an awards dinner canceled his speech and went back to Gettysburg. Pictures on T.V. showed the Kennedys arriving in Dallas that morning with happy crowds to meet them; Jackie looking precious as always, carrying an armful of red roses.

My blood ran cold to see the sudden spurt of the presidential car racing out of the parade line toward the hospital. And the panic of people on the sidewalks when the crack of the rifle was heard. We discussed briefly the possibility of going down to Washington since we were so close (where history was being made) but knew it would be useless to try to get hotel or plane reservations.

The next morning we drove through abandoned streets to the airport — many of the shops had already dismantled their windows and had draped them in black surrounding pictures of the President.

From Cleveland where we had left our car, we drove to Oberlin to pick up our grandson Chris. Classes had been suspended and students were going home for the weekend. The dreadful events had sobered young as well as mature citizens and during the long drive to Grayling we listened constantly to the radio. At one point our senses were again shocked to hear that the President's accused assassin was in turn murdered while being transferred from one jail to another. It all seemed incredible."

Fred setting up his camera to photograph the fury of Murchison Falls on the White Nile in Uganda.

Offering a bunch of green leaves, Fred makes friends with a young giraffe at a Wildlife Refuge.

On safari, Algot, Henrietta and Kamizee standing beside the Land Rover in a sea of six-foot elephant grass.

Earlier that same month, one of Fred's British Columbia grizzly hunts was the subject of a five-page feature article in *LIFE* magazine authored by Don Moser, with photography by Robert Halmi of New York. In the article, Don Moser described their awe of the rangy woodsman as he searched the forest for grizzly bear.

The Crawford County Avalanche
Thursday, October 31, 1963 — November 8th issue
Life To Devote Nearly Six Pages
To Fred Bear's Grizzly Hunt

The November 8 issue of *LIFE* magazine will carry a five and one half page feature spread of pictures and story concerning Fred Bear's 1963 grizzly bear hunt in British Columbia, just completed.

The article is to contain 3,500 words and tremendous full-color photos of the hunt.

Don Moser, *LIFE* Associate Editor and Bob Halmi, *LIFE* photographer, personally accompanied Fred on this latest trip. No less than 23 grizzlies were seen and photographed on this thrill-packed wilderness expedition. Mr. Halmi is the same photographer who accompanied Mr. Bear on his tiger hunt in India. The two men were houseguests at the Bear home before the start of the British Columbia trip.

This is the finest advertising for the sport of archery ever published and a feather in the cap of the local industry.

One of Fred's stories that came out of this hunt concerned their outfitter, a capable, completely honest and upright fellow who had never been more than 100 miles from his home in British Columbia. One night around the campfire, this guileless fellow remarked that he could use more business and wondered if they would advise him to place a half-page ad on behalf of his guiding service in Moser's *(LIFE)* magazine — utterly innocent of the fact that the cost would run into the thousands!

A year after the tiger hunt, Henrietta accompanied Fred on a three-week photographic safari to Kenya and Uganda before he joined Arthur Godfrey and others for an elephant hunt in Mozambique. The other members of his hunting party were Dick Mauch of Nebraska, Ken Knickerbocker and Virginia and Jim Crowe of the *Detroit Free Press*.

Crawford County Avalanche
Thursday, May 7, 1964
FRED BEARS GO TO AFRICA

This Friday Mr. and Mrs. Fred Bear leave for Africa flying from New York. The first two weeks of the trip will be spent in Kenya and Uganda to see and photograph wildlife in the National Parks of those areas. One of the highlights of the trip will be a night spent at TREETOPS, an English Lodge built high in a tree over a waterhole. From a balcony, guests watch wild animals, including elephants and rhinos, as they come in to drink at dusk and on through the evening.

On May 30th, Mrs. Bear will go to Europe by way of Egypt and the Holy Land to visit interesting places on the continent and visit relatives and friends in Norway and Sweden.

Mr. Bear will continue south in Africa to Mozambique where he will join Arthur Godfrey, Peter Barrett and Robert Halmi for a hunting and photography safari during the first weeks in June. Peter Barrett, who is outdoor editor of *TRUE Magazine* will write of their experiences for this monthly publication.

It is not generally known that Arthur Godfrey is an expert with the bow. He will do some hunting with this weapon and some with a gun and will tape his daily radio shows from their safari camps. They will then be flown to New York for airing. It is expected that these programs will be heard on his morning shows beginning about June 8th.

Robert Halmi, the photographer who did the pictures on the Grizzly Hunt for *LIFE* Magazine last fall, has been working with CBS script writers and Mr. Godfrey's producer in preparing an outline of a film for a television show of the hunt. In addition to the TV film, Bear and Halmi will make one or perhaps two films for the Bear Archery Company's film library.

On June 26th, Mr. Bear and Mr. Halmi will join another safari party for two more weeks of hunting in southern Tanganyika. This group will include Sam Snead of golfing fame and Douglas Kennedy, editor of *TRUE Magazine*. Following this hunt, Mr. Bear will join Mrs. Bear in Europe for a ten day holiday before returning home.

The Bears' pre-hunt trip with a professional hunter and two natives in a Land Rover was anything but luxurious, but spending three weeks in a safari limousine was not Fred's way of doing things. The Land Rover could take off from the usual path at any time, cross the veldt, ford small streams, or cruise up to herds of elephants for his camera.

The trip was a giant step for Fred's wife who asked for and was granted, only one concession — that they sleep in a bed at night, under a roof. For her the thought of a camping safari, endured and enjoyed by many women all over the world, was unthinkable. One of the reasons, aside from her natural timidity, was that a hunter's wife she had met in Wyoming, describing a recent safari to Africa, said that going into her tent one day she found a yellow and black snake stretched down the length of her bed.

Surprisingly, it was not impossible to find reasonably comfortable accommodations (vintage of the 1800's though they were) and reservations were arranged for every night at one of the English Inns scattered great distances apart through the two countries. They traveled long, tiring miles to reach them, but their quarters consistently proved to be off the ground and under a roof. (Excerpts From Henrietta Bear's Journal are found in the appendix).

The first entry of Fred's field notes for this trip said:

"In Flight, Dar-es-Salaam-Tanganyika. Kissed my wife goodbye in Nairobi before boarding this flight to Salisbury via African Airways, where I will meet our safari group to continue on to Biera for our Mozambique hunt."

The party had diverse missions: Godfrey was there to attend ceremonies related to his gift of an airplane to the African Medical Research Foundation. Fred wanted to test his bow against an elephant. Halmi would take the pictures and Barrett wanted a story of the adventure. Godfrey and Barrett would also do a bit of trophy hunting.

Camp Ruark was situated on the Save River, a delightful spot in the vast hunting concession of Mozambique Safarilandia. Wally Johnson, Sr., Wally, Jr. and a young Portuguese named Amandeu Peixe were their outfitter guides. Peixe means "fish" in Portuguese, so 'Fish' became his name among the hunters.

The camp was clean and tidy. All the buildings were of masonry with thatched grass roofs. The surrounding veldt and rough scrub country contained great numbers of game. There were warthogs by the hundreds, impala by the thousands and in less numbers, waterbucks, bushbucks, zebras, wildebeest, hartebeest, kudu, nyala, sable, eland, reedbuck, forest hogs, dikdik, Cape buffalo and, of course, the mighty elephants. A herd of these actually passed within 200 yards of the camp one night.

It was good bowhunting country, gently rolling and lightly forested with occasional clearings. The grass that soon would be burned off by the natives to promote fresh green growth, provided cover for both game and hunters. Even so, it was rare to get closer than 40 yards and at that distance several misses were chalked up. But slowly, Bear's trophy list grew — two warthogs, a waterbuck, two impala, a record-class nyala and a fine kudu bull fell to his arrows.

Despite the abundance of game, encounters with elephants for some reason eluded Fred, who with Fish, his personal tracker, Halmi and two native trackers scoured the countryside daily on foot and in a Toyota Land Cruiser, ever alert for an opportunity. Finally one came.

Word was received that elephants were watering near a native village early every morning, but the report proved false. From there the men continued cruising through the bush, stopping at every settlement to ask about elephants. At the end of the day the results were favorable. They came to a village near a forest through which feeding elephants had passed, knocking

Before the hunt, an African witch doctor puts a 'charm' on Fred's bow and arrows.

down so many trees it appeared that a tank battle had been fought on the spot. The hunters were on the trail at first light next morning and soon found fresh droppings, still steaming in the cool morning air.

Savo, the village witch doctor, stopped the cars as they drove by, proclaiming the necessity of making sure there was no curse on their weapons. In a scene immensely enjoyed by the hunters and recorded on film by Halmi, he laid Fred's 70-pound bow and hunting arrows beside Fish's .375, got out a small flask of snuff, propped a cracked, red tail light against the gun and bow and with muttered incantations, sprinkled pinches of snuff over all to ward off evil spirits. The ceremony over, the hunters once more set out on the track left by the elephants.

Taking the trail on foot now, their excitement grew and soon they started running. Alternately trotting and walking for three and a half hours, they covered approximately 12 miles, knowing that moving fast was their only hope of catching up to the herd.

One of the trackers who was in the lead stopped suddenly, holding up his hand. The men eased out of the forest into an area of chest-high bushes and saw elephants on every hand, singly and in groups, for a third of a mile. It was

Close quarters! Fred attempting to close within bow range of Tembo.

Fred and the 4-ton bull elephant he bagged after an arduous hunt.

Field notes were written where and when.

a sight to make the neck hair bristle.

The hunters bent low and circled to get downwind of the nearest animals, then began stealing up, trying to get close to a large bull at the rear of the group. But when the bull turned toward them, it was discovered he had no tusks.

Abruptly two cows that had been acting as scouts near the rear of the herd either sensed or saw the men and cut back to get downwind, trunks raised. Then they changed course and headed straight for them, big ears flapping, trunks reaching, not making a sound but getting closer every second.

The trackers broke and ran toward the forest, taking the .375 with them. Fish snapped his fingers and led Halmi and Bear hastily out of the elephant's line of approach. The hunters had barely found shelter behind some bushes when Fred turned around and saw more elephants moving in. The men now experienced real fear. They were in the middle and completely surrounded by elephants.

Without warning, the trackers reappeared. They firmly declared there were too many elephants and that everyone would be killed and then vanished again. The hunters followed them back to the forest edge, knowing that the trees wouldn't offer real protection but that hiding was better there.

Immediately upon reaching the forest, five elephants led by a large bull began drifting their way. Fred suddenly felt that this might be his chance. Presently the animals stopped. The bull was behind some brush with only his tusks protruding into the open. Fish whispered to Fred to shoot, completely forgetting that Fred wasn't using a rifle and dared not risk an arrow through the brush.

The bull seemed to stand there for an eternity. Finally he moved, coming into the open slowly about 40 yards away. To the man with the bow, who also had stepped out in the open, he looked colossal. For a moment the elephant hesitated and Fred shot, the arrow almost disappearing into the bull's side.

Bear knew he had placed a killing shot, but did not know how far the bull could travel. The hunters rounded up the natives and sat down to rest and cool off. After about 15 minutes, they resolved to take up the trail. He had fallen without rolling over, one tusk buried in the earth.

Word was sent back to the village and soon the entire populace was on hand. Every man had a knife with which he hacked the carcass at top speed, hoping to get a large share before it was all gone. The women carried the meat off in woven baskets. Some was eaten raw, but most was smoked over open fires.

Fred wanted the head mounted so the head, trunk and tusks were loaded into the hunting car.

The arrow that had downed four tons of elephant was a standard four-blade Razorhead but weighed nearly two-ounces, about 75 percent more than usual. Fred had given the arrow extra weight for better penetration by inserting an aluminum arrow shaft inside a shaft of fiber glass. The arrow had gone in about twenty-four inches and had done its work quickly.

As he so often did, Fred immediately shared the good news with his friends in Grayling in this letter:

Beira, Mozambique
June 22, 1964

"To the employees of Bear Archery Company:

Hunt is finished. It has been successful from every point of view. Leaving here for Salisbury today. Overnight there, then to Nairobi where Jomo Kenyata will have a celebration for Godfrey relating to the latter's gift of a small plane for the African Medical Foundation. Going then to Dr. Wood on the slopes of Mt. Kenya for a few days. To Rome about the 30th when I will leave party to join Mrs. Bear in Copenhagen.

If you got my two cables and are hearing Godfrey's shows, you have at least a brief account of activities. I will enlarge somewhat here. A full accounting will be contained in my field notes.

We should have a fine film. Ten thousand feet exposed. Some very good action of game and shooting same, including elephant. This latter was very exciting and not without hazard. I have shot my first and last pachyderm. It was a big one, but tusks not impressive. Will have head mount.

Also have good film of Godfrey shooting bow.

I shot lousy the first day. After success with the elephant, however, I settled down again. Total bag for the first 10 days is as follows: elephant, 54" kudu, nyala, waterbuck, two impala, two warthogs. Pete Barnett says nyala and one impala are record book. One warthog big tusker for head mount. The kudu is quite a prize. It had been beyond my fondest hope to get one. The nyala is impressive and beautiful, too.

This racy start came to a sudden end. Going through tall grass about 10 miles an hour and looking ahead for game one day, we

Fred with the dangerous Cape buffalo that fell to his arrow in Mozambique, 1965

nosedived into a wash five feet deep and six feet wide. The stop was abrupt to say the least. I was in front with the driver in the open jeep, Halmi and two natives in the back.

Halmi landed head first in the ditch. Why his neck was not broken, I will never know. I was thrown into the dash and cushioned Babuda's flight forward who then continued to roll like a rubber ball into the grass beyond.

When the dust cleared, I was half in and half out of the jeep. A cracked rib and a wrenched back. All the rest OK except for cuts and bruises. Equipment scattered all about. Peter (tracker) carried my movie camera with him all the way. No damage except stock broken off. Halmi's big lens was broken.

Have been licking my wounds more or less since then and doing little hunting. Never did get to try for buffalo, although there are many here. Godfrey happy and agreeable. He has a good collection of trophies. Barnett shot some good game also.

See you later, Fred

After a day in Rome with Godfrey, Fred left for Copenhagen to join his wife. From there the Bears went to Oslo, Norway, where Henrietta's relatives were hosts for a week's tour of the mountains and fjords of that magnificent country. Fred declared upon boarding the plane for home that in his opinion, "Norwegian girls are the prettiest in the world."

In 1964 Fred had succeeded in downing the world's largest land animal with his primitive weapon. During the summer of '65, he returned to Mozambique with a party of friends for a fine hunt with Safarilandia outfitters, directed by Werner Von Albenslaven, operating at that time in the Save River region, one of the greatest game areas on the African continent. Wally Johnson, Sr, was Fred's guide and shared with his client the excitement of collecting both the fierce Cape Buffalo and a large, full-maned lion with the bow and arrow. Henrietta also traveled to Europe again that summer, this time in the company of her daughter, Julia and granddaughter, Hannah (age 17). Upon arriving in Bergan, Norway, the first lap on their summer's travels, the women received a telegram from Fred, who had gone on ahead:

Telegrafverket June 8, 1965
Lourencomarques Via Osloradio

Mrs. Fred Bear
Hotel Bristol, Bergan, Norway
   Have fine buffalo. Everybody happy, have fun. Looking forward to
   meeting you all in Madrid.

Love, Fred

The following is a Press account of the buffalo hunt:

FRED BEAR HAS DONE IT AGAIN

The much traveled archery manufacturer and renowned bowhunter safaried through Mozambique, Portuguese East Africa again this summer and added a brace of mammoth Cape Buffalo and a lion to the extraordinary list of big game trophies he has taken with bow and arrow.

Last year, Fred, holder of numerous Pope & Young records, brought down a four-ton bull elephant with a single arrow in the same country — among the dozens of trophies bearing testimony to his prowess as a hunter are a towering Kodiak Bear and a Bengal Tiger.

Fred, president of Bear Archery Company, Grayling, Michigan,

Fred Bear and Arthur Godfrey attending ceremonies in a Masai village, relating to Godfrey's gift of an airplane to the African Medical Research Foundation.

Godfrey recording some safari highlights to be mailed to the States for use on his radio show.

Surveying the damage after the safari car upended in a grass hidden gully.
Fortunately, none of the riders were seriously hurt.

along with eight other Americans, including James Crowe of the Detroit NEWS and New York photographers Robert Halmi and Zoli Vidor, set out in early June to film a sequence on hunting Cape Buffalo. They were assisted by a handful of white hunters from Safarilandia, Ltd., which has exclusive hunting rights in Mozambique.

The Cape Buffalo is rated by experienced hunters as one of the most dangerous beasts of the veldt. Fred found out why on the first day of the hunt.

His party was trekking through the high grass when a charging bull scattered the natives ahead. The animal turned on Fred and guide Wally Johnson, Sr. Wally dropped the buffalo, moving at express train speed, with a quick shot over the lowered horns. The beast collapsed a scant 10 feet from the pair.

On the second day, Fred brought down his first buffalo with one arrow.

They were traveling through the brush in their Toyota (hunting car) in an area natives described as good buffalo country. It was fairly open. A small scattering of bushes and an occasional thicket were broken here and there by dongas or creek bottoms, heavily timbered and brushy.

Suddenly, Fred caught a glimpse of buffalo in a thicket. They circled the area in the car and found tracks of two buffalo leading into the donga. Wally told Luiz, his native tracker, to take his rifle and flush them out while the main party got over to the other side. They no sooner got there than a pair of huge bulls came charging out, heading straight for the car.

What ensued was a mechanized bullfight fought at 20 miles an hour. The little hunting car bounced over the rough ground, pursued by the larger of the two buffalo.

Juca, one of the natives, was sitting on the backseat holding a camera and rifle when one buffalo charged from the right and hit the car on the back panel. The charge jolted the rear end, jerking it over about three feet and ripping off the spare tire. The impact threw Juca off on the side toward the buffalo. Wally brought the car to a screeching halt, but Juca jumped up and ran for safety.

Fred's cameraman on many of his most famous hunts around the world was Robert Halmi,
now a well-known television producer in New York.

Fred and his warthog. Africa, 1965.

Fred, his outfitter and camera-crew head for Cape Buffalo country. Africa, 1965.

Fred Bear, describing what followed, says, "I jumped out on my side of the car and got an arrow on the string as the buffalo galloped past me headed for the bush. He was quartering away at about 35 yards when the arrow hit him, going into the rib cage. We found him dead 300 yards away with green paint from the Toyota ground into his horns."

Getting the desired films, the primary purpose of the safari, took several weeks of intensive stalking and observing waterholes from a blind. The payoff came at the end of this period when Fred was able to approach an isolated bull near a herd of 60. Shooting down an alley in the high grass, Fred bagged his second Cape Buffalo of the safari while the big movie cameras recorded the event.

Each of these bulls weighed over 1,000 pounds and had horns wide enough for a man to ride on."

His plans that year were to hunt both Cape buffalo and lion. Originally there had been eight in the party, but after a month of hunting and filming, all were gone except Fred and Dick Mauch, a hunting friend from Nebraska.

When the rest of the group disbanded, Mauch set out to try for a leopard, while Fred and Wally prepared to encounter the "king of beasts." Excerpts from Fred's field journal carried the resulting story:

"Last Wednesday night I had the thrill of a lifetime."

"Wally, Luiz, Juca and I drove to Alois Delima camp on Sunday afternoon. We stopped at a native village en route and picked up another native tracker named Paulo, whom Wally said had been a poacher of vast experience before they converted him into one of their best game wardens. At this camp also, I saw Tisus, a strapping young native whom I'd met before. On that occasion I'd given Tisus some candy wrapped in cellophane which he shared with a younger sister. The little girl appraised the gift for a few seconds and then popped it into her mouth, wrapping and all. Tisus, who could speak some English, was embarrassed and said with great authority: 'You've got to skin it first!' "

"We have just finished such an exciting lion hunt that I'm afraid the story will call up suspicions that I am stretching the truth. It is the bow that brings on these unusual situations. With a gun, my hunt would have been over quite some time ago. The first lion we saw would have been shot, the buffalo sequence over in less than a week and we would now be on our way home. But the range limitation of the bow makes it necessary to get so close before shooting that almost anything can happen, so at the risk of claiming too many thrilling hunting episodes, I'll chance one more.

"Monday we roamed the country looking for lion tracks and scanned the skies hoping to see circling vultures that would pinpoint a lion kill. Tick birds lead one to buffaloes, but it's the vultures that tell where a lion has made a kill.

"We traveled around for several days until we found a spot well marked with lion tracks. We shot a wildebeest for bait and dragged it around behind the car to lay a scent trail. That done, we chained the carcass to a lonely tree eighteen yards from a thicket-like grove of trees growing in a twenty foot circle. We planned to build a blind here if the lions found the bait. Wildebeest are almost always used for lion bait in this area where there are thousands of them. To take wildebeests for bait may seem like wanton killing, but when one considered that the lion would kill one for himself anyway, the odds are about even. Lions appreciate bait either fresh or in any stage of aging — up to several weeks. We kept the vultures away (vultures find carrion by sight only) by covering it with leaves and branches.

"Wednesday morning we were ecstatic to discover that two lions had been feeding on the carcass. A discovery like this is sensational in itself. Only some unusual turn of events would prevent their coming again in the evening.

"It was reasonable to expect the big cats to come in silently within eighteen yards of my arrow. If we were lucky, they would come early while there was still shooting light.

"We planned a sleep-out now with great anticipation. We went back to camp for blankets and food and returned in the afternoon to build our blind. No attention need be paid to the wind since lions, like leopards and tigers, have a very poor sense of smell. Luiz, Juca and Paulo began clearing out within the circle of trees. We planned to drive the hunting car inside and use it as part of our barricade. The three men chopped and grubbed at the undergrowth and bushes while the rest of us got everything in readiness for spending the night in the blind.

A wild shriek from Luiz stopped all operations. Backing away in haste, he pointed to a python coiled up on the ground. The snake had been hiding under a clump of bushes that Luiz was chopping out. There was time to get a blunt arrow though its head and I thought with some satisfaction, that it would make a fine trophy. We looped the twelve and a half feet of python over the limb of a tree nearby and went back to our work of building the blind.

As we cleared the ground, we piled the brush around the edge in a circular fence, providing a limited measure of security but no obstacle at all if a lion chose to leap over the top.

There were just two trees large enough to climb, one on the bait side where Wally and I would be, the other opposite, where Luiz, Juca and Paulo would spend the night. The tree on our side was a thorn tree that offered poor possibilities for climbing.

An hour before dark we ate a snack and stretched out on our blankets. We had two .375 caliber rifles with us.

As the sun began going down, we were lying flat, silent and motionless. The hour was five-forty when we heard a sudden cracking of bones, which gave us a jolt since we had not heard anything come in. My 66-pound Bear Kodiak bow lay at my feet, an arrow nocked on the string. I eased to my knees, keeping low and got into shooting position. The light was poor, but good enough — eighteen yards is not far. There were two lions, both males and both of them saw me. Both cats stopped feeding. One, almost broadside, was facing me slightly and the other one was behind him staring at me head-on. I felt an urgency to shoot quickly…The light was too poor to see the path of the arrow or exactly where it hit, but there was no doubt it did strike home when no time elapsed between the hit and the first vicious snarl. Both lions sprang up and the one in back shot off to the left. The hit lion, growling and snarling at every bound, curved toward us for a second and then swerved away to the left also, passing very close to the blind.

The lions gone, there was complete silence except for the whispered speculations of Wally.

"Where did you hit him?"

"I don't know," I told him. "Right behind the shoulder I think, but I can't be sure how high or low."

There was silence for another ten minutes. Ten ears straining for the slightest sound. It was dark now. There is not much twilight in Africa.

We were not long in learning where at least one lion was. A shattering roar seemed to rattle the leaves of our blind, the walls of which now seemed so thin they would not keep out a rabbit. One of those lions, maybe both, was out there twenty yards away in the black night.

Lions are fearless at night and it is difficult to remember that they can see as well in poor light as we do in the daytime and a wounded lion is not to be trifled with even in the daylight. We could only guess that this was the hit one hell-bent for revenge. He must be sitting out there in the dark, studying our leafy barricade and selecting the best spot to leap in and land on this concentration of human beings. I clutched my .375 and Wally held his. All safeties off. If he came in our first sight of him would be his silhouette against the faint light of the sky.

Lying half slouched against the thorn tree, I covered the area behind Wally who was facing me. He covered the area behind me and Luiz took charge of his end of the compound. If the lion came in we would be lucky to get off a shot in time, luckier still to hit him and it would be nothing short of a miracle to get a killing shot. In any case, we would have a lion upon us, dead or otherwise.

There was another mighty series of roars and snarls from the same location, followed by deadly silence both in the blind and out in the darkness.

I can vividly remember all the details now — a week later. Nobody said a word or laughed or coughed or cleared his throat at any time. I remember asking myself: What am I doing here? My insurance company had told me before I left for this trip that it would reduce my rate by five dollars a thousand if I'd quit this crazy business. Now, for the first time I was beginning to see the sense of it.

There was another half hour of agonizing silence. Then a lion, a half mile away, gave the low half-purring, half-moaning 'get-together' call that lions use for communicating. Another answered from somewhere. In the safety of camp I had found this interesting, but out there that night, it made the hackles on my neck stand up like porcupine quills. My legs were cramped and stiff. It was cold, but no one so much as touched the corner of a blanket to relieve this condition. The tension in that blind filled the air like dense fog.

I began to worry, seriously now, how long the natives could stand it, or myself and Wally, for that matter. And, as if to test us, another roar like the vibrating, bone-shaking blast of an ocean liner came through the night.

Luiz suddenly broke down. It was eight-thirty by the luminous hands on my watch when he crept over to Wally and whispered:

"Boss, Paulo is mighty scared, says he's going to climb that tree."

"You tell him to keep still and quiet," Wally whispered back fiercely. "If he tries to climb that bloody tree, the lion will be in here on us before he can get one leg up."

Luiz knew from experience with the boss that Wally was holding him responsible for what Paulo did.

We waited even more expectantly after this stirring around in our blind, quietly done as it had been. For another hour, no one allowed himself so much as a satisfying deep breath.

The night was getting colder. The temperature must have been down to 50 and each roar of the lion seemed to send it down an additional degree. At nine-thirty, Luiz risked Wally's wrath, his job and everyone's safety by inching over to our side of the blind once more.

"Boss, I can hear that lion tearing flesh. I think he's feeding on the dead lion."

"Wally made no reply, but we all listened intently. Following another raging blast from the dark I, too, could hear the ripping of flesh and clicking of teeth.

This was a stimulating development. For the first time, we had a valuable clue. It was highly unlikely that a wounded lion would be eating anything and a lion that was not wounded would certainly be less of a problem to us. With indescribable relief, we put our guns on safe and I quietly slid my aching muscles down into a more comfortable position.

The sky was beautiful. The Southern Cross made a brilliant display in the velvety night. A large bright satellite raced across the heavens. The moon, in its first quarter, was due to appear at midnight. We waited eagerly for its light.

At ten o'clock, Luiz whispered again.

"Boss, that lion out there is tearing up the skin of the dead lion. It

Fred and Wally Johnson with Fred's lion taken during a harrowing night when they were pinned down in their thornbush blind.

Twelve and a half feet of python!

won't be any good. Maybe if you fire a shot, it might scare him off."

This brave show from Luiz didn't fool anyone. Luiz was worried about his own skin.

Wally asked my opinion. I thought it was worth a try. If the lion was bent on doing us in, it might be better to have the showdown now rather than later when our reflexes would be less keen from loss of sleep and the cold.

The streak of fire and boom of Wally's big gun was comforting, but only for a split second. The defiant reply from out in the darkness was the longest and loudest we had heard so far. And the silence that followed was ominous.

These outbursts continued at about 15-minute intervals. I thought of the possibility that my trophy was being ruined. Lions will eat another lion carcass, Wally assured me. I knew that bears consume their own kind. Was the agony of this long night going to go unrewarded? The thought of losing my lion made my skin feel icy cold.

I grasped at the possibility that the roaring lion was eating the dead python hanging in the tree rather than my lion. Wally said, "Could be." Luiz said, "Maybe."

At eleven forty-five, right after another roar outside the blind, Luiz pronounced his ultimatum.

"We go home, or we all going to climb that tree."

Wally considered this for a few minutes, realizing I'm sure that the small tree could hardly hold all three natives anyway. He asked what I thought of making a break for it in the car. It had never occurred to me to try to get away in the open hunting car. But any risk seemed less than being pinned down in this blind.

We took nothing but our guns. It was difficult getting into the car quietly with all the brush and branches piled over it for camouflage, but the car started at first try. Wally switched on the lights, gunned the motor and bulldozed through our barricade with a burst of speed that almost threw us out on the ground.

Fortunately, the country was open and fairly flat. We raced out for 200 yards and then made a tight circle, sweeping our backtrack with light to make sure we were not being followed before heading for camp.

Early the next morning, we returned to the battleground. The lion had eaten most of the python, but the loss of that trophy seemed trivial compared to the relief of finding my lion dead not far away.

The arrow had entered low, back of the foreleg and pierced the heart. It was a beautiful animal, a full-grown male, weighing 460 pounds and measuring 10 feet in length. Hung up in camp, he reached far above my head with the tail touching the ground.

Dropping Paulo off at the village on the way back to camp with the lion, he had one final remark.

"Boss, next time you stop by and ask me to go lion hunting, I say, No thank you!"

Fred and his hunting companion, Bob Munger, Paint Barrow, Alaska, 1966. At the time, Munger was one of Fred's partners in the ownership of Bear Archery.

CHAPTER 12

Fred had twice tried for a polar bear, in 1960 and again in 1962. During one of these hunts he had placed what should have been a fatal arrow in a good bear, but the enraged animal charged at close range and had to be shot by the Eskimo guide. The bear dropped 9 yards from him.

He was anxious to succeed in this challenge, however, in April of 1966 found him headed north once more to the mouth of the Colville River, 150 miles east of Point Barrow, Alaska, with a group that included film star Cliff Robertson. He was doubly on the spot this time, since an ABC television camera crew accompanied them out on the ice to record the hunt for the weekly "American Sportsman" television series. Cliff Robertson was to hunt with a rifle and Fred would hunt with the bow.

For Fred, the exact date of departure for a hunting trip was never delayed. Once the airline tickets were on his desk, he was on that plane. There were times when Fred's wife and indeed his doctor, would urge him to wait a few days before leaving, but broken bones, malaria, pneumonia or migraine headaches had no effect on stopping him.

"I'll be all right as soon as I hit camp," he would say and was off.

On the first lap of this third Alaskan trip he set out with a bad sore throat. A postcard back home en route said:

"My throat is cured. Am feeling fine and looking forward to the hunt. We are almost to Fairbanks. Just finished showing two of our films on the plane. Alaskan Airlines public relations men aboard as well as a Seattle newspaper man. The films were well received."

Fred

He never missed an opportunity to promote bowhunting.

Fred, Cliff and crew arrived in Alaska on April 13 and for almost a month they camped on the ice, seeing no bears. They weathered storms with 30 knot winds and temperatures of thirty below zero. Living in double thermal tents pitched in the lee of a great wall of ice, they staved off boredom by playing cards, staging archery contests, building an igloo and sculpting a polar bear from a large cake of ice.

Cliff had to leave on April 28, but Fred and the rest stayed on. To attract bears, the hunters dragged seal carcasses around the camp area and cooked pots of seal blubber 'round the clock. Finally on May 11, Fred got his chance, this was before hunting on the same day as flying was banned.

Fred was determined, long before the banning of hunting with a plane, to make every attempt to get a bear by camping, in tents, well out on the ice pack. This effort was abandoned only after 25 days of frigid cold when they took the plane and finally found a bear.

Quoting from an article published in *Hunters of the Frozen North*, "Since 1973, all use of aircraft for hunting these animals has been prohibited. Nevertheless, the 'kill statistics,' such as they are, continue to rise. This is true partly because many Eskimos have taken to driving motor sleds over the frozen wastes and some of them are not reluctant to use these vehicles in pursuit of bear. Visitors also find it easier and safer to go hunting across snowblanketed regions with motorized transport and as a sad consequence, the number of polar bear shot illegally has been climbing steadily."

"In Canada, where two separate populations of polar bear exist, one on the Arctic coasts, the other in the Hudson Bay region, the authorities try to enforce a quota system. All bearskins, including those acquired by Eskimos, have to be indelibly marked. Whether the decline in the polar bear population can be effectively checked by this and similar methods is questionable." Fred's account of the encounter with the bear is from his Field Notes:

"I found a place on a pile of ice and Bud and Bob found cover about twenty yards back of me to cover any action with the cameras. We were all clothed in white from head to foot to blend in with the snow.

We waited for an hour and a half, cramped, uncomfortable and cold before we saw him coming about a half mile away. He showed up faintly against the bright snow, shuffling along in an aimless way with his mind on a good seal dinner, I suppose, as he investigated piles of ice and cracks in the snow.

At first he appeared to be coming straight by at close range, but he swerved away from the ridge to choose a course through rough ice that would put him one hundred yards away as he passed me. We decided to move out in front of him and again found cover with the cameras in position as before.

The bear came into sight very quickly. Three hundred yards, two hundred, one hundred...coming on a course that would pass me at twenty yards or even closer. But the wind was not good in our new position. At fifty yards his nose went into the air and he stopped to look toward us. Not sure, but suspicious, he turned sideways looking our way and sniffing. Having been charged before at much closer range than this, I felt sure he was trying to make up his mind whether he would come for us or run off, so I rose from behind my cover and released an arrow.

It looked good all the way. He went down in the loose snow, recoiling from the hit and snapping at the arrow. Then he was back on his feet like a cat and took off over the pressure ridge where he went down, this time for good.

A handsome trophy. After 25 days of bad weather and rough luck, we found ourselves with perfect conditions and bagged a polar bear just 12 miles from camp. We should have a good film."

Fred made eleven 16-millimeter hunting and bowfishing films in sound and color before 1960. By 1970 another nine had been added to the Bear library, films of hunting Stone sheep ("North to Adventure"), Alaskan brown bear ("Kodiak Country"), whitetail deer in Pennsylvania ("The Oldest Game"), African elephants and lions ("Mozambique Game Trails) and Cape Buffalo ("Year of the Buffalo"), tigers in India ("Land of the Tiger") and three films made by ABC-TV for their *American Sportsman* series, featuring Fred hunting Alaskan polar bears, British Columbia grizzly and New Mexico mule deer.

In filming the background camp scenes during the ABC grizzly hunt, the script called for an exchange between Fred and one of the outfitters, Bill Love. Fred was to step out of the hunting cabin carrying a knapsack and Thermos jug, walk over to where Bill was saddling a horse and ask, "How do you want your coffee, Bill?"

Bill was supposed to answer, "I'll have mine black." It was an uncomplicated scene, but things just didn't go smoothly. Each time, Bill (who was very conscientious but extremely camera-shy) misspoke his line, or something else occurred to mar the scene.

Take number five: A member of the ABC crew inside the cabin once more fed fresh balsam boughs into the wood stove to provide picturesque white smoke for the chimney. Fred, on cue, Thermos in hand, opened the cabin door and stepped out, this time tripping over the lintel. When he did not hear the expected, "Cut!" he knew the director intended to use this segment even though it showed him at a disadvantage and like all "movie stars" Fred decided this must not happen. So he took matters into his own hands, ap-

Making a bowhunting promotional film at the top of the world.

After 25 days searching on the polar ice cap, Fred finally located this great polar bear and claimed it with his bow.

Fred doing some trick shooting for TV cameramen during filming of the 1966 grizzly hunt.

Outfitters Bill Love and Jack Lee are pleased with Fred's success on the grizzly hunt. Kispiox River, British Columbia, 1965.

Fred Bear instructing film star, Fess Parker, during an ABC-TV grizzly hunt in British Columbia.

proached the outfitter on cue, but changed the script, hoping to break up Bill's composure and thus spoil the scene. The dialogue came out as follows:

"Bill, would you like some moose droppings in your coffee this morning?"

But Bill, determined to do it right, thought only of his line and with no change in expression firmly answered, "I'll have mine black."

This grizzly hunt was shared with Fess "Daniel Boone" Parker. The day before he left camp, Parker got a bear with a rifle, but he told Fred, who had introduced him to archery, that from then on he would hunt with the bow if possible.

More insight into filming with a big city television crew is found in this letter that Fred wrote to Mrs. Bear during the hunt:

September 16, 1965

Plane coming in tomorrow. Hope this gets to you before you leave for Wisconsin.

Almost no time to write. Three cameramen have exposed 10,000 feet of film in five days. A great break in weather. Today is the first bad day. A black sky and a few snowflakes. Have had no rain to date.

It is 10 a.m., I am in the cabin. A poker game going on. Big stakes.

244

Fess and Ted (Fess Parker's stand-in) are going strong for the bow. I have a target set up here at camp with an assortment of bows and plenty of arrows. Have Fess shooting discs in the film. Until making this picture, he has done very little hunting or fishing! Nor has Ted, who is his stunt man and double in the Daniel Boone T.V. series — Fess is getting good at fishing also, although fish have been scarce.

I have been pleasantly surprised at the quality of the ABC crew. No heavy drinkers, all business but a good sense of humor. They are clumsy in the bush, but fortunately the pair of bears we have been working with on the creek have been most cooperative. We frighten them off the river (filming activities) into the bush, wait 10 minutes, go up or down the river 100 yards and there they are again. This can be repeated just about as many times as the light holds out.

Had hoped to find a bigger bear for Fess, but it looks like he will have to take one of these. Raining now and dark. May not get the shooting done today. ABC plans to do a big promotion on this, their first 1966 show. Several days ago they sent a still photographer up here from L.A. to get pix and story of this Parker and Bear hunt for magazines and for Sunday newspaper supplements.

Two days after Parker left, Fred stalked to within 25 yards of a large grizzly while dependable Bill Love backed him with a gun. The script called for Fred and the bear to be in the same frame when the arrow sped toward its mark. In a breath-stopping scene, the two men managed to get close enough without alerting the bear. Fred shot — and missed.

"Will the bear be back tomorrow?" asked the frustrated director. Fred, who was supposed to know all about wild animals, boldly said, "Yes."

For the retake, the script was changed to require that the bear stand up, the better to be seen.

Miraculously, the bear was back the following day and stood up when Fred whistled. The arrow went exactly where aimed and the entire scene was captured by the cameras and viewed later by millions on national television.

Bill Love and his venerable fellow outfitter, Jack Lee, later said of Fred, "Anytime we think of a true outdoorsman and a person with great hunting skills, our thoughts are always with Fred Bear. He is a wonderful companion to be with on an outing. His interests certainly aren't just in hunting, as he enjoys everything about the wilderness. One simply could not find a truer sportsman or finer companion."

Fred Bear with ABC camera crew after a successful hunt for mule deer on the Jicarilla Apache Reservation in Arizona, 1966.

(The following is a copy of an amusing letter sent to Fess Parker by Burr Smidt, who was the writer with the ABC-TV crew that accompanied Fred Bear on his hunting trip in British Columbia. Parker had to leave as soon as his part of the picture was finished because of his "Daniel Boone" TV commitments.)

Land of the Grizzly
September 23, 1965

Dear Fess and Big "T": (Parker's stand-in)
Leaving camp a bunch of the boys came in whooping it up and Terrace will never be the same, mainly because we hit the town smelling like reclaimed bear bait...the bathtub (at camp) got colder every day...But as they say, 'all's well that ends well' and I packed out 10 year's supply of Lil's oatmeal cookies.

As these things usually go, the day after you left a brace of 1800 pound Ursus Horribilli (grizzlies) hit the area. Fred got a crack at one right away...it was a beautiful stalk, the cameras were set up perfect, even Allen had it framed. Twang, the lanky coot missed: of course he says, 'I did it on purpose' but I know for a fact that he stole out of camp at nightfall and tore up five acres of prime timberland practicing.

It paid off though, because two days later Fred nailed one dead at 25 yards...a brisket, lung and aorta shot...frankly I think it was more likely an accidental death. Fred will naturally come up with some tall lies and I feel that you are entitled to the true story...so here goes.

Fred will claim that the bear will go about 650 pounds (untrue). Bill, Jack and I agree that it was more like 450 and in as much as it had just finished off about 350 pounds of moose meat, you could loosely call it a hundred pound bear.

Also, F.B. will likely mention the beautiful stalk he made (untrue). Actually he stumbled in the brush and when Bill helped him to his feet...there, sitting in a wide-open space, too full to move, was this bear...

Fred got off eight arrows in slow succession and the last one caught 'teddy' in the right hind foot...When he turned to see what hit him, he knocked himself unconscious on a low-hanging hemlock limb... Bill had him skinned out before he came to... and only then did F.B. come up close enough to see what he'd shot. You can ask Jack if this ain't a true account, or you can wait for the release and see the whole thing yourself on TV.

We really missed you both; the camp wasn't the same after you had gone...but we stumbled onward and I really mean it, we are going to get a fine show out of all this effort...I am sure you will be delighted with it. Fess, am equally sure you will come out 'smelling like Dan'l Boone' and the biggest and best biggest of them all...and that's a fine compliment...

Regards et al, Burr

In 1966, ABC's "American Sportsman" series made a film of Fred hunting mule deer on the Jicarilla Indian Reservation in New Mexico. He was made a member of the Apache tribe there and found himself in the peculiar position of teaching American Indians how to shoot a bow and arrow! The venture was a success in every way, including Fred's taking a fine trophy mule deer for the film.

A brand new Fred Bear Museum at Bear Mountain, Grayling, Michigan,1967.

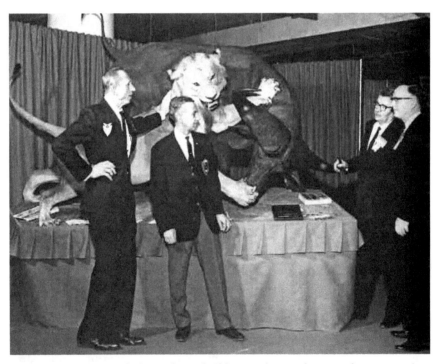

Fred's museum mount of a lion and Cape buffalo in combat was the center of attention at the 1966 NSGA Show in Chicago. Ben Pearson is second from right.

CHAPTER 13

Since the 1952 fire in the Grayling plant destroyed or severely damaged Fred's accumulated trophies, he had gradually rebuilt the collection and it suddenly became a problem. By 1966, the mounts of game taken on Fred's many hunts completely filled the plant's reception room, which by now had became known as the "Trophy Room" and attracted scores of visitors. The W. B. Wescott collection and a wealth of artifacts donated by others were in storage for lack of appropriate display space. It became apparent that a separate and permanent place was needed in which the public could enjoy these exhibits. Therefore, plans were made for a Fred Bear Museum to hold Fred's own collection and items that other archers sent in for display and safekeeping. In September 1967 the museum opened its doors.

It was erected on a picturesque woods-bordered tract in the Grayling Winter Sports area, a short distance from town and a mile and a half from the Bear Plant. This area soon became known as "Bear Mountain" and the name was on a large sign over the entrance road.

The museum building was 170 feet long and 50 feet wide. The entrance was flanked by two totem poles of western cedar, carved in Alaska especially for the museum. Full life-size fiberglass sculptures of polar and Kodiak bears guarded the area.

In addition to the museum, the building contained an archery pro shop, a gift shop and an air-conditioned theater with 70 seats. The pro shop had one of the world's largest and most complete displays of modern archery tackle. The gift shop's merchandise was related to archery, Indians, Eskimos and life in the outdoors. Among the items for sale were authentic Indian chipped arrow points of flint and obsidian, turquoise, gold and silver jewelry, items of ivory and jade, moccasins, native pottery and books.

Visitors to the museum were transported immediately to another world, the world of wildlife and nature. The walls were decorated with mounts of large and small game from four continents, many of record size. One wall was devoted completely to African trophies, including a full-head mount of the 4-ton bull elephant brought down by Fred with one arrow in Mozambique. A few other prominent species in this group were the eland, kudu, sable, nyala, impala, topi, oribi, waterbuck, bushbuck, wildebeest, hartebeest and the fierce Cape buffalo.

In the center of the floor were full mounts in natural postures: Fred's African lion in deadly combat with a Cape buffalo, a leopard attacking a baboon, the

Bengal tiger from India, an Alaskan moose, a polar bear with one foot resting on his life sustaining quarry (an Alaskan seal), Yukon wolves, a muskox, a Barren Ground caribou and others. A full mount of Fred's world-record Kodiak bear, standing nearly nine feet tall, was in a position that allowed visitors to be photographed posing against its massive frame.

The remarkable animal mounts shared space with items of historical significance such as the collection of bows, arrows and other archery equipment from Tibet, Mongolia, China, Japan, Persia, India, Turkey, Arabia, Africa, South America, the Malay Archipelago and the South Pacific Islands.

Undoubtedly the finest individual collection of ancient archery artifacts in the world was on display: native tools, weaponry, decorations and art from Eskimo to Hopi, Iroquois to Yahi and Masai to Bushmen and Pygmies. There were relics of the Stone Age from North America, Europe and the Japanese islands, bronze bodkin arrow points taken from the remains of Persian warriors killed in the Battle of Marathon in 490 B.C. and ancient Oriental thumb rings. The data on ethnology and wildlife classified it as a valuable source of natural history information. Despite the rather off-track location, more than 100,000 people visited the museum every year. Many of them knew little about Fred Bear and asked such questions at the desk as, "Who *is* Fred Bear?" Others wanted to know, "Is he still alive?" and "Is it true that he was a full-blooded Indian?" and on and on.

Of course, the majority of visitors were people interested in archery, many of whom knew the name Fred Bear and wanted to meet him in person. One woman, the story goes, did not dream of meeting him but, when she visited the museum nonetheless asked timidly, "Does Mr. Bear ever come out to the museum?" The girl behind the desk replied, "Of course, as a matter of fact, he is standing over there right now." The woman turned to look and gasping and groping in her purse for a pencil and paper for an autograph, she said unbelievingly, "Why, I saw that man in the restaurant this noon, eating an ordinary ham sandwich, just like anybody else!"

In 1967, after much deliberation, Fred sold his company to the Victor Comptometer Corporation, a Chicago-based firm with wide interests in recreation (including Daisy Air Rifles, Heddon Fishing Tackle and PGA Golf Co., etc.). Very soon the new owners greatly expanded the plant to meet the growing demand for Bear products. Fred remained as division president with an active day-to-day interest in the operation of the business. The year of the sale, the company began to export its products worldwide. It was by now the world's largest manufacturer of quality archery tackle.

"The *Grayling Avalanche* reported on October 18, 1967, "Bear is stirring up this little town. Yesterday a big jet carrying six officials of Victor Comptometer flew in from Chicago and landed at the Grayling airport..." This landing strip, built for planes to protect the Straits of Mackinac during World War II, was long enough to accommodate the Victor plane. Nothing but private planes were ever seen out there, however, so when the big jet set down the entire town was alerted. One person said he thought that war had been declared.

Early December of 1968 found Fred on yet another continent, South America, where he hunted on Brazil's Marajo Island in the 200 mile wide mouth of the Amazon River. His longtime friend, Bob Munger, of Charlotte, Michigan, was again his companion on this trip. Original plans had been for a jaguar hunt on the island, but heavy rains, the earliest rainy season in twenty-three years, ended all hopes of that. Fortunately an interesting alternative developed and although the climate and topography made it one of Bear's toughest expeditions, he succeeded in bagging a tremendous Asiatic Buffalo bearing a 5 foot sweep of horns. These buffaloes had been transplanted to South America from Asia where plans for domesticating them had not materialized. Decades later, the wild inbred creatures lived in the foreboding swamps of Marajo Island, ferociously defying any adversary in their paths. They proved to be as skittish and wary as whitetail deer. The tropical heat and impenetrable jungles were in their way as stern a test of the hunters' endurance as the Arctic ice fields had been. So far as is known, Bear was the first modern bowman to hunt this type of terrain and species of game. Pages from his notebook record the route to Brazil and some highlights of the hunt.

BRAZILIAN HUNT — 12-6-68

New York — Barbados — Port of Spain — Georgetown — Paramaribo and on to Belem.

Short sleeve weather and 9 out of 10 cars are cabs, madly trying to run down pedestrians who are the lowest form of life in the cab driver's opinion.

Those hit are lucky to be killed. Those who recover face a lawsuit for damages to the car.

Got in late last night. Met by outfitter Richard Mason. Took cab to Vanja Hotel. Lucky to have air conditioned room.

Continental breakfast this morning — sightseeing and to the zoo and botanical gardens.

This was Fred's transportation on Marajo Island, off the coast of Brazil, while hunting wild Asiatic buffalo, 1968.

Asiatic Buffalo taken by Fred on the Island of Marajo, located in the mouth of Amazon River. Estimated weight is 1800 pounds. The horns span five and one half feet.

Shaving in the Brazilian jungle camp.

Fred's Marajo Island camp.

Fred Bear proving that archery is a great recreation for entire families.

Repacking gear to reduce total weight. Must go light as trip to hunting grounds (after plane flight) is four hours by horse and bullock through mud into the swamp where the buffaloes are. No chance for jaguar.

We leave for the island at 8 a.m. tomorrow.

Belem is very old. Mostly one-story buildings and most all need paint and repairs. People are small and many remind me of Mexicans. Very pleasant and nobody in a hurry except the cab drivers.

Outfitter says don't wear your camouflage until we are out of town. Natives might think another revolution was starting.

Saturday, December 7th — 7 p.m.

What an evening. Temperature just right and a gentle breeze bringing mixed sounds from the swampy meadow beyond the open-thatched hut we sit in. Howling monkeys set up a clatter just before dark and now the night voices have taken over.

We flew to this Island of Marajo this morning. Landed at the home of a cowboy. Sent a note in a can to be dropped by our plane at a ranch about five miles away saying we were here and to bring the horses.

Left there at 2 p.m. and got here at 6 p.m. Bob and I rode horses. Dick, a cowboy and our tracker rode bullocks (Brahma bulls). Two more of the bulls were pack animals.

Travel was chiefly through marsh either open or wooded in water up to three feet deep. Temperature about a hundred between showers.

The tracker, a mixture of Negro, Indian and Portuguese, lives here with his wife and three small children. Dick says he is a great woodsman, can call in monkeys and that we will eat some! We will also eat parrots here in this jungle camp.

After a week or more recording full hunting days, the diary finally comes alive with the story of success.

We got up at 3:30 a.m. to be about three miles from camp at daylight. Travel was through the bush. The moon had waned and the very first signs of day unveiled a mist that reduced visibility to a hundred yards. Suddenly, the sound of splashing hoofs reached our ears. It could only be buffalo and they were coming our way.

We quickly got ourselves into position and the splashing died into a beat of feet as they came to the hard ground of the wallow area. Looming up out of the mist were two ponderous bulls with massive horns that swept back like the wings of a jet.

Their crafty caution was forgotten as they lumbered toward our ambush, thinking only of the pleasure of submerging themselves in the yellow mud ahead. We had gotten to our machan from the rear and there was no scent in their path. The situation was perfect except that they were about 40 yards apart — only one of them within bow range. Bob had sensed this and exchanged his bow for Dick's .416 rifle. This left me with no problem and I could choose the timing of my shot. I let the first one go slightly by and put my arrow deep in the area of the heart from about 15 yards, an awesome and unusual specimen for the museum.

Also in 1968 the first of Bear's books, *The Archer's Bible*, was published by Doubleday & Company. During the next 15 years more than 400,000 copies were sold. In addition, Fred teamed with sportscaster Curt Gowdy to record an album entitled, "The Secrets of Hunting." The record's 40-minute discus-

Fred often talked to all his employees to let them know how things were going.

Aerial view of the Bear Archery Plant in Grayling. The Bear and Kroll homes are in the background, along the AuSable River

sion revealed much of the lore accumulated by Bear during his more than 50 years of experience in hunting.

Around this period, Bear Archery introduced their revolutionary Converta-point arrow system, which permitted instant interchanging of various points or heads on the same arrow shaft.

1969 was the year he appeared on the Mike Douglas television show while wintering in Florida; sharing the spotlight at Cypress Gardens with "Gentle Ben," the large black bear that was the star of the well-known television series. Feature articles written by or about Fred were appearing regularly in *Outdoor Life, Field & Stream, Time, True* and many other national publications. Columns concerning his various exploits ran in hundreds of newspapers and he was the "star" of many a Sunday supplement story.

In the fall of 1969, Ray Kennedy, a writer for *Time Magazine*, accompanied Fred on a deer hunt to St. Martin's Island in Lake Huron for the purpose of getting a story.

Kennedy's day-by-day account, entertainingly written, appeared in the magazine during December.

Fred's fame spread in ever-widening circles. Stories and articles such as this from the *Franklin News-Herald* in Ohio appeared frequently in newspapers and magazines:

A Column For Outdoorsmen
By Steve Szalewicz
Safari to Sharon

"One recent Saturday afternoon as our auto skidded and slid over the squeaky ice on Route 62 near Polk, we wondered to our companion, Wade 'Smokey' Wagner of Hasson Heights, Oil City, whether the man we were to see and possibly meet would be worth the 50 mile trip.

The Western Reserve Fish & Game protective Association of Sharon, for its 25th annual banquet, had attracted Fred Bear of Grayling, Michigan as its principal guest and speaker. The Shenango Valley sportsmen every year get the biggest names in the outdoor picture.

The invitation said he was a nationally famous archer, big game hunter and president of Bear Archery Company. That much we knew because the name Bear is to archery what Winchester is to firearms or Mitchell is to fishing reels..."

Fred had seen the splendor of plains, deserts, mountains and for-

The Fred Bear Sports Clvb Patch. Worn around the world as a symbol of the wearer's commitment to conservation and outdoor ethics.

ests. He encountered thousands of game animals on four continents, but it had always been important to him to see and know most song-birds, small rodents and mammals, reptiles and other forms of life. He talked with Indians, Eskimos, Africans and people of other lands, seeing firsthand the interrelationship of man and nature. He realized that man, the dominant species of the earth, must develop a new morality, accepting responsibility for the condition of his environment and using every resource, including plants and wildlife, wisely. He further realized that if man continued to despoil his planet, he would surely end in destroying himself as well. Fred felt obligated to use his position of leadership to reform man's attitudes.

As a result, over the past 30 years he has concerned himself more and more with the game management problem of our country. A firm believer in the Pittman-Robertson Act, which levies an 11% tax on guns and ammunition and sets the proceeds aside for conservation, he campaigned to have archery equipment subjected to the same tax. Some segments of the industry opposed the tax, but it was approved in 1971."

Astronaut Joe Engle, left and Daisy Air Rifle Chairman, Cass Haugh, right, flank Fred during an early 1970's visit to the Fred Bear Museum in Grayling.

Fred's interest in ecology and conservation led to the formation of the Fred Bear Sports Club. This national organization, originally suggested in 1967 by Dick Lattimer, Bear's advertising head, was founded in 1970 when ten prominent Americans with high standards as outdoorsmen and an interest in protecting America's ecology and wildlife were invited to join Fred in his conservation endeavors. These ten original members of the Fred Bear Sports Club were Astronauts Joe Engle and Walt Cunningham; Astronaut trainer, Joe Garino, Jr.; television stars, William Shatner (Star Trek) and James Drury (The Virginian); and five of the country's best-known professional archers of the day; Vic Berger, Frank Gandy, Vince DeLorenzo, John Klemen and Clarence Kozlowski.

Fred invited this group to attend an archery tournament at Cobo Hall in March of '70. The following letter was posted for the employees of Bear Archery a few days prior to the event.

Fred and sports-caster Curt Gowdy recording "Fred Bear's Secrets of Hunting" in a Hollywood Studio in 1968. It sold 60,000 copies over the next few years, as a highly successful sales promotion tool.

Two bears getting acquainted at a Sport Show.

Original members of the Fred Bear Sports Club. Cobo Hall, Detroit, 1970.

Fred talks archery with two of the Astronauts who were shooting bows for Bear Archery at Cobo Hall, Detroit. Left to right: Walt Cunningham of Apollo VII and Joe Engle, Commander of the second Space Shuttle flight.

NOTICE TO EMPLOYEES
3/17/70

Wednesday, March 18, James Drury, "THE VIRGINIAN" of television fame will tour the plant and talk with some of you in the various departments. Mr. Drury is stopping in Grayling on his way to the 12th Annual American Indoor Archery Championships this weekend in Detroit's Cobo Hall. He and other personalities will be shooting in the team match Friday Evening with members of the Bear Archery Advisory Staff. The following teams will compete, using the Bear "Tamerlane" Take-Down Tournament Bow:

James Drury, *"The Virginian"*
&
Victor Berger, Current PAA Champion Bear Advisory Staff

William Shatner, *"Captain Kirk" of "Star Trek"*
&
Clarence Kozlowski, *Bear Advisory Staff*

Joe Garino, Jr., *Astronaut Physical Fitness Coordinator*
&
Vincent DeLorenzo, *Bear Advisory Staff*

Walt Cunningham, *Astronaut — First Manned Apollo Flight*
&
John Kleman, *Bear Advisory Staff*

Joe Engle, *Astronaut*
&
Frank Gandy, *Bear Advisory Staff*

On Fred's 70th birthday, the organization was opened up on a selective basis to the general public. Its stated objectives were to protect outdoor ecology, to promote proper wildlife management in our woods, fields and waters and to bring together people who believe in these things. Members are required to uphold the Rules of Fair Chase, their state game and fish laws, the restrictions under which they compete in outdoor sports and the Fred Bear Sports Club

Creed, which reads:

"We believe that man has a right to use his natural resources but that he has a duty to use them wisely, carefully and with reverence.

We believe that wildlife of all sorts must be intelligently managed in a natural environment and we will work to make it happen.

We believe that clean, pure water is essential to the well-being of all creatures and we will not pollute it.

We believe that clean air is vital to the survival of all and we will constantly be alert to those who would have it otherwise.

We believe that litter and waste are spoiling our heritage and we will not tolerate it.

We dedicate ourselves to these goals for our own generation and for the generations to come. For we believe this to be the fulfillment of the American Dream."

Within five years, the organization burst its national boundaries and had more than 25,000 members in more than twenty countries. By mid 1987, the club had grown to over 40,000 members in forty-three countries.

The Fred Bear Sports Club (FBSC) is involved on all levels in active promotion of scientific wildlife management and opposing the anti-hunting, anti fishing movements. The Club, along with the National Rifle Association and the American Archery Council, helped launch "The American Outdoors" television project in 1977, a series of 26 half-hour shows for national television featuring all types of outdoor recreation. The films were designed to educate the public on the pleasures of such recreation and on the state of the nation's wildlife, fish and other natural resources. "The American Outdoors" was televised in nearly 50 states. In 1978 and 1979, 26 segments of the show were seen on 54 television stations nationwide, reaching approximately eighty million viewers of all ages.

In 1982 the FBSC joined forces with the Izaak Walton league in fostering a National Outdoor Ethics program to stimulate the creation and dissemination of materials and programs supporting the ethical behavior of everyone who shares the outdoors.

In addition, each year FBSC and IWLA jointly sponsor the Annual Outdoor Ethics Media Awards among the nation's fisheries and wildlife management professionals to encourage the broadcast and print coverage of the outdoor ethics idea. This is done in concert with the Association For Conservation

Information.

Since 1978, the Club has reached 27,000,000 television viewers with over 7,000 telecasts of its film "THE GOOD EARTH" starring Fred Bear and Astronaut James A. Lovell. The film promotes bowhunting, fishing, shotgunning and other outdoor activities.

And also, since 1978, "THE GOOD EARTH" has been seen by 897,000 individuals in 13,270 locations (668,000 students in 10,110 schools and 228,000 people at 3,159 community groups).

To further bowhunting education, Bear attaches an "ABC's of Bowhunting" booklet to every bow shipped and since 1978 has given away over 1,754,000 of them (many of these went to state hunter education classes).

To help public awareness and understanding of hunting's place in our society, the Club has circulated 1,575,000 copies of its BEAR FACTS cards since 1973.

The Fred Bear Sports Club also brings matters of concern in wildlife, ecology and related issues to the attention of Congress, state governments, various wildlife agencies, outdoor writers and the public.

Fred and Astronaut Jim Lovell during the filming of "The Good Earth." This scene is in Bear's living room in Grayling. Film creator and producer, Dick Lattimer, is 'slating' the scene for editing, 1977.

The Club has also helped in the A.W.A.R.E. (America's Wildlife Association for Resource Education) public education program of the International Association of Fish & Wildlife Agencies (IAFWA) for the future of Wildlife education and conservation. Organized in 1902 as part of Theodore Roosevelt's new conservation movement, the Association has played a major role in the evolution of our national conservation affairs ever since. Its leaders, with headquarters in Washington, D.C., include the directors and associations of the 50 state Fish & Wildlife Departments, each Canadian Province, Commonwealth of Puerto Rico and the federal wildlife agencies of the United States, Canada and Mexico. For many years, Dick Lattimer, the Fred Bear Sports Club executive director, served, at Fred's request, as Co-Chairman and Vice Chairman of the IAFWA Communications Committee.

During the 1980's the FBSC helped produce over $4,000,000 of free/air national television time for IAFWA on Glen Lau's Sports Afield television series in support of proper wildlife management.

DRY CREEK, ALASKA 1971 HUNT

In the late 1960's, Fred began rewarding the top half of his sales force with yearly hunts to Canada and Alaska. These district managers exerted all their energies and sales skill to win a place on one of the coveted trips.

Typical of these hunts was one made in September 1971 with Alaskan outfitter Bob Buzby. The hunting territory was on Dry Creek about 80 miles south of Fairbanks. Center of operations was a cabin of spruce logs built by a prospector back in the early thirties. A large wood-burning cookstove and big table identified it as the dining cabin. It was also the living quarters for the outfitter and cook.

Scattered about were nine by twelve foot tents, on wood frames over wood floors, in which the hunters were housed. Each contained a stove and an ample supply of split dry spruce.

A small creek ran from a slope nearby. Its clear, sweet water was just the right temperature for cooling butter and other food.

Equipment consisted of a Swedish Snow Track machine to which a four wheeled, rubber-tired farm wagon could be attached. It had a hand winch and could retrieve an entire moose, carrying it, if necessary, across miles of tundra. It was also used to haul and take gear and supplies to and from the airstrip to which hunters were flown from Fairbanks.

A Caterpillar bulldozer pulled another wagon and was used to transport supplies to higher sheephunting camps and to keep the trail, which crossed

Care About America's Wildlife. We Do.

A well meaning person gave this conservation officer what they thought was an orphan fawn.

Don't pick up fawns. In most cases their mother is watching nearby, waiting for you to leave.

Ads created and produced by the Fred Bear Sports Club and distributed nationally for use by State Fish & Game Departments in wildlife conservation. The Club also spearheaded getting wildlife and conservation coverage on television.

Clare Conley, Editor of Outdoor Life Magazine, accompanied Fred on his 1971 Alaskan hunt.

Fred and friend. Alaska.

A fine Alaska moose taken at the Dry Creek camp.

Fred and his horse "Flicker" about to set out for a day wandering over the Alaskan tundra.

Fred and Astronaunt Joe Engle at Dry Greek Camp, Alaska, 1971. Engle later was the Commander of space shuttle missions in the Columbia and Discovery.

Dry Creek twenty-one times on the way to sheep country, cleared of rocks and slides.

The hunting party was made up of Astronaut Joe Engle, an X-15 pilot who later commanded several space shuttle missions; Clare Conley, then editor of *True* magazine; Bill Wright, a friend of Fred's from San Francisco, plus two Bear Archery district sales managers, Frank Scott and Henry Fulmer, who had won places on the hunt. All of the men were bowhunters.

They ventured out at dawn each day fortified by a lunch consisting of a sandwich of cold moose or caribou meat, four cookies, a candy bar, an orange, a stick of gum and a napkin. A camp anti-litter rule decreed that the plastic lunch bag, orange peels, gum wrapper and napkin were to be exchanged in camp for their lunch the next day.

The first five days of the hunt were marked by rainy weather and low clouds. But since the bad weather had little effect on the activity of game, the hunters ignored it. Joe Engle and Bill Wright decided to concentrate on hunting Dall sheep. The others set out in search of moose and caribou from the main camp.

The nomadic caribou had not yet reached the territory in any numbers and were hard to find. As for the moose, plenty of cows and calves were about, but the big bulls evidently were still in the Wood River tundra flats to the north.

Departing hunters had left the group some caribou meat, but this gave out after three days, leaving the outfitter embarrassed without meat. The higher terrain continued to be blanketed in fog, rain and occasional snow, foiling stalks on rams sighted briefly through holes in the overcast.

Because of the scarcity of game close by, Fred chose to scout farther out by horseback. His horse, Flicker, was a good mount but had an insatiable appetite and tended to be lazy unless bribed with a few leftover pancakes from breakfast. To Flicker the woods were full of demons. A crooked stick was a deadly snake. A plane sitting on the airstrip was a dread monster, a porcupine was a grizzly bear and even a flushed ptarmigan could bring on a mild attempt to unseat his rider. Fortunately Fred was an accomplished horseman and got along very well with the otherwise dependable Flicker.

On the fifth day of the hunt, he rode out to Newman Creek, in an adjoining drainage basin. By noon he could see the valley and, topping a hill, saw a bull moose slowly making its way up the side of the opposite slope. By the time Fred crossed the stream and tied his horse in a clump of spruce, the bull was out of sight. With his binoculars, however, he was able to locate him lying down in thick brush.

Some willows screened him as he crept up and he spent an interesting three hours with the bull in sight at all times.

He debated whether to risk crawling through the brush to get closer to the moose or detouring around the creek bottom and come in from above. Meanwhile the moose got up once or twice and moved a short way before lying down again.

Suddenly the thicket showed some action. Two cows and a calf appeared and started to feed. The bull got up grunting and began tearing into the willows about him. His heavy antlers threshed the brush with tremendous force and after about fifteen minutes of this uproar walked over to the cows to look them over. They appeared totally unimpressed. The bull started fighting willows again until he tired and once more lay down. The cows and calf began feeding downhill, making their way toward a mineral lick. Fred now was confident that he could get a good shot at the bull because he was sure it would follow the cows.

Another half hour passed. The bull got up to tackle the dead willows once more, this time with a racket that was almost deafening. Ten minutes later he started down toward the cows, lurching from side to side to destroy any brush that got in his way. He was approaching the hunter at a very slight angle, making the only possible shot head-on. At fifteen feet, Fred rose, drew and released in one fluid motion. The arrow went true, sank deep and cut the jugular vein. The moose bounded 50 yards and collapsed. His antlers measured 55 inches. The hunting party's meat famine was over.

In the next two days, Joe Engle bagged a fine Dall ram with a thirty-seven inch curl on the horns, Henry got a bull moose with a fifty-six inch spread and Frank Scott collected two fine Barren Ground caribou.

In camp that evening, Joe reported his hunt for a trophy caribou. He had bagged it quite some distance away and had a five hour hike back to camp with the antlers, cape and a load of meat on his packboard.

The final evening of this hunt was climaxed by a profound display of northern lights, twisting, shimmering beams and streaks of glorious colors melting in and out across the awesome dome of sky. As Fred noted in his diary, "It was impossible to witness this spectacular auroral display without an over whelming sense of a power greater than man..."

Fred had gone on other hunts with Bob Buzby. "Bear never ceased enjoying every day spent in the open," said Buzby. "Hunting to him was merely a way to an end. Many times he had opportunities to kill and did not. There was never a time when he wasn't concerned with the welfare of his companions

Another even larger moose taken by Fred near High Lake in the Interior, 1966. This moose weighed 1500 pounds and stood 7 feet at the shoulder.

and he was always happy when a fellow hunter came in after a successful day. In our 40 years of guiding and outfitting, we rate Fred as one of the family — a friend first and a client second."

Fred had organized similar hunts for top Bear dealers and sales representatives in Alaska's interior, east of Mt. McKinley between the watersheds of the Susitna and Tulkeetna rivers. Their outfitter there was Ken Oldham. Headquarters was Oldham's comfortable lodge on High Lake in the middle of good moose, caribou and bear country. This is Fred's story of a moose hunt with Ken Oldham that appeared in the ALASKA BOWMAN, 1980 edition.

BAREFOOT MOOSE HUNTER
by Fred Bear

"The train departs Anchorage at 9 a.m. Arrives Chulitna at 2:15 p.m. It has dining car and club room. Most of the conductors are well dressed in local color and will contribute a great deal to your trip.

You pass through the edge of the famous Matanuska Valley farm district, past Independence Mine, into the new farmland of the

Susitna Valley with the world's largest stand of birch.

The train stops at Tulkeetna, originally a Tennah Indian village but now a trade center for the mines across the Susitna and the local farmers and fishermen. Then you plunge into the gorge of the Susitna and through the tiny stations that served the mines of fifty years ago. Chulitna, population five, is the head of navigation on the Susitna and is now the terminal of the Silver Dorne Mining Company. You get off the train here and I'll take over."

The above was a letter from Ken Oldham in July of 1966. Who could resist the prospects of such a trip? I needed a good specimen of moose for a full mount for the museum and the time was right in every way. In August, Bob Munger of Charlotte, Michigan, joined me and we found the train as comfortable and the scenery and local color as interesting as Ken had said it would be.

Ken met us in Chulitna and we flew into his High Lake hunting camp to begin a 10-day hunt for moose and caribou. High Lake is not as high as its name suggests. It is surrounded by mountains grown over with black spruce but much of the area is bare or grassy. The mountains are gentle and the tops rounded or flat. The lake itself is about a third of a mile wide and a short mile long. The air strip is located next to the lodge and cabins and a Cessna 172 rocks lazily on floats at the dock on the lake.

As we stowed our gear in the Cessna next morning, Ken informed us that the caribou had not yet moved into the area. We decided to try for moose in the meantime, in an area seldom hunted before. That was a thought to tingle the blood of any hunter. After a 10 minute flight, we sat down on a lake. A cabin hugged the shore and beside the cabin was a small track machine that would serve as our transportation into an area that was accessible only by this method or by horses.

Six hours and five miles later, over some rough going that seemed almost impossible at times, we topped a ridge that overlooked a valley of the Susitna. It was the most likely looking place for moose I have ever seen.

The valley floor was covered with spruce that fingered up into draws. This growth gave way to willow that fringed the entire bottomland, creeping up the hillsides a few hundred yards before tapering to buckbrush and finally the grass on which we stood.

As the morning progressed, the weather turned cooler and it was more comfortable to move about. By early afternoon I found myself in the midst of a dozen or so moose. One of these was a good bull, but he was 80 yards away and there was heavy brush between us. Two smaller bulls and a cow were between me and the big fellow and since they were staring at me, I could not move. The big bull was lying down. For the next half hour I knelt in the grass, well out of sight, not daring to move.

Finally the bull roused himself, got to his feet and started off. I ran toward the cover that separated us, skirted the corner of it at a trot and came up sharply with the bull standing broadside, 60 yards off and looking my way. I drew an arrow and released. As we discovered later, the arrow went through his heart. He fell less than 100 yards from where he was hit.

During this activity, the other moose stood calmly and watched. They did not leave until I started calling for Bob.

We field dressed the bull and headed toward camp. As we emerged from the timber and climbed above the brush, Bob put his glasses on a suspicious looking object in the willows about a mile down the slope. He decided it was a bull moose of shootable size.

"Let's go get him," he urged. I declined, saying that I preferred to find a comfortable spot where I could watch the activities with binoculars.

I could still see the moose long after I lost sight of Bob, whose camouflage clothing melted into the willows. I kept watching. At last the bull left his bed, looked to the left and ran into the spruce.

Bob Munger is not known for great accuracy with the bow. But he is a persistent hunter and a fine stalker and he has the eyes of an eagle. In this case I assumed he had shot an arrow at the moose before it ran off into the timber, unscathed. With no great urgency I made my way up the mountain toward camp.

Twilight was well gone by the time I'd done some camp chores and had the gas stove going. The coffee was about to boil when the tent flap opened and a familiar voice asked sadly, "Is this a shoe store?"

It was poor Bob, looking dejected and uncomfortable. His feet were bare, blue and bleeding. I put a cup of steaming coffee in his hand and brought a bucket of warm water for his aching feet while he told his story:

"I had no trouble finding the moose and had made a good stalk to within a hundred yards when I decided to take my boots off for a quiet approach. I removed my socks too and hung them on a willow bush as an aid to locating the boots later...

"At 30 yards the bull saw me. After I shot an arrow into him, he trotted off toward the timber. He ran a short way, stopped broadside and looked back at me so I hit him again. This time he made his way to the spruce and I followed. He ran about a quarter of a mile before going down.

"Now I had time to think about my boots. It was getting cold and ice was forming in wet places. I was sure I could go right back to the spot, but all success eluded me. I searched for an hour in an area that looked entirely unfamiliar. Nothing seemed the same and there was no sign of my socks. My feet were bruised and getting cold and I had to make a firm decision. It was an hour to camp. An hour of daylight remained. Should I spend the hour looking for my boots with a good chance of not finding them and have to face traveling after dark bare-footed, or should I start now and have daylight to find the best places to set my tender feet down?

I chose the latter and I don't mind saying there were times when I wondered if I'd make it..."

Ken came back to camp in the track machine from a scouting trip. He was surprised to learn that our licenses were filled and the moose hunt was over. That was good, he said, because the Nelchina caribou migration was expected to pass only a few miles away. Now there would be time to see this spectacular sight. The caribou, he said, would be enroute from Mt. McKin-ley to Lake Louise.

Ken's track machine was a great piece of equipment. It had a 4-cylinder, V-type engine that would go all day on five gallons of gas. It also had a winch on it. The winch gave me an idea.

When a deer is brought into camp, it is usually hung in a tree or from a pole for pictures. But moose are too heavy to handle that way — or were they? I asked Ken if with the winch we could string him up on one of those spruce trees. Just for a picture. He said it could be done. He found a sheave in the tool box and shinned up the nearest tree and wired it in a crotch.

The operation was doomed to failure. After precise planning, we fastened the loop around the antlers and Ken started the winch...but as the poet said, "the best laid schemes o' mice and men..."

The moose was heavier than the machine. We got a picture of a moose winching a track machine up a tree.

In a letter Ken Oldham wrote to a friend he said, "I could say a lot of things about Fred Bear — honest, hard-working, enjoys life; but the aspect of his life

This moose, taken by Fred's companion, Bob Munger, proved to outweigh the vehicle they tried to lift it with. Bob Munger is at the left and outfitter Ken Oldham is next to him. 1967

that I'm best qualified to judge was his hunting. Fred is the finest natural hunter I've ever known. It didn't take fancy equipment or gimmicks for him to be successful. He always carried a good quality bow and arrows, cheese and bread and a can to boil his coffee in. I went with him sometimes but more often than not he'd tell me to drop him off on some lake and not come near him for four or five days — he didn't even want to hear an airplane engine. I'd worry the whole time. Sure, he was in good moose country, but it was also good grizzly country and he was armed with only a bow. If he didn't get something after the first day or two, he was out of food. That didn't seem to bother him. Our base camp pantry overran with canned goods and special camping equipment, but he didn't want to be bothered with what he didn't need. Fred didn't worry about bears. He usually knew they were in the country before they knew he was there."

In the early '70's a bestselling novel "DELIVERANCE" appeared in the bookstores — it was a story written by Pulitzer Prize-winning novelist, James Dickey of Columbia, South Carolina about four young men canoing down a wild Georgia river. Warner Brothers made a movie of the story starring Burt Reynolds and Jon Voight. It was an extremely thrilling and well done film.

Dickey, in addition to his fame as a poet, lecturer and professor is an ac-

Fred and poet, James Dickey, inspecting a Bear take-down bow during a visit to Bear Archery by the Pulitzer Prize author of "Deliverance." Dickey is an archer and a bowhunter.

complished archer and his book has a strong archery thread running through the story.

Jim Dickey is also a friend of Fred Bear's. On a visit to Grayling just before the new compound bows were launched, Fred showed him a model and asked him to draw it back. When Dickey experienced the characteristic "let down" of the new bow, he said firmly and without hesitation, "I want one for myself. I want one for my son and I want one for my wife."

Being aware of Dickey's artistic tendencies and love for the beautiful bent bow of the ages, Fred had been certain he would scorn this clumsy, wired and wheeled model and throw it down in disgust. Instead, Dickey was impressed with the ease with which one could draw it back and after his declaration of intent, Fred said later, "I decided to go into the compound bow business with confidence."

Warner Brothers were established on location at Clayton, Georgia when Hugh Blackburn, southeastern regional manager for Bear Archery's sales department, found a note on his desk one day. It was from James Dickey. Blackburn returned the request to call and Dickey said, "You'd better get up here to Clayton right away. We're in a hell of a mess. They've got some old wooden arrows they picked up in a dime store and a bunch of assorted bows

Fred writing his field notes at sunset. British Columbia, 1964.

they don't know how to shoot."

So Blackburn went to Georgia and was introduced to the cast as the technical director from Bear Archery Company.

Keeping in mind that *Deliverance* was slated to be the most powerful archery movie ever made, Dickey was anxious that the archers in the cast, particularly Burt Reynolds and Jon Voight, were completely schooled in the art of shooting a bow. So Bear Archery became the advisor and supplier of equipment for the film. *Deliverance* made a distinct impact on the sport of archery, introducing it to thousands who had never before been aware of its wide use among hunters.

CHAPTER 14

Fred's association with his grandson, Chris Kroll, was warm and close. On one occasion Fred was in the hospital in Grayling for a few days, in a room that looked out over the AuSable River. Every day after school Chris made it a point to visit his grandfather and then go down to the river to fish at a spot where Fred could see him from the window. They'd exchange waves of recognition and then, with binoculars, Fred followed Chris's fly hitting the water.

Another time when Chris was in his early college years, he played King Henry in "A Man For All Seasons." The family attended the performance and a few days later Fred sent his grandson a wire: "Observed your King Henry performance last night. Congratulations! Are you interested in signing contract for a hundred thousand grand?

Metro Golden Bear

During the time that Victor Comptometer's fortunes had dwindled drastically — from $84 to $4 a share, a note from Chris to Fred said:

> "Have your letter concerning affairs at Bear Archery Company. It seems unfair after a lifetime of work to see a fortune dissolve so. I can only say that if you look back, your goal was never to amass a fortune. Never did I hear you speak of 'getting rich'. What you set out to do, you have done. You have done it with integrity, with love and with flourish. That will always remain. You created and you are, Bear Archery Company and the whims of a spastic stock market can never change that. I hurt for the disappointment I know you feel, but I am literally overwhelmed by the joy and pride that we, not just family, but all archery feels for you."

When a story about Fred's grizzly hunt in British Columbia came out in *LIFE* magazine, Chris wrote him from school in Oberlin,

> "...From your notes I'd say you had a grand time in British Columbia. I am looking forward to the next issue of LIFE and have alerted half the campus! I am really proud of you, PB. (Papa Bear), you'll never believe how proud."

Christopher Kroll, Fred's grandson, accompanied him on an Alberta hunting trip and took this fine mountain goat, which was the bowhunting world record for several years.

Chris's life ended in tragedy. The farther Chris progressed in years the more deep-seated his problems became. He was a product of the sixties when the lives of so many promising young men were cut short as a result of the lifestyles and unrest of that era.

The end of Chris' life came close to the Christmas holidays, just before the beginning of the second semester of his junior year in college. Things, for Chris, had been on the upswing for some time; he was on the Dean's list at school and appeared to be looking forward to returning. But it was not to be. Fred, who loved him so dearly was the one who found him dead from self-inflicted carbon monoxide poisoning.

The family mourned and grieved as families must do at those times and on a misty, rainy Sunday afternoon they drove to Bear's Bend and scattered his ashes over the scene of happier times.

One year later the family gathered again, this time in Ann Arbor when Fred received the Regent's Citation of Honor from the University of Michigan.

They listened to the words of the Citation which had its roots in a letter Chris had written to the University calling attention to his grandfather's accomplishments (see below) and suggesting that he be recognized for them. (The family had no knowledge of this until notice of the award came after Chris' death.)

University President Robben W. Fleming presented the award during the commencement luncheon held at the Michigan League. It was a graceful and dignified event. Fred stood with President Fleming before tall, rain washed windows while one of the regents read the Commendation:

FRED BERNARD BEAR
MANUFACTURER, SPORTSMAN
AND CONSERVATIONIST

YOUR CAREER AS MANUFACTURER, SPORTSMAN AND CONSERVATIONIST REMINDS US THAT A STRONG AND IMPERISHABLE LINK WITH NATURE IS ONE OF MANKIND'S SUREST DEFENSES AGAINST THE PANGS OF SPIRITUAL ISOLATION.

YOUR LIFESTYLE HAS PROVIDED THE NATION WITH INCENTIVE TO ENJOY OUTDOOR INTEREST AND YOUR CREATIVE IMAGINATION HAS PROVIDED SUPERLATIVE EQUIPMENT TO PURSUE THEM. THE NAME FRED BEAR HAS BECOME A LIVING LEGEND, A TRADEMARK OF EXCELLENCE.

BEAR ARCHERY COMPANY OF GRAYLING ROSE TO WORLD LEADERSHIP OUT OF THE GREAT TRADITION OF THE ARTISAN AS A CORNERSTONE OF CIVILIZATION. HAVING ADMIRED THE ANCIENT CRAFT OF BOWYER, YOU ASSUMED ITS MANTLE AND BROUGHT TO YOUR CRAFT A THOROUGH GRASP OF MODERN TECHNOLOGY. REVERSING THE CUSTOMARY ORDER OF HISTORICAL DEVELOPMENT, YOU UTILIZED EXPERTISE GAINED IN THE MANUFACTURE OF AUTOMOBILES TO REVOLUTIONIZE THE MAKING OF BOWS AND ARROWS. YOUR FIRM WAS FIRST TO MASS-PRODUCE ARCHERY EQUIPMENT SUPERIOR IN DESIGN AND WORKMANSHIP. YET YOU HAVE UNSELFISHLY SHARED YOUR DESIGNS WITH OTHERS.

Fred Bear receives University of Michigan Regent's Citation from President Fleming at the Commencement luncheon held at the Michigan League, Lansing, May 1, 1976.

A LIFE LONG SUPPORTER OF CONSERVATION, ACTIVELY INVOLVED IN LAND AND WILDLIFE PRESERVATION, YOU WELL DESERVE YOUR REPUTATION AS ONE OF THE OUTSTANDING SPORTSMEN OF THE CENTURY.

THE UNIVERSITY OF MICHIGAN IS PROUD TO ACKNOWLEDGE THE GREAT CREDIT YOU HAVE BROUGHT OUR STATE. WE TAKE PLEASURE IN PRESENTING TO YOU, THIS REGENT'S CITATION OF HONOR.

As the reading of the Citation came to an end, the family, through bittersweet tears silently raised their glasses to the empty chair where Christopher might have been sitting.

Fred's postscript to this painful era of his life was written at a time when he was summing up the notes from a few of his hunts. He mentioned that during a hunt in Alberta he had not kept a journal:

"My seventeen year old grandson, Chris, accompanied me on his first big game hunt in 1956. He was a fine bowman, having been schooled in the sport by both his father and myself and our plans were that he would "take over" for me when he finished school. He had dreams of the Ovis Poli and other achievements I might not get around to.

We talked of these things on the long plane trip to Alberta where I broke several ribs soon after arrival and was out of the hunt. But Chris saved the day by taking a first place Pope and Young Club mountain goat.

It was his finest hour and he had time for no more. He died while yet in his twenties and shattered both our dreams."

Following is the letter Chris had written to the University.

Mr. Robben W. Fleming, President
University of Michigan
Ann Arbor, Michigan

Dear President Fleming:

I am writing on behalf of a University recognition for Mr. Fred Bear of this state. It is my understanding that the procedure is to state one's case and present it to the faculty for consideration.

To begin with, I am his grandson and naturally biased. But everyone who knows him shares that bias as well. What started this idea in my mind was a meeting of the Ivy League Club where he was a speaker. He had invited me to go along and when it came time to sign the book with our respective schools, I saw an expression on his face that has haunted me ever since. A wistful sort of sadness and regret over his neglect of higher learning.

You see, he quit school at the tenth grade level in Carlisle, Pennsylvania where he grew up, the nephew of Daniel Drawbaugh over whom the New York Court took three separate trials to decide in favor of Alexander Graham Bell for the invention of the telephone. At this early age, my grandfather was too consumed with nature and wild things to tolerate school any longer. He went to work, making up his High School diploma at night school and learning the trade of pattern making in the railroad shops of Carlisle. He started up a little archery business in a Detroit basement after learning about Pope and Young, the men who are called the fathers of modern archery. In those days all bows were made by hand, by a master bowyer. It was a very slow process, but the way it was "always done." He began thinking about how it could be done by machinery but no machinery existed. So the almost impossible prospect of making a new product by first making another new product lay before him. He, like every other bowmaker for centuries had studied the bows of the fantastic ancient Turks, trying to duplicate them. My grand father today has done that and made it possible for others to do the same. He converted the mystery into a modern composite weapon. He has revolutionized the industry. He took it out of the basement and put it into a factory. A visit to the Bear Archery Company is an experience in learning what can be done with dreams and ideas alone. The machines for making bows, the jigs, the processes, the ovens, the miracle that stamps out the inventive Razorhead would not have existed without this man. In lieu of a visit to Bear Archery Company, one of the best industrial films ever made is entitled RU-RAL ROUTE ONE, GRAYLING, MICHIGAN dealing with the workings of this remarkable company.

In all about 32 films have been made of his hunting trips to all parts of the world. In many of these he is joined by celebrities such as William Shatner, Cliff Robertson, Arthur Godfrey and astronauts, Deke Slayton, Joe Engle and Walt Cunningham. These films are shown on television stations far and wide. He has been written up in *Life, Time* and many, many other magazines, not to mention the Sports periodicals. He has been used in ads by Canadian Club, Lincoln Mercury, banks and never fails to be recognized when he travels. No matter how tired or late or busy, he would stop to talk to people who blurt out from crowds: "Aren't you Fred Bear?" He's been on all major television shows. The Smithsonian has a Bear Bow displayed as an a example of the most perfect form of technology and art of its time. He supplies countless orphanages and poor or troubled young people with archery sets.

During his groping years, he consulted another archery enthusi-ast, W.B. Wescott, incidentally the co-inventor of Technicolor. Mr. Wescott was so impressed by his imagination and practicality, he made my grandfather his protege of sort and when he died he left his entire collection of rare archery books and artifacts to him with the hope that one day they would be incorporated in an Archery museum. That museum has been a reality for about six years now and thousands of people go through it every year, learning about and seeing things they could never see anywhere else. A great deal of research has gone into making it a genuinely educational experience.

Well into his seventies, a recent heart attack, with the factory in good hands, the hunting days over, but duly recorded, the museum paying its own way, his interests have narrowed more on conservation and humane hunting practices. He founded the Fred Bear Sports Club, a national organization dedicated to conservation, clean hunting, dignity and honesty. He is in Washington often sitting in on legislative sessions. He cares about animals. He cares that they be hunted with knowledgeable sportsmen who respect the rules of fair chase. He realizes that human encroachment necessitates the hunt.

But above all the publicity, the recognition, the accolades, he is the best human being I have ever known. He is a legend to millions. His contributions to sportsmen and a bright shining new field of endeavor cannot be counted. His genius is two-fold, an innate understanding of engineering and a boundless love of living things. He has had many personal heartbreaks poured on him, mainly by me and I have a heartfelt desire to see this man recognized by our great university.

Sincerely,

Christopher Bear Kroll

Chris' sister, Hannah, was her grandfather's delight and he had to have her with him on the initial trip of a new snowmobile he'd bought. They set out in high spirits, with a fresh snow falling. Five minutes later they were back, Fred with a broken leg. His number thirteen boot had caught on a sapling close to the path, twisting his leg to the breaking point. This ended his love affair with the snowmobiles that were sweeping the country at this time.

During Hannah's college years in Ann Arbor, someone took a picture of her admiring a picture of French film idol, Belmondo, she had tacked up in her room. The picture ended up in PARIS MATCH and later on in the pages of LIFE MAGAZINE — indicative of her 'serious' years at the university.

By the eighties great-grandchildren had been added to the Bear Family and the following letter Fred wrote to his great-grandson and namesake, Taurin Bear McGrath, is an example of the love and attention he paid to them all –

Dear Taurin:

Having come into this world in rather small size as most us have, it seems most appropriate that you should have weapons of survival.

The enclosed hunting knife is a gift from your great-grandfather. It will be handy for freeing yourself from wet diapers and may be useful in defense from whatever wild animals you meet along life's way.

The teeth on the rear of the blade can be used to saw bars from your crib when you want to escape.

On your first birthday, I will send you a bow and some arrows along with a complete camouflage outfit.

In the meantime, eat well, grow strong and come to see us often.

Papa Bear

Taurin's sister, Anna MacKenzie McGrath, was born on her great grandfather's eighty-second birthday and Fred's pleasure on this occurrence knew no bounds. Taurin and Anna are Hannah's children and live reasonably close by.

CHAPTER 15

Fred had successfully built his company from a 1930's workshop operation at his home in Detroit into the largest archery company in the world by
1970. His philosophy was 'to build a good product and stand by it'.

His efforts materialized through his many films and countless articles down
the years, as well as his field notes, typed for his friends around the country.
These field notes eventually culminated in a book — a collection of fifteen of
his most famous hunts, published in 1976. Some of the reviews for this book,
now in its fifth printing, appear below.

SPORTS ILLUSTRATED BOOKTALK
May 1977
by Michael Marsh

"Archery enthusiasts now number about three million worldwide
and within that group the growing popularity of hunting with bow
and arrow is in large part the result of the activities of an archer
from Grayling, Mich. named Fred Bear. It was Bear who developed
the wood-and-Fiberglass-laminated bow back in the '40's, a break-
through allowing mass production of bows formerly painstakingly
constructed by hand (SI. Sept. 27, 1976).

Bear, who is in his mid-70's has written an autobiography of sorts,
Fred Bear's Field Notes, a day-to-day record recalling 15 of his more
memorable hunting trips. The book covers the years 1955 to 1967,
though Bear's career as a bow hunter has spanned half a century and
encompassed four continents. In that time, more than 125 big game
animals have fallen to his arrows. A book must be taken more or less
on its own terms and Bear makes something of a case for his chosen
life-style, which has to do with being an archer and the cat-and-
mouse style of hunting that archery imposes.

To assure clean kills, says Bear, you must of necessity be a white-
of-the-eyes hunter. Where a modern, scope-sighted rifleman is in the
chips at ranges in excess of 100 yards, a bow hunter's effective range
is often mere feet. Bow hunting, the author says, has reintroduced
the art of stalking game, which is what hunting should be all about.
By choosing to hunt with the bow and arrow, the man enters the an-

imal's world. He must match his skills more directly to the animal's instinct; the hunt becomes a more equal contest, a sort of one-on-one confrontation between man and animal.

If the game happens to be dangerous, the hunter, by choice, puts his own life in jeopardy. To Bear, this fair-chase ethic is the hunter's ultimate concession to the dignity of the animal he is trying to kill. But, he says, the kill itself is secondary. He writes, "A downed animal is most certainly the object of a hunting trip, but it becomes an anticlimax when compared to the many other pleasures of the hunt. A period of remorse is in order. Perhaps a few words asking forgiveness for having taken a life. After this, there is a self-satisfaction for having accomplished a successful stalk and a good shot."

For the archer, naturally, the odds of taking game are greatly reduced by the very nature of the primitive method of hunting and Bear has pushed the art of stalking game, especially dangerous game, to the point of brinkmanship. He has taken Alaskan brown bears and African lions at such close quarters that one wonders if he didn't smell their breaths. In 1962 on the Alaskan Peninsula, Bear shot an 810 pound Kodiak bear on an open beach at a distance of 20 feet. His subject wasn't killed on the spot, running 90 yards — fortunately, not in Bear's direction — before succumbing. Two years later, in Mozambique, Bear bagged a large bull elephant with one arrow. The number of times this particular feat has been accomplished in recent history can be counted on the fingers of one hand. The late Howard Hill did it in 1950. Bob Swinehart, a protege of Hill's accomplished it the same year Bear got his elephant. The author thinks there may have been one or two others.

Bear has been charged twice by enraged polar bears. About polar bear hunting, he observes "...man will never know whether he is the hunter or the hunted."

Throughout his journal, Bear is attentive to the many rewards hunting brings: the opportunity for solitude and self-examination and for observing wildlife in its natural habitat, the comradeship of friends, the enjoyment of campfires, sunsets and good horses. The reader is made more fully aware of the restrictive and often frustrating nature of hunting with the bow. One spends day upon day with Bear in storm bound cabins and tents, accompanies him on countless unsuccessful stalks.

Fred reviews the galleys for his new "Field Notes" book with his editor, Ferris Mack at Doubleday, 1976.

And as if the limitations of the bow were not enough. Bear assumes the additional burden of filming his hunts. Long, uneventful hours drag on in cramped camera blinds. Potentially marvelous photos are lost because the camera is not properly set up or an uncooperative cloud covers the sun, or the moment the camera whirs the alert quarry bolts to safety. Then another animal must be located, another stalk executed. The book becomes, at times, an exotic travelogue and here the author's observations are perceptive and often charming. We learn that during a successful 1966 polar bear hunt, Bear and his guide landed their plane undetected at a DEW-line outpost, to the consternation of the radar operation. "How did you get here?" asked the technicians. Bear writes, "We wondered how efficient our Distant Early Warning system is. We had flown straight in front of their screen coming in and had, for five weeks, been flying 25 miles north of their site." But the most effective passages of the book are Bear's accounts of close encounters and narrow escapes. The *Field Notes* are a welcome addition to outdoor lore."

The woodsman on 5th Avenue during the editing of his "Field Notes" book. New York, 1976.

SPORTS AFIELD
by David Harbour
BOWHUNTING CLASSIC PUBLISHED

"Fred Bear has done more than any other single hunter to prove that bow-hunting is an effective and humane method for taking any kind of game, up to and including brown bear, lions and elephants. During each of his exciting and often dangerous exploits from the frozen Arctic to the steaming jungles of Africa and South America, Fred kept careful notes. At last his 50-year journal of bowhunting history is available in a superb hard-cover book.

This first edition of *FRED BEAR'S FIELD NOTES*, Doubleday and Company, is sure to become an important hunting classic and valuable collector's item. With real authority, the 288-page book documents the evolution of America's fastest growing sport and at the same time, projects the reader from one spine-tingling encounter with wild game to another. You relive nights with Fred when lions are roaring only feet away and days when you wonder who will win when mammoth brown bears charge. You also share this sensitive sportsman's love and respect for the game he hunts, the entire outdoors and those he has hunted with. "I feel like one of God's chosen people, having had the opportunity to share, with many fine companions, these varied and lovely realms of our natural world."

THE MAHARAJAH VISITS GRAYLING

Fourteen years after the tiger hunt, the Maharajah of Bundi visited the Bears in Grayling.

They had kept in touch in the meantime, although with the restrictions and changes in government in India, Bundi had found it difficult to do much traveling.

The thought of a Maharajah as a house guest filled Henrietta with trepidation. But that all went well with what proved to be a memorable occasion, was recorded in an account of the visit she wrote some months later.

"I never quite believed His Highness would come and wondered what I would do if he brought more than one servant. We have only two guest rooms. The Maharajah has twenty...Fred's quarters at the Phoolsagar Palace consisted of two enormous rooms and two baths. His bed was more than king-size and the adjoining room was furnished as a parlor with upholstered lounges and chairs, a handsome desk and other priceless items. In the ceiling, great white fans whirred softly day and night and at the rail of the porch outside his rooms, cascades of water tumbled over a thick mat of vines — a perfect air conditioning system.

What should I feed him? I felt comfortable with lamb, but not sure of beef and had no idea of pork. Was he accustomed to dropping his clothes on the floor at night, knowing white-clad servants would be in later to pick them up for laundering...

Word came that he would be here in July. Faced with it at last and not knowing what to expect, I simply gave up and decided to treat him as any other guest in the long line of visitors we have had through the years. Fred met him at the Saginaw airport on July 7, expecting to be back around 7:00 p.m.

I planned a typical Michigan dinner for this first night. Fresh brown trout, wild mushrooms cooked in cream and sherry and blueberry pie. The table was set and ready when Fred's 'arrival toot' told me they were here. I went to the door with misgivings, but at first sight of the handsome dark man who, but for the tunic type jacket over expensive but rumpled trousers, looked almost as if he might live next door, I felt at ease. He responded to my words of welcome with a smile and kissed me on the cheek.

His Highness traveled alone, with one bag, an ample red case with

The Maharajah visits the Fred Bear Museum in 1977. Here he stands with Fred before the tiger taken near Bundi's palace in India.

Fred and Bundi discuss the new Bear compound bows.

The Kroll's entertained His Highness with a champagne reception in their home. Julia and her mother on either side.

Fred and Bundi take a turn in Fred's canoe on the AuSable River.

his initials on the side. We followed him to his room. He chose the bed next to the windows and, after checking the towels, we left him to settle in before joining us in the living room. I had hoped we could go to the dining room by 8:15, but by the time he had drunk a cup of tea and two rounds of scotch and water, it was 10:00 o'clock when we sat down to dinner.

I watched him from the corner of my eye, wondering if he would refuse this food sans curry and fiery spices, but although he ate sparingly, he seemed to enjoy everything. The Maharajah suggested that we call him Bundi. On occasion, though, we felt called upon to refer to him as Your Highness, although for the most part we used the familiar and relaxing "Bundi". An eight year old grandson visiting us one day during this time asked Bundi what his subjects called him back in India. Bundi replied, "They call me Sir." Young Heath, managing a polite, sidelong glance, responded, "Oh, I thought they would call you Master."

Among the preparations made for Bundi's visit, one of the most pleasing according to His Highness, were the red and orange Bundi flags Fred had made up in triplicate by a local 'Betsy Ross' (Ruth Cruz Feldhauser). One was displayed from the bank, one from the factory and one from our flagpole at home. He also had small flags mounted on black and gold standards for the Chamber of Commerce luncheon held in the Maharajah's honor and for our farewell dinner party at home. Bundi was extremely touched by this gesture and every morning, padding down the hall carpet in his dark-skinned bare feet and flowing blue silk robe, he stood by the window and looked out for long periods at his flag ruffling against the blue sky at the end of our dock. It occurred to me while preparing the hot milk and sugar he liked with his breakfast, that he must be lonely in this strange country where men hang up their own pajamas and busy themselves manufacturing commodities by way of earning a living. The flag must surely have reminded him of the luxurious life back home that his family has enjoyed for the past thirteen hundred years.

The days went by. Bundi spent hours with Fred at the Bear plant. A gun hunter himself, he'd been fascinated with bowhunting since Fred took a tiger in his realm by that means, the only bowhunting done at the palace in modern times. He went to the Fred Bear Museum to see the Bundi tiger, where we took many pictures. His

Highness' presence boggled the minds of visitors when they became aware that an Indian prince was in their midst.

We introduced the Maharajah to our Grayling friends at a champagne reception hosted by our daughter and husband at their home next door. He was gracious and charming and posed for innumerable pictures. His Highness drank neither too much nor too little and Grayling's first and probably last encounter with a Maharajah was an evening to remember.

Bundi and I had time for many visits and he was generous in answering my questions. I was saddened to learn that Rosie, the elephant featured in the film of Fred's tiger hunt, had gone to her reward at the age of 67! We had all come to love her for her part in the farewell ceremonies when, with her trunk, she dexterously laid a garland of golden flowers around Fred's neck and accepted his trunk-shake of thanks in return.

The Maharajah was very pleased with Fred's newly published Field Notes and took many copies with him for friends. A telephone call came from London, England, one day and another book was needed for that visit.

The time came for the friends to part. Their hunt together in India had been gone over many times. Fred took Bundi to the airport and I went into the room he had occupied during his visit. The only sign of occupancy was a streak of fine ashes down the front of an antique chest where Bundi had forgotten to remove the small incense stick wedged into the lock of the top drawer. A poignant reminder, I thought, with its tiny curl of ash still clinging to it, that someone from a distant land and culture had momentarily been in tune with his homeland in my guest room.."

We missed Bundi after he left. I'd come to understand somewhat this gentle, dusky man from a world I knew so little about. I sometimes tried to remind myself that this was a potentate straight out of fairy tales, but actually, he seemed more like an old friend."

A newspaper account of that time sheds further insight on Bundi's personality and lifestyle.

The Herald Times
Gaylord, Michigan
July 21, 1977
by Jackie Bonkowski

Grayling: His Highness, the Maharajah of Bundi, is everything an awestruck American would expect of a prince of India.

A handsome gentleman of indeterminable age, His Highness has the manners and bearing of a monarch and a nearly poetic command of the English language.

While spending a four day reunion in Grayling last week with his old friend, Fred Bear, the Maharajah took time from a busy schedule to talk to the *Herald Times.*

But what does one say to a Maharajah? Better yet, how does one address a Maharajah? His degree of perception was both unnerving and comforting as he chuckled reassuringly, "Don't be nervous. 'Your Highness' will do fine."

And His Highness did do fine as he chatted amiably about the United States and his friends here, his homeland and palace in Bundi, the changes he has observed in both countries and himself.

Bundi, the Maharajah's ancestral city, is the capitol of a 3,000 square mile territory in the Province of Rajasthan in northwest India. It has a population of 60,000; has been ruled by the Maharajah's family from the 14th century through India's independence and still houses the old palace which was built in 1323.

Home to His Highness now, however, is a new palace which he constructed in 1947 two miles from Bundi. It was at this residence, the Phoolsagar Palace, that Fred Bear spent eleven days as a guest of the Maharajah in 1963.

During these days, His Highness said, the 14-year friendship between him and Bear began. The Bengal tiger Bear felled during that stay is preserved in the Fred Bear Museum, a fact which obviously pleased His Highness.

According to the prince, the Bear Museum is "a fine monument" to the skill of his friend. A skill he recalls from first-hand experience as Bear's rifle back-up on the hunts.

"I was responsible for his safety during his stay with me," he explained, "so I stayed back with a rifle in case he missed." His High-

296

ness smiled as he added, "But he didn't need me because he never missed."

The Maharajah spoke repeatedly and warmly of his friends in America. Many, he said, he has known since World War II when he served with the famous Bengal Lancers in North Africa and Burma.

One such friend is Dr. J. Hubbard whom His Highness first met in the Pacific during the war and who later served as U.S. Education Aide in India. The prince will visit Hubbard, who is now president of the University of Southern California, before he returns to India.

Prior to that he will spend some time with his friend, Julian Levi, president of the University of Chicago.

'New York,' he explains, 'is the base of my operations while I am in the United States.' This base is also the home of his friend, William Wasserman, who lives on the former estate of Theodore Roosevelt on the Hudson River.

His Highness received the Military Cross during World War II, the honor having been bestowed by King George VI. He served thereafter as an aide to King George, a position he maintained until the coronation of Queen Elizabeth II in 1952.

The termination of his service to the English throne, the prince explained, came with India's independence from Great Britain.

A few weeks after Bundi's departure from Grayling a shocking and sad epilogue was written to the story. Word came from England that the Maharajah had suddenly died while visiting his old friend, Lord Mountbatten, at Broadlands. The letter to Fred, written on engraved blue stationery, said in part:

Dear Mr. Bear:

I expect you will have heard from Bill Wasserman of the tragic news of Bundi's death on November 24, but I wanted to write and tell you of his last moments, knowing how fond he was of you and how much he appreciated the honors with which you greeted him in Grayling...

Mountbatten had asked him to plant a tree to commemorate his visit. They returned to the house to talk when suddenly Bundi collapsed and died of a massive coronary..."

Two clippings from London papers were sent to us. One, from the *London Times*, listing his achievements, stated: ...he took part in the militia drive against the Japanese as tank commander and was sorely wounded...For his conduct he was awarded the M.C.

The other, from The Sunday Telegraphy, read: Maharajah dies at Earl's home. The Maharajah of Bundi, 57, has collapsed and died after lunching with Earl Mountbatten at his home, Broadlands House, at Ramsey in Hampshire. The Earl and the Maharajah...had been close friends for many years...

In reply to the letter from England, Fred's wife wrote:

"...my husband has asked me to acknowledge your letter of November 28th. We very much appreciate your kindness in writing of the circumstances of our friend's death...We had received the word previously at our winter home in Florida early one morning through the Wasserman's in New York...It was a great shock to us...Bundi was a charming house guest. In this country we are not used to the ways of royalty. However, he put us at ease from the start, entering gracefully into whatever we planned for him.

I hope the tree he planted for Mountbatten will wax and grow into an everlasting memorial to their friendship..."

CHAPTER 16

1976 witnessed trouble at the plant, which was struck by members of the United Auto Workers Local 1903. The union claimed that Bear's management refused to bargain, but the UAW had conducted an election among the non-union Bear workers that Bear officials maintained was improper. After a year and a half, a federal court ruled the election invalid since it was not conducted by secret ballot. Bear had continued full scale operations throughout the walkout.

Grayling is a small, close-knit community and the majority of its people worked for Bear Archery or for the companies that were established because of its presence. Often more than one generation of a family worked for the company and many employees were torn between friends and family and between the union and management. Lifelong friends and even families were separated by the strike. When the business moved to Florida several years later, many families were further separated as some went with the plant and others stayed behind.

The Bear's move to Florida was, for them, personally, both good and bad. Fred would miss his favorite sport of fly fishing in the fast, clear waters of Michigan's streams. Thirty years of friendships in the small town of Grayling were disrupted and the Bear's daughter, Julia Kroll, had to abandon her work at nearby Camp Shawono, a state facility for distressed young men she had been working with for some time. Fred was involved with this project also and gave one of the best speeches of his career at a 'graduation' day exercise at the camp.

The year before they left, just at dusk on Christmas Eve, the Bears heard music outside their home and turning on the lights, found a group of young men from the Corrections Camp standing in the freezing snow singing Christmas carols...

When Chris died, the family gave his memorial gifts to Camp Shawano for a new athletic field.

Victor Comptometer was taken over in 1977 by Kidde, Inc., a widespread conglomerate headquartered in Saddlebrook, New Jersey. Bear Archery became one of the company's most prominent subsidiaries.

That year the new owners approved a further expansion of Bear Archery as well as a move from Grayling to Florida. Fred stepped up from company president to chairman, which freed him from the daily concerns of business and

Fred Bear supported by Fred Sullivan, Chairman of Kidde, Inc., cuts the dedication ribbon for the new Bear Archery plant in Gainesville.

gave him time to do what he enjoys most — promoting the sport of archery and developing new products.

After much investigation of labor markets, local taxes and school systems in a number of areas, Gainesville, Florida was chosen. Its chamber of commerce worked hard to show Bear officials that the community was extremely interested in them, that it had an eager and hard-working labor force and that the University of Florida could provide much in the way of research and development aid for the company. A prime location along major Interstate 75, reasonable utility rates and the availability of twelve trucking lines were also advantages. The final factor was that Gainesville is oriented toward outdoor recreation and is a nice place in which to live. In addition, the city built a new access road for the plant, connecting Archer and Williston roads, naming it "Fred Bear Drive."

Gainesville is an unusually lovely big (university students) 'small' town.

Although not everyone there is a native southerner, people are hospitable and friendly. Long streets are bordered with dogwood, a breathtaking sight in spring. Azaleas bloom in nearly every yard. The crepe myrtle's pink blossoms, the lavender of wisteria and the orangey red trumpet vine brighten the landscape in every direction. Furthermore, the whole city rests under a mantle of magnificent live oaks and Spanish moss.

Gainesville's welcome to Bear Archery started off with a flourish in the form of a dinner at the Hilton with Governor Reuben Askew among the guests. Fred was asked to speak and in his usual charismatic style made friends on the spot.

There followed a well attended ground breaking ceremony and in due time a gala open house after the plant was in operation. This affair was held in May, under a red and white circus tent pitched on the green, landscaped lawns of the factory.

On this occasion Bear Archery Company was honored to have its parent company, Kidde, Inc., choose Gainesville and the date of Bear's open house for its annual stockholders' meeting. The weather was glorious and Florida smiled on the entire proceedings.

Since Bear Archery had established a partially-trained work force at the new location in cooperation with Santa Fe Community College, it was able to adjust rapidly to full production which was achieved by the beginning of 1979.

The new plant houses an environmental control system to regulate temperature and humidity, a mighty dust collection system and an electrostatic varnish device that moves drying bows through two floors on more than

301

The Bear Archery facility covers 165,000 square feet on 35 wooded acres bordering Interstate 75, in the rolling hills of northern Florida.

1,600 feet of elevated track.

One of the most interesting features of the plant is an elevated walkway overlooking the production areas where visitors are able to watch the stages in bow and arrow construction while visiting the Fred Bear Museum. Since more than ten million vehicles pass by the plant each year, visitors to the new Fred Bear Museum are numerous.

In mid-1979, Doubleday published Fred's third book, *Fred Bear's World of Archery*, a definitive overall view on the subject to which he has devoted a lifetime, this four hundred page volume covers all aspects of archery: its history and folklore, physical and mental shooting preparations and techniques, competitive shooting, the Olympics, technical aspects, industry standards, bowhunting and the preparation involved, as well as archery around the world.

At various times in the early history of the company, Bear temporarily manufactured products other than archery tackle, such as skis and television cabinets, but for many years there had been no time for this. In 1979, however, General Motors asked Bear, the archery industry's leader in fiber glass technology, for assistance in producing prototype fiber glass springs for the suspension system of motor vehicles. The springs received an acid test in the fall of 1980 when they were used on vehicles in the famous Baja Peninsula Road Race.

Although Fred spent the 1950's and 1960's globe-trotting with bow and cameras, he spent much of the 1970's perfecting the inventions he had field-tested.

His bowhunting exploits are well known among fellow outdoorsmen, but few realize the tremendous impact Bear has had on the sport of archery in general. Any composite-limbed bow made today is built on principles he discovered and on which he acted. Most modern bows owe their existence to Fred's innovative patternmaking.

Despite the fact that other manufacturers were by this time bringing out take-apart bows, Fred was still deliberating with his own process. He had started work on such a bow in 1943 and continued designing one at odd times through the years.

He used his latest take-down design on the 1964 African hunt and, although the bow was efficient, it presented some production problems as it would have been too expensive to mass-produce. When he returned to Africa the following year he used a revised model which, with further slight modifications, became the final design. In 1966 he tested it successfully against polar bear, moose and caribou and in 1967 used it on the Asiatic buffalo in Brazil. He insisted, however, on yet another three years of testing before he would announce it to the public.

It wasn't until 1970 that Fred was fully satisfied and marketed his final version. Other manufacturers had bows whose limbs separated from the handle, but each had to be put or held together with anything from an oversize pin to a series of nuts, bolts and wrenches.

Fred's new model came in three sizes and gave the archer convenience and versatility never before possible. The main feature was an ingenious steel latch by which limbs could be attached instantly to the handle, in much the same way a fine shotgun works. The limbs were made in three lengths and a wide range of draw weights. Any pair of limbs would fit any handle. The longest model for target archery was the Bear Tamerlane Take-Down, while the shorter hunting and all-purpose versions were called simply the Fred Bear Take-Down. These bows rapidly became the favorite of archers everywhere

Fred at his workbench in Grayling, designing refinements to his Take-Down bow. Various interchangeable limb designs can be seen over his shoulder.

and remained so until the advent of the new compound bow revolution. Even today they are greatly in demand, particularly by bowhunters and the older versions have become valuable collector's items. At present, Bear Archery is still producing the Fred Bear Custom Kodiak Take-Down in answer to customer demand as the top of its recurve bow line and Fred still hunts with this bow himself. He is often asked why he does not hunt with one of the newer compound bow models his company produces. His answer is always prefaced with a shy grin, "Because I can't hit anything with them." And then he goes on to explain that his unique snap-shooting style is thrown all out of whack when the compound bow hits its let-off point. Hence he stays with his take-down recurve.

Fred introduced many other innovations in his products during this time period, two of the more important being a bowsight and adjustable arrow plate built into the sight window as an integral part of bows.

The Bear plant had grown steadily in size through the previous two decades, with increased number of employees and productive capability. The number of bows produced yearly had increased from 7,500 in 1947 to 360,000 in 1976. In addition to bows, Bear turned out millions of arrows and a full line of archery accessories each year.

Early in 1980, Fred announced an event long awaited by archery buffs and collectors; the introduction of a limited edition of the Fred Bear Signature Bow. He designed this hunting bow for the archery connoisseur. It commemorates more than a half century of his leadership in the sport.

The Signature Bow is his favorite take-down recurve model. The latches by which the limbs are instantly attached or detached from the handle are of the design Fred spent so many years perfecting and have been used on his own hunting bows through the years. On the Signature Bow these steel latches are plated with 22 carat gold.

The exotic rosewood and ebony handle is trimmed with brown and white fiber glass. The limbs have clear glass backing and facing, under which the rich grain of seasoned yew wood is displayed. Fred Bear's signature appears on the handle.

Other details include a scrimshaw African-ivory Bear medallion set in the riser and a hand made Flemish splice bowstring. The bow comes in a lined and decorated walnut case.

Fred and Michigan Governor, William Milliken, during a Bear Archery Open House.

CHAPTER 17

Fred Bear's exploits in both fields of industry and bowhunting brought him many honors over the years. In 1955, the year of his first African safari, he was awarded membership in the Adventurer's Club and two years later in the New York based Explorer's Club. Both memberships were offered in recognition of his world-wide expeditions with resulting publicity in scores of publications, thus forwarding the cause of exploration and adventure. The latter endeavor also resulted in 1960 in an invitation to join the Outdoor Writer's Association of America.

In 1964, Fred was given the Compton Medal of Honor, the National Field Archery Association's highest award, for lifetime achievement in the promotion and support of archery.

The Compton Medal is not a competitive award, but one presented to a person who has made an outstanding contribution to archery. It is not given annually, but only to persons worthy of the honor. The medal bears on its face the profile of W. J. "Chief" Compton. He was the last of the "Immortal Three" of archery - Saxton Pope and Arthur Young being the other two. It was the "Chief" who interested Pope and Young in archery and taught them to shoot. Fred was the eleventh recipient of the award. The plaque is inscribed as follows:

CITATION

"Whereas Fred Bernard Bear has unselfishly given of time and money for more than three decades to the betterment of Archery, as evidenced by the following achievements and contributions -

Winner - Instinctive Division -
1939 Michigan State Field Tournament.

Winner - Numerous Art Young Awards -
National Field Archery Association.

Honorary Life Member of the Michigan Archery Association.

First Midwest Representative to N.F.A.A. in 1940.

Charter Member, Archery Manufacturers and Dealers Association.

In 1961 held five world records from the Pope & Young Club in North American big game Competition.

Fred is presented with the Compton Medal of Honor in 1964. It is one of archery's most prestigious awards. Gilbert Boening, President of the N.F.A.A. made the presentation.

Whereas Fred Bernard Bear has shown his absolute dedication to archery as evidenced by the following:

By his genuine interest starting in the early days of the National Archery Association when A. J. Michelson, John Yount and others were groping for ideas to further the cause of archery.

By his desire to make better archery equipment — using all available technology for better craftsmanship and performance – insisting upon proving equipment in the field and being satisfied with only the best.

By his promotion of archery, especially in the bowhunting field, which has been unparalleled. This has been done in a most dignified and sportsmanlike manner which is the very image of the man himself.

By his production of movies on hunting of big game, he has done much to popularize bowhunting. His television appearances have

In 1968 Fred, shown with Governor Romney in the front of the Capitol in Lansing, was given the State Governor's Award. The citation stated in part: "In recognition of Bear's invaluable aid to the state in the field of public relations...in the interpretation of its resources, culture and history...and in the exemplification of its hospitality and friendship to the people of the nation."

brought archery into thousands of homes. His promotion through the media of national magazines has brought archery to millions. This has helped to relieve us all of pressure brought about by unwarranted attacks upon the sport — mainly in the direction of bowhunting. In his quiet, gentlemanly way he has gained the confidence of magazine editors and been able to prove to them the error of their thinking and eventually turned them completely around and made them our friends.

In the final analysis the untiring efforts of Fred Bernard Bear have made archery equipment better — have made all archery equipment sell easier — Conservation Departments everywhere are more easily convinced that they should have a bowhunting program — and the sport of archery enjoys greater stature in the world.

NOW, THEREFORE — In response to the unanimous selection of the Compton Medal of Honor Committee and on behalf of the National Field Archery Association, Fred Bernard Bear is hereby granted and awarded the Compton Medal of honor in recognition

Fred Bear is inducted into the Archery Hall of Fame.

of outstanding and unselfish contributions to archery in any and all phases.

All of the nation's archers join in congratulating Fred Bear as the recipient of the greatest honor that is within the power of the National Field Archery Association in field and hunting archery. Finally, we wish for you, Fred Bear, countless blessings as you continue to pursue the sport you so dearly love."

Gilbert Boenig President, N.F.A.A.

The following year he was presented with the National Leadership Award by the National Sporting Goods Association and in 1966 he was inducted into the Industry Hall of Fame as the leader of one of their most successful and fast-growing branches.

Crawford County Avalanche
Thursday, February 3, 1966
Bear Named To Hall Of Fame

Fred Bear of the Bear Archery Company has been named to the Sporting Goods Industry Hall of Fame. This is the highest honor that can be given to a sporting goods manufacturer.

William E. Talley, Senior Vice President of Winchester Group (left) presents the 1976 Winchester Western Outdoorsman of the The Year Award to Fred Bear.

Only twenty-eight pioneers in sporting goods manufacturing have received this honor since 1956. Among them are John M. Browning of the Browning Arms Company; Ole Evinrude of the Evinrude Motor Company; Albert Spaulding of the A. G. Spaulding Company; Howard Head of the Head Ski Company; William Shakespeare, Jr. of the Shakespeare Company and Samuel J. Colt, Colts Patent Firearms.

In 1968 the State of Michigan gave Fred its Governor's Award. The presentation was made by Governor George Romney in recognition of Fred's invaluable aid to the state in the field of public relations. "For distinguished service in Michigan — in the interpretation of its resources, culture and history; in the exemplification of its hospitality and friendship; and in the promotion of its attraction and advantage to the people of the nation and the world."

Gordon Bentley, left, American Archery Council President and Fred Bear, receive a Leadership Award honoring the AAC and The Fred Bear Sports Club, 1980.

Ex-Governor John Connally of Texas and Fred Bear at an SGMA Industry breakfast at the Sheraton Center in New York, where Fred was presented with the "Extra Mile Award", 1982.

Inductees into the North Florida Sports Hall of Fame, 1981. Left to right: Fred Bear, Percy Beard, Jack Gaither, Bobby Joe Green and TB. McPherson.

In 1972, Fred was named in the first group of inductees into the new Archery Hall of Fame, joining such notables as Maurice Thompson, Dr. Saxton Pope and Arthur Young. The plaque given him on that occasion read:

"His pioneer work in the art of archery manufacturing is matched only by his world-wide contributions to the art of bowhunting."

An award that afforded Fred particular pleasure was the Winchester Western Outdoorsman of the Year for 1976. He was introduced at a special luncheon at McCormick Place in Chicago by William E. Talley, senior vice president of the Winchester Group, who presented him with a special plaque and a custom-built Winchester Super-X Model I autoloading shotgun.

In making the presentation, Mr. Talley cited Bear's 50-year crusade for good sportsmanship and a better understanding of environmental and conservation practices among millions of sportsmen around the world. This particular award is selected by a national poll of outdoor writers and professional conservationists. Previous recipients include Jack O'Connor, Congressman John Dingle, Roger Latham, Lee Wulff, the late Nash Buckingham, the late John Alden Knight, Stewart Udall, the late Robert Taylor, General James Doolittle, the late Warren Page and Ted Trueblood.

In the fall of 1979, Fred and Gordon Bentley, president of the American Archery Council, were awarded the Hunting Hall of Fame's "Leadership in Action" award in Washington D. C. This high honor was paid to the Council for its actions in promoting hunter education and the sport of hunting. The

Fred Bear Sports Club and the other archery organizations played a major role in the 1970's during a period of communications crisis for the sport of hunting in answer to numerous national network television attacks by bringing the true story of professional fisheries and wildlife management to the attention of the American public.

Additional honors and awards have continued to come Fred's way through the years. In 1981, he was guest speaker at the annual dinner meeting of the exclusive Boone & Crockett Club in New York. Following this event, held in the Hall of North American Mammals at the Museum of Natural History, he was invited into membership of that organization, composed chiefly of gun hunters, which had been established by Teddy Roosevelt back in 1887.

October of 1982 he received the "Extra Mile Award" during the Sporting Goods manufacturer's Association industry breakfast held at the Sheraton Center in New York.

Just recently Fred received two prestigious awards from Safari Club International. In January 1987, he was inducted into the Safari Club's Hunting Hall of Fame and was the first inductee into their newly-formed Bowhunting Division Hall of Fame.

Also in 1987, he was presented with a Conservation Career Achievement Award by the National Wildlife Federation and the Minnesota Conservation Federation.

Perhaps one of the finest tributes ever paid to Fred and that places him in historical perspective, occurred in 1976 when he was inducted into the Hunting Hall of Fame. He was sponsored by Congressman John Dingle of Michigan who asked Virginia Kraft, Associate Editor of SPORTS ILLUSTRATED, to present Fred on this occasion. She said, in part:

"In this age when man set out to conquer space and did, when he turned from earth's green fields to heaven's vastness for his quarry, one man, as unique an adventurer in his own right as those whose sights have been on the stars, turned back instead to a period of man's history that was perhaps his most basic. Fred bear, who learned to hunt with a gun, put it away more than 50 years ago and took up instead one of the oldest weapons known to man, the bow and arrow."

Fred Bear explaining how he cuts down his arrow rest on his favorite hunting bow to Jim Dougherty.

Fred's bow.

APPENDIX

To help round out the life of Fred Bear, we are including here some of the interesting material that surfaced during the writing of this book. A person in the public eye still has a personal life and we thought you might enjoy a few brief glimpses into Fred Bear's.

(EDITOR'S NOTE: Before he joined Arthur Godfrey for the successful hunt in Mozambique in 1964, Fred and Henrietta took a three week photographic safari through Kenya and Uganda. Her journal provides an interesting insight into the personal side of Fred's life during that time period.)

"It was 8:45 a.m. African time and God knows what time in Michigan. Numb with fatigue and loss of sleep I stood under a fern tree outside the Nairobi Airport while four or five natives carried in our luggage. A short time before, as the plane rolled to a stop on the tarmac, I looked out my window straight into the unflinching eyes of a gray baboon sitting in the grass.

We had been prepared for the changes in this part of Africa since its independence six months before we arrived. Africans would be in charge, many places, they told us, endeavoring to learn how to run their country.

We had a day of rest before continuing our schedule. Our room was cool and comfortable at the New Stanley Hotel in Nairobi and Fred was asleep in five minutes. Before I could settle down, however, our wardrobe had to be sorted leaving everything in storage here except what was needed for traveling in the Land Rover on safari. In addition, before I could go to sleep, I tried to get some drinking water brought to our room. I had read that one should not drink or even brush his teeth with the tap water in Africa.

Getting pure water took almost an hour. No one at the desk, if they answered the phone at all, could understand what I wanted. On the first trip the waiter brought a bottle of soda water. The second trip produced a bottle of gin! (It was between 10 and 11 a.m.) and on the third he brought a bottle of un-corked, warm Coca Cola.

Making myself understood at last, a carafe of fresh water came up on a tray and all that was left was to know how much to tip in African money. Fred had left a pocketful of change on the dresser and I scooped up a handful and presented it to the over-worked waiter, expecting him to take an honest fee. Instead, he took it all, looking very pleased as he departed.

The safari was to start in Uganda, an hour's flight across Lake Victoria. I hate flying over vast expanses of water and cringed at the prospect of coming down over a jungle full of boa constrictors on this late night trip. Our plane was late leaving Nairobi so when we arrived at Entebbe there was no one to meet us, although our schedule read clearly: Depart 11 p.m. from Entebbe where transportation will be furnished to Kampala.

Fred left me with the luggage while he went out to find a tiny bus about to pull away into the darkness. He talked to the driver and learned that there was no hotel in Entebbe, that no one was likely to come to our aid and that his bus was full. Fred disregarded this and motioned for help to carry our luggage. The poor driver tied pieces on fenders, over the hood and on top and we then squeezed in with already too many passengers for the long ride to Kampala where everyone goes from Entebbe.

We were extremely hungry by the time we checked in at the Grand Hotel at 2 a.m. and I inquired at the desk for some food. Impossible at this hour of the night, the clerk assured me, but on second thought, perhaps he could send up some tea and biscuits. Gratefully consuming it all we fell into bed and went immediately to sleep hoping to be rested for the start of the safari in the morning.

One night, our destination was a small inn thirty miles or so from the Queen Elizabeth National Park which was anything but a park with its hundreds of unfenced miles where Fred would photograph elephants for several days. Algot, our white hunter, seemed to be lost. We were not supposed to be out after dark, but this night a storm was brewing and night fell early. The narrow road twisted through the endless ranges of the Mountains of the Moon with thunder roaring and lightning darting like golden fangs about the peaks.

Algot looked nervous. He drove with pursed lips and had nothing to say. We had been in the Land Rover with him and his two native assistants since early morning and wondrous and beautiful as that day had been, we were bone weary and ready for bed.

We eventually got under cover, but not before the heavens opened up in a veritable Noah's Flood. We were obliged to sit in the steamy, closed up cab of the land Rover until the rain relaxed enough for the manager to send out escorts with enormous black umbrellas to rescue us.

We slept several nights at this place, The Margharita, by far the most modern inn we came across during the next weeks. Even so, in the shower the first night I saw, and knew I'd have to live with, a sizeable lizard climbing the wall beside me. Little handlike feet clinging to the tiles and bright eyes fixed on the intruder in the shower. These little creatures were so commonplace that white mosquito netting was draped from the ceiling in most places, completely encasing the bed against whatever crawled or flew in through the unscreened windows.

Another stopover was at the Paara lodge near Murchinson Falls. Our quarters here turned out to be a thatched cottage with an open air space between the walls and floor! I squirmed and protested that I could not sleep here, but there was no other place and within half an hour an earthmover couldn't have taken me out of that fairy tale room I grew to love.

We had walked from the main lodge with a warning sign confronting us to "Beware of elephants on the path," and my complaining all the way that I could never sleep here. The men paid no attention, jingling their keys as we approached two cottages, one for us and one for Algot. I followed Fred up on the little porch and from the moment the door opened my complaining ceased.

The most pleasant and attractive of clean rooms greeted us, just big enough for two beds, a chintz draped dressing table and two chairs. Each bed was enclosed in a snow white, lacy mosquito net. The nets hung from a loop at the ceiling and swept over the beds engulfing them completely. Despite elephants roaming at will along the path to the lodge and hippos grunting in the Nile below our cottage, Paara Lodge remains in my memory as a jewel in the wilds of Uganda.

The Jolly Farmer in the chilly hills of Mau Mau country in Kenya was another story. In spite of its sturdy red brick construction, it was run down and very uncomfortable. Inside was a dusty, dingy lounge with the inevitable bar and a splash of faded, torn cretonne. A gigantic fireplace furnished the only heat. The manager's wife ushered us down the hall to a room at the end, furnished with cheap unattractive pieces. The floor was bare and the windows barred (we were to find out why all too soon). The saving grace of the room was a tiny fireplace before which stood two easy chairs and a low tea table. The wife said that someone would be in soon to light the fire and that there was hot water.

We shivered through changing for dinner in the antiquated bathroom with the usual giant, brownstained tub and cracked washbowl. At the end of the dark tunnel of hall, Algot was waiting for Fred to play a game of darts before we ate. The manager behind the bar, clad in baggy pants and slouch hat before dinner, was spruced up now in stiff collar and tie. He was talking to two men, obviously travelers, telling them about life at the Jolly Farmer during the Emergency (Mau Mau uprising). Those farmers who dared stay on their farms, trying desperately not to lose two or three generations of work and fortune, he said, came to the Inn every night to sleep armed with a good gun. It was then that the windows were barred and double locks put on all doors. He continued, glancing over his shoulder as all whites do in Africa now, about the murders and betrayal of houseboys who had been with English families for years. One word from the chief of the tribe and he would slit the throats of his lifetime employer and all of his family as they slept in their beds.

What tales these walls could tell, I thought, shuddering over the terrible dinner and the very large picture of Jomo Kenyatta on the wall over our plates.

In contrast, in this land of contrasts, one of the next places was probably the most alluring of them all, food wise at least. Barry's Hotel at Thompson's Falls. We made a lunch stop here, finding a large and beautiful dining room beautifully equipped way out at the end of nowhere in Africa. There were starched white cloths on the tables, a bowl of fresh flowers on each, linen napkins and heavy silver place settings. But, the miracle of all was the sweet fresh butter, straight from the churn, passed with oven-warm bread.

The only flaw here was that being directed to the ladies' room at the end of a very long, outside porch, it was necessary to walk under some wooden rafters from which hung, swaying in the breeze, the dried skin of a three foot snake shed sometime before my arrival..."

Henrietta broke her promise only once about accepting any kind of accommodations that were off the ground. It was at Amin's Lodge at the foot of the Semliki Valley where Fred had plans to fish for the famous Nile perch found only here at the south end of Lake Albert. Semliki Lodge where one would usually stay was closed during May, the folder said and the Bears were shown to quarters in Amin's Lodge.

"No one had told me about Amin's Lodge," Fred's wife wrote in her story of the trip, "But no one needed to tell me that I wouldn't be staying there. My first glance at this place filled my veins with vinegar and I knew that catastrophe had finally caught up with me. Love and sympathy for my husband's desire to fish for these renowned perch soared out over Lake Albert and disappeared.

The accommodations consisted of a thatched building with two beds, a cupboard of dishes, a bench stacked with canned goods, a pink refrigerator and table and chairs all in one room. There was an open space of at least ten inches between the thatched roof and the tops of the walls. There were big holes in the roof as well and a communal washbasin and an outside tin toilet up on the hill. Poor Fred didn't know what to do and I wished that the earth would swallow me up for thinking I should ever have made a trip to Africa.

Algot, with venom in his heart, admitted that he knew of a hotel at Fort Portal where I could stay and wait for them. And Fred, crossing his palm with silver, persuaded him to drive me back. The thought of staying in Fort Portal alone was almost as bad as staying here, but I had to make a choice and decided to leave. I did not like myself. I was filled with remorse and shame and wondered why Fred ever married me, but I climbed into Algot's Land Rover nevertheless.

Following a two-hour ascent, back tracking up the narrow rough road of the beautiful valley, Algot's car sputtering and the engine overheating, we eventually saw the New Ruenzori Hotel standing on a hill surrounded by tea and coffee plantations. A long wooded drive led to the one story stucco building with a wide veranda running along three sides. I invited Algot to have tea with me before he started back. There were no other guests that I could see and the evil-eyed proprietor who resembled an enormous cat and his strange, blackhaired wife disappeared as soon as they assigned me my room. All night I heard eerie sounds from the jungle and sinister scrapings on the veranda outside my door. The lights went out at midnight so I lit the smoky kerosene lamp and burned it the rest of the night. I slept a couple of hours after daylight. First extinguishing the lamp that was out of oil in any case.

In spite of my fears I actually survived three nights alone at this place. I rolled up a rug against the crack under the door to keep out snakes or whatever nocturnal beasts might want to get in. But it was hard to keep back the tears of joy when Fred finally returned..."

Fred was due to leave for his hunting safari the day before his wife left for Cairo. That last afternoon, while packing to leave, her room phone rang. Two young archers from Australia, in Kenya to hunt, had read in the local paper of Fred Bear's visit to Africa and called his hotel in hopes of possibly meeting him and shaking his hand. Since Fred was gone, they enthusiastically accepted Henrietta's invitation to come up. From accounts in her journal, it would be difficult to determine who enjoyed the afternoon more; the young archers who had endless questions about life in the United States, bowhunting there and the activities of archery clubs and tournaments, or Henrietta, lonely and apprehensive about the start of her long trek alone the next day.

FAN LETTERS TO FRED BEAR

Every day's mail brings letters to Fred. Many from foreign countries, as well as from old and young alike here in America and his autograph is eagerly sought wherever he goes. "Hero worship is funny", Fred once told an interviewer. "It surprises me and I don't understand it. When a man starts to believe what his Ad Department says about him, he's had it."

It is to Fred's everlasting credit that he does not understand this sort of thing. Many men in his situation would have used it to advantage. But Fred never ceased to wonder at the many letters and items that came to his desk.

At a meeting in Milwaukee some years ago, archers lined up with copies of the Field Notes book for autographs from the author. One little girl had only a piece of paper and approached Fred timidly asking for his autograph. Fred, always anxious to put children at ease, asked what her name was in order to make the inscription more personal. The girl told him her name; he wrote it down and then, to inject a little humor into the situation he said: "Now I don't remember my name." The youngster, forgetting her shyness, said promptly, "Fred Bear."

An hour or so later she was back with a friend for another autograph. Fred heard her whispering as they approached. "You might have to tell him his name, he sometimes forgets."

There was a youngster from Pennsylvania who said: "Thank you for your time and bother of writing me a letter. I have the letter in a frame in my bedroom. You are the first great man that has ever written me a letter."

A three page letter from another boy, fourteen years old, giving every lurid detail of the movie Big Foot, warns Mr. Bear to be careful if he has any plans to ever hunt in British Colombia again!...

Another young boy wrote: "I bet you can shoot a bow and arrow better than anyone in the world. I am pretty good, but I will never be as good as you and never will be. You're tops with John Wayne."

Then, from a serious adult archer:

Dear Mr Bear:
Sitting down to write to you is like writing a letter to superman or Daniel Boone — I have trouble believing that you really exist. Although during the past several years I have come to know you through your books, magazine articles, etc. Foremost in future plans is a trip to Alaska or British Columbia. Harsh reality, however, is

complicated by an ever increasing inflation. I am concerned but not discouraged. Why? Because I HAVE BEEN THERE! Many times with you through your writings. I have shared the cold, wet, disappointing days as well as your finest hours afield. And for this I am grateful indeed. Thank you for sharing these times with me.

A lad from Philadelphia once wrote:

"Thank you for the autographed picture. My archery dealer thought you would never answer my letter and laid out $25 for my picture. I told him what he could do with his offer.

PS. Mr. Bear you got real class. Not even President Carter wrote back when I needed his letter to pass a history test with an 'A'...I was forced to settle for a lousy 'C'."

In a slightly different vein and intention, a letter from a lady in Colorado states:

"I used to live in Michigan and was wondering when I read about you in our paper, if you're alone, like I am, if you would care to write to me. I get so lonesome for that part of the country. But I don't want to make any trouble. If your wife is still living just forget about it."

"Yesterday's mail left me speechless!", said another. "The autographed picture you sent simply floored me. I still find it hard to believe. You must be some kind of man! I am nobody but you answered my letter. All of my life and I am 48, there are only three people to impress me deeply, Harry Truman, John Kennedy and Fred Bear. If Fred Bear had been on the scene in or before the '60's Custer would never have crossed the Mississippi."

A schoolboy's letter from Wisconsin said:

"I am 15 years old and in the 9th grade in high school. I live with my mom and brother and sister. My dad left us when I was 11 and we don't see him. I really love camping and hunting. Mom gave me the Adventures of Fred Bear for Xmas and I really love it. I am a scout and working on my Eagle Award and am also in archery and got two first places last summer. Your book talks about how you always thought more about the outdoors and I can't think of anything else. School is getting so hard and Mom says archery is getting ahead of my studies. How did you get through school without thinking of the outdoors? I want to get into some kind of work outdoors. Have you any advice for me?"

Fred's reply was typical of his relations with young folks and said in part:

"I want to say I sympathize with your love for archery and desire to be outdoors. However, you are in the years when you are building for your future and it is becoming more and more important to carry a degree in some field when you get out in the world trying to find a job. One can't study all the time and with diligence, your homework coming first, should take up only part of your weekends, leaving free time to be out of doors. They say that the more you have to do, the more you can do.

Have you thought of preparing yourself to work with the Fish and Game department? Or some branch of engineering that would take you outdoors? Very best wishes and keep in mind that the school years are but a short segment of your life, but they mold whatever you do with the rest of it."

One of Fred's fans appeared in person one day. He was from Iceland and spoke fairly good English. Fred asked him where he had learned to speak our language so well and his reply was:

"Some I learned in school and some I learned from reading the Archer's Bible."

In November of '83, Robert Lesher, president of the United States Chamber of Commerce in Washington, D.C. wrote:

November 21, 1983

Dear Fred:
Your impressive success with Bear Archery demonstrates that despite its problems, the American private enterprise system still provides exciting opportunities for those with creative ideas in products, research and marketing.

The story of your achievements is told in the current issue of Nation's Business, the U.S. Chamber's monthly business advocate magazine. I have enclosed a copy of this issue.

I am confident it will be a source of great interest and inspiration for our readers.

Best wishes for continued success.

Richard L. Lesher

Fan letter from Gisborne, New Zealand.

5-11-52

"Sincerest greeting and hearty salutations to you sir from "Down Under"...I can't delay any longer to report upon performance with that stupendously beautiful KODIAK bow and how tremendously grateful I am to you, Sir, for your kindness in providing me with such a remarkable specimen of craftsmanship. None can approach the KODIAK it is just perfect and does not vary at all in weather changes. By Jove! I am so deeply grateful to you."

And from a friend of more that thirty years from Fred's home town in Michigan.

Grayling, Michigan
March 82

MY FRIEND FRED

The relationship between Fred and me is probably unique. We both loved to hunt and fish. We never hunted together and never went fishing together.

He was a hunter, I was the conservation officer. Our paths crossed often during a period of many years. His office was always open to me, as was my office and Fly-Tying Shop open to him.

We had breakfast together in downtown Grayling hundreds of times and had coffee more times that I could estimate.

We spent many hours swapping stories, I am not sure they were all true, but interesting.

I have a tremendous admiration for the man and have always considered Fred to be a very, very dear friend.

Clarence Roberts

A recent letter in June 1987 from a well known wildlife artist:

Dear Fred,
Many thanks for sending me the book on your hunting experiences. It will be highly prized by me forever. As I briefly told you in Tulsa, you have always been a personal hero of mine. I was once asked who I would invite over for an evening of stories from anyone in history. I picked a rather unusual group:
    Carl Rungius the great American big game artist.
    Wilhelm Kuhnert the African wildlife artist.
    Lewis and Clark (counted as one)
    Jim Corbett legendary tiger hunter and of course Fred Bear.
    That would be an interesting evening.
                                        Best wishes, Mike Sieve

The following is a tribute from Ferris Mack the Senior Editor at Doubleday where three of Fred's books were published:

Doubleday & Company, Inc.
245 Park Ave.
New York, NY 10167

Dear Friends at Bear Archery:
In the business that I'm in, which is described as book publishing, I spend 82% of my time talking to or writing to authors and defending myself and my company. "Where are the full page ads in the Times? (I'll talk to the advertising people.) Why are there no books in Chicago? My wife's aunt can't find any. (Where did she look and when?) When does my (promotional) tour start? When can we get worth while appearances on network TV? Why don't you put out more copies of my book? (Because stores have to order it and pay for it.) Why did you contract my book if you weren't going to promote and sell it? (No response)."
Does this describe a conversation with Fred Bear? Never. Fred is an author who makes it all worthwhile. He expects publicity and promotion but not miracles. He is modest and unassuming, with

no sign of the big ego one would expect in a man of his accomplishments and fame. Fred has been a joy to deal with and a pleasure to know. He deserves the best of everything.

Sincerely, Ferris Mack

FRED'S 80TH BIRTHDAY ALBUM

What had begun in a snowstorm in Pennsylvania 80 winters before was remembered with affection and warmth by Fred's friends who had gathered secretly for the occasion. His wife, "Hank", later wrote an account of the party.

REFLECTIONS ON AN 80TH BIRTHDAY
by Henrietta Bear

Gainesville was a rainbow of flowers on March 5 when Fred Bear celebrated his 80th birthday. At no time of the year would our friends from all over the U.S. have found a more beautiful setting for a visit.

We celebrated for five days, not intentionally, but it so happened. At the end of this unheard-of pace in our quiet lives, I was completely crossed out and Fred left for the Morman Ranch near Orlando to hunt wild turkeys with his friend, George Eidsen.

The festivities started on Thursday with a party at the factory, all 350 employees participating. The cafeteria was decorated with signs, pictures of F.B.B., streamers and flowers on the tables. An enormous birthday cake, enough to share with everyone and more, took up most of the coffee table. It was frosted in white with a complete Michigan hunting scene laid out in green, blue and brown icing. Tiny fir trees, farms and boundary line fences, miniature deer and shining rivers – all in stunning relief. It was a crime to cut into it.

Flashbulbs flared as different departments posed for pictures with 'Mr. Bear'. One got the feeling that whoever was in charge of the time clock today set it back since there was time for everyone to enjoy every phase of this lovely party before the bell rang. This particular celebration ended when a young girl appeared carrying eighty gasfilled balloons tethered with multicolored ribbons, to lead the assemblage in singing Happy Birthday!

The main event took place the following evening. A dinner for more than a hundred people at the Hilton, across the lake from our home. This gala was kept a complete surprise from Fred. When we left the house at 7 p.m. he did not know where we were going except that "they were celebrating his

Fred is shown with two hunting companions – (left) Les Line, Editor of Audubon magazine and FBSC Member #360 and Jerry Anderson of Anderson's Archery in Grand Ledge, Michigan.

Astronaut Joe Engle displays his gift to Fred, a collage of mementos from his Space Shuttle Columbia flight in 1982.

birthday." Upon arrival, the wide doors of one of the banquet rooms were thrown open to a dazzling scene of bright lights and smiling faces.

There was no denying Fred's surprise. He saw dear friends and hunting companions, some of whom he had not seen for many years. They came from north, south, east and west and the pleasure on his unbelieving face was nice to see.

The dining room appeared to be an enormous bouquet of flowers. Armfuls of daisies, tulips, forsythia, etc., on every table, crowned with placards commemorating a favorite hunting ground of past years Little Delta, Mozambique, Phoolsagar, Arctic Circle, Grousehaven, etc., designated seating arrangements.

First of the after dinner speakers to be introduced by Dick Lattimer, head of Advertising at Bear Archery and Master of Ceremonies, was Merrill "Pete" Petosky, Director, Natural Resources Unit, U.S.D.A., Washington, D.C. Pete had his roots in Michigan and was part of our early days there. I hardly heard his speech for thinking of the time, long ago, when he and Fred were hunting rabbits with our ten year old grandson. Chris, walking fast to keep up, got his foot tangled in a vine and was thrown violently to the ground. His further misfortune was to fall on a sharp stick that lodged solidly in the roof of his mouth. Pete, taking charge of this bloody, frightening event, told us later how Chris, tears running down his cheeks, looked squarely into his eyes as he painfully removed the shaft and rushed him to the hospital...One remembers old friends for many things.

Astronaut Joe Engle, commander of the space shuttle, Columbia, when it was hurled into space for the second time, was applauded and cheered before he spoke a word. His reminiscing of hunting trips with Fred and the fact that he was a charter member of the Fred Bear Sports Club, made his talk extremely entertaining.

Colonel Engle then presented Fred with a collage of mementos that had accompanied him and Dick Truly on their extraordinary journey aboard the "Columbia". Joe also brought along a second collage, gift of astronaut "Deke" Slayton who had flown the first International Apollo Soyuz Spacecraft (U.S. - U.S.S.R.) on that historic joint mission.

In his remarks, Engle said: "There's a large percentage of the guys in the Astronaut Office that flat idolize Fred Bear. We idolize Fred because he represents just about everything that can be represented as a hunter, as a conservationist, an outdoorsman, but mostly, as a human being."

In making the presentation to Fred, Joe said, "You represent everything

Frank Scott, Curator of the Fred Bear Museum and Bear Archery's longest term employee, gives the gathering some highlights of Fred's career. Scotty went to work for Fred in 1940 at the age of 17.

Mr. and Mrs. Glen Lau of Glen Lau Film Productions enjoy visiting with Mrs. Bear during the festivities.

A humorous anecdote recalled by one of the speakers tickles Fred's funny-bone.

Fred reminiscing with Charles Haller and Ray 'Hap' Fling, Bear Archery's National Sales Director. Gawayne Kinsey, advertising artist, is in the background.

Dr. Rex Hancock and son, Brian, present Fred with a waterfowl print, in honor of his generous contributions toward saving the Cache River Basin in Arkansas.

there is American and Dick Truly and I want you to have this Flag and our Patch that flew on the Second Shuttle Mission...the First Reusable Flight of a Spacecraft."

Many, letters and cards came in to honor the occasion and Dick Lattimer read one to the guests. It was from Skylab Commander, Astronaut Jerry Carr:

> Dear Fred,
>
> Late in life on the occasion of one's birthday when one is suddenly confronted with the years he has spent on this planet Earth, it's natural to want to assess results. The trouble is, there are still a few "arrows in the air," and the One who will determine the score is in no hurry to tally up.
>
> I daresay that your life has consisted of a lot more bullseyes and nines than misses. You have been an enthusiastic sportsman and businessman, a patriotic American and a good friend to many. To those of us who managed to ride an "arrow" into orbit and to those who aspire to do so, you have been a spirited supporter. Your phi-

losophy has influenced our sons and helped make up for the times when we couldn't be with them to enjoy the outdoors.

So, let me take this opportunity to sincerely wish you a most HAPPY BIRTHDAY!

Sincerely,
Gerald P Carr, PE.
NASA Astronaut (Retired)

Clare Conley, Editor of *Outdoor Life* magazine, brought a handsome, framed sketch of Fred, the original of a full-page likeness that illustrated Conley's profile, commemorating Fred's 80th birthday, in the magazine.

Dr. Rex Hancock, president of the Citizens Committee to Save the Cache River in Arkansas, not only added spice to the evening, but brought along his winsome twelve year old son who carries the title of Champion Duck Caller of the World in his age group. (A substantial purse for the Cache River cause was presented by the guests in honor of Fred's birthday.) Rex displayed a birthday gift, a beautiful numbered print entitled, 'Cache River Memory' by Lee LeBlanc with an engraved brass plate on the frame:

'One of man's greatest obligations is to serve God as a wise steward of earth's resources. Fred Bear has fulfilled this obligation. Rewards from his actions as a sportsman and conservationist will long be reaped by his fellow sportsmen, generations yet unborn and wildlife.'

Among the guests were Les Line, editor of AUDUBON magazine and John Mitchell, author of the best seller, "Bitter Harvest".

Finally it was Fred's turn to speak:

"I'm overwhelmed", he said, "this place is full of celebrities and I mean they're great people...Actually, I don't deserve this. All my life I have been having fun...all my life I have done jobs that I liked to do, the only times that I worked on any kind of a job that I didn't like was when I was hungry. I'm honored that all you people showed up to celebrate my 80th birthday. And really I feel like a kid who is given candy for being naughty — that's the way I feel about it..."

The party broke up late and we drove home in a downpour of Florida rain.

The next day, Saturday, we held open house for those who could stay over. Midway on this happy day with people coming and going, visiting and eating in all corners of the house, I met eye-to-eye in a hallway with our two and a half year old great grandson, Taurin Bear McGrath. From all reports he had sampled every variety of food on the trays and was in remarkably good humor. Upon seeing me he elevated his tiny shoulders and with a deep breath and happy smile said as he exhaled, "FUN!"

Kidde not only sent Harvey Ekenstierna and his wife from that company, but a photographer as well, who was commissioned to take pictures throughout the occasion. The complete photographic record was put in an album and presented to Fred as a treasured birthday gift.

Members of the Bear Archery staff who worked so hard to make this affair outstanding, compiled a book containing tributes and letters that came in from friends unable to attend, as well as some who did. Quotes from these letters plus some birthday cards, are part of the record:

From Fred Sullivan, chairman and president of Kidde, Inc.:

"...Your place in American folklore and sport and industry are secure. Also, you are a towering human being that I am proud to be associated with and call my friend."

Robert Marston, president of the University of Florida here in Gainesville, said in a greeting from his family:

"...legendary figures are measured by many yardsticks...How did they change the course of history in their chosen field? What was the import of their writings? Those who have known you longer than the Marstons have passed judgment already on your contributions in changing forever the concept of bowmanship and its relation to good sportsmanship..."

Congratulations were received from the President and Mrs. Reagan.

From our thirty-year span of friendship, our family physician in Michigan, Dr. Elmo Henig, wrote:

"Grayling has never been the same since you left! The coffee shop lacks the tall tales of its senior sportsman. The swans have left the river at Fred Bear Drive and the trout population has increased two-fold since your departure. I have a feeling that you have a great chance of becoming a centenarian now that you are no longer fracturing legs on snowmobiles or hunting ferocious wild animals with your bow and arrow."

From Robert Tapley, one time manager of Bear Archery:

"Fred Bear, the Man...Hunter, Grandfather, Inventor, Friend, Entrepreneur, Conservationist, Archer, Writer and Moviemaker.

Percentage of Nominal Human Allowances (NHA)

Bravado	.*	Originality	.700
Common Sense	.500	Perseverance	950
Humor	1300	Vision	650
Malice	.*	Stamina	350

*"Contains less than 2% of the NHA of this trait."

An old friend, Dr. Paul E. Klopsteg, one time Director of Technological Research at Northwestern University, wrote:

"We met first when the National American Archery Tournament (its 50th) was held in Chicago...about the time you were getting into the archery business in the thirties...Possibly, just possibly, you and I may see our hundredth birthdays...To have known you through the years...has given me much satisfaction."

One of the employees who worked for Fred in Michigan said on her birthday card:

"Five times I came back and worked for you (Time out for five babies). It was a great honor when my husband became supervisor and we got to attend the special Christmas time dinners at the hotel. We loved all the adventures you wrote about and had them printed for the employees. You have been a true friend and set an example of love, forgiveness and generosity"

Close-up of the collage presented to Fred by Joe Engle. It comtains the flag that flew on the Columbia flight in November of 1981.

"It's been a long time", wrote Astronaut Walt Cunningham, "since you gave Joe Engle and me lessons (in archery) and made us char- ter members of the Fred Bear Sports Club. I will never forget the time on Florida's St. Vincent Island when you, as a seventy-year-old, broke trail for this forty-year-old novice hunter."

Billy Ellis, bank president, poet and official of the Mississippi Bowhunters Association, dedicated a whole page to Fred's birthday in that organization's newsletter. There was a picture of Fred in hunting shirt and hat and Billy wrote in part:

"Happy Birthday Fred Bear. We don't know how old you are and it really doesn't matter. To us you'll always be as young and change-less as a craggy mountain peak. Your glacier blue eyes have seen the aspens turn gold a goodly number of seasons. You have introduced several generations to the greatest sport on earth. You have done more than any other man to promote bowhunting and we love you for it. An Arabic saying pretty well sums up your life: 'When you see an older man, amiable, mild, content and good-humored, be sure that in his youth he has been just that, generous and forebearing. He does not lament the past, nor dread the future, he is like the evening of a fine day.'"

Karl Palmatier, Director of national archery tournaments for years on end said:

"Your continuous research produced archery products of superior quality. Your business acumen warranted the respect and goodwill of archery manufacturers. Your interest in hunting and conservation gained respect from layman and governmental departments alike..."

Elisha Gray, past president of Whirlpool Corporation and longtime hunt-ing friend remembered a time they sat on top of a mountain together:

"...I recall as if it were yesterday, the time you and I struggled to the very top of a mountain while sheep hunting and sat down to catch our breaths. I asked you if you thought a couple of guys our age should be doing such things and your reply was classic. Holding out your hand you pointed to a tiny blood vessel and said something like this, 'You see that little capillary, Bud, well it hasn't had blood in it for a long time and this exercise has put it back in condition...'"

One of the last letters to come in told about a meeting of some Alaskan bowhunters. They had planned their get together for Saturday night, March 6, but when they heard that Bear was to celebrate his 80th birthday on Fri-day, March 5, they changed the date and celebrated with him over the miles. Ninety signatures were on the birthday greeting they sent.

Dennis Arrowsmith presents Fred with a fancy hatband fashioned from exotic game bird feathers.

A visit with two of his long-time Bear employees, Dennis and Donna Patton.

Two old friends, Bill Boyer, owner of Grousehaven and Fred Bear.

Scores of old friends were on hand. Here, Fred is greeted by Bill Earl, Sharon Sheridan and Dennis Arrowsmith.

Clare Conley, Editor of Outdoor Life magazine, presents an artist's portrait of Fred to Mrs. Bear.

Dick Lattimer, Bear's 'in-house' Advertising Director for many years, served as Master of Ceremonies for the 80th Birthday Party.

Fred's secretary, Shirley Bonamie, led the Bears into the surprise party awaiting them.

Fred greets well-known author, John Mitchell, retired General Motors Vice President, Bill Boyer and Keith Salmon of Rose City, Michigan.

Fred congratulates newlyweds Dick and Carol Mauch. With them are Keith Salmon (left) and Bob Munger (right).

Merrill 'Pete' Petoskey, Director of the Natural Resources unit of the U.S.D.A. in Washington, D.C., had some comments concerning Fred's life-long efforts in conservation.

MILESTONES IN THE LIFE OF FRED BEAR
AND BEAR ARCHERY

1983 marked the 50th Anniversary of the official founding of Bear Archery and to mark the occasion the following list of milestones was published in the Bear Archery catalog for that year:

1902   Fred Bear born March 5 in a farmhouse near Waynesboro, Pennsylvania during the worst blizzard of the winter.

1915   Fred's father, Harry Bear, took his 13 year old son on his first deer hunt.

1916   Fred Bear shot his first deer with a firearm.

1918   The Bears moved to Carlisle. Here he watched the famous Olympic athlete, Jim Thorpe, play football at the Carlisle Indian School.

1919   Fred Bear served on active duty with the Carlisle National Guard Cavalry in the Cherry Valley coal field.

1920   Fred Bear's wages were 17 1/2 cents per hour as a patternmaker at the Carlisle Frog & Switch Company.

1923   A few days after his 21st birthday, Fred Bear left home on the train for Detroit where he began work as a patternmaker for Packard Motor Car Company. He attended night school at the Detroit Institute of Technology.

1926   Fred Bear became Plant Manager of Jansen Manufacturing Company, making spare tire covers for the auto industry.

1927   Fred Bear saw Art Young's film, "Alaskan Adventures" at the Adams Theatre in Detroit. He later met bowhunter Art Young at a Rotary luncheon and the two became friends. They built archery equipment in Fred's basement and began shooting together.

1929   Fred Bear went bowhunting for the first time in a cedar swamp near St. Helen's, Michigan.

1930   Revival of target archery competition in U.S. Indoor archery lane shooting began.

1931   F.I.T.A. (International Archery Association) organized.

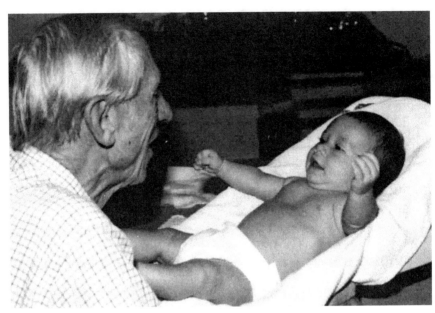

Fred Bear with his great-grandson and namesake, Taurin Bear McGrath.

For smome reason, Fred's childhood had not included Hans Christian Anderson, but the grandchildren he acquired through his second marriage saw to it that he learned the subject well.

1933   Fred Bear and Charles Piper founded Bear Products Company. Their
        primary products were silkscreened advertising materials. Off in a corner
        of the small building Fred made archery equipment, it soon became a
        fulltime business.

1934   Fred Bear won Michigan State Target Championship.

1935   Fred Bear shot his first deer with bow and arrow.

1937   First bow and arrow deer season in Michigan. (2 Counties)

1937   Fred Bear patents were granted for the modem shooting glove.

1937   Fred Bear won Michigan Field Archery Championship.

1939   Fred Bear won Michigan Field Archery Championship, again.

1939   National Field Archery Association established.

1942   First Fred Bear bowhunting film produced with Jack Van Coevering
        (Sports Editor of the *Detroit Free Press*).

1943   Fred Bear began work on his first take-down bow.

1945   Fred Bear's first bow and arrow big game taken other than deer
        (Canadian Moose).

1946   Fred Bear's first black bear.

1946   Fred Bear patents use of fiberglass as bow backing.

1946   Fred Bear secures first bow quiver patents.

1946   Fred Bear's father, Harry Bear, won N.A.A. Mail Matches at age 68.

1946   "Moose Diary" Fred Bear's second bowhunting film produced.

1946   First National Field Tournament held in Allegan, Michigan.

1947   Bear Archery plant opened in Grayling, Michigan.

1948   Bear Archery produced TV and record cabinets for Admiral Corp.

1949   Fred Bear developed new bow bonding process.

1949   The first year that Bear bows carried a written registration and warranty.

1949   Bear Grizzly bow introduced.

Taurin Bear McGrath and his great-grandfather's giant Kodiak bear. Taurin's mother is Hannah, Fred's Grand-daughter.

1951	Fred Bear developed special presses for bow bonding.
1951	Unidirectional glass developed and patented; for use as bow backing and facing.
1951	Fred Bear's first western bowhunt.
1952	Fred Bear's first elk and first antelope taken in Wyoming.
1952	Fire nearly destroys Bear Archery.
1953	Plant repaired and first addition completed.
1954	Bear produced first working recurve bows (Kodiak II) .
1954	Fred Bear's first successful western mule deer hunt.
1955	Fred Bear became a member of Adventurer's Club.
1955	Bear plant is up to 100 employees.
1955	Fred Bear's first overseas hunt in French Equatorial Africa.
1955	Fred Bear's first western Canada hunt (moose and caribou).
1956	Second addition to Bear plant - 200 employees.
1956	Bear Archery markets new Bear Razorhead hunting points.
1957	Fred Bear took world record Stone sheep in British Columbia.
1957	Fred Bear made member of Explorer's Club in New York.
1958	Bear hosted N.F.A.A.'s 13th National Championships.
1958	Bear hosted first large Money Shoot, following Nationals.
1958	Pope and Young's first Awards Program held in Grayling.
1958	Little Delta hunt (Alaska).
1959	Little Delta hunt (Alaska).
1959	Bear film library expanded to 13 subjects.
1960	Bear hosted N.F.A.A. Nationals with 26 field ranges.
1960	Fred Bear took world record Kodiak bear in Alaska.

Barbara and Michael Steger on a visit to Grayling in the 1950's.

Fred's foster son, Mike Steger and a fine mule deer taken with his bow near Vandenberg Air Force Base, where he was stationed in 1967. Mike was comptroller of the Los Angeles Air Force Base in the 1960's and served as SAMSO Chief of Staff at Vandenberg.

1960	Bear developed clear "Crystalight" Bearglas.
1961	Bear introduced "Fox" line of solid fiberglass bows.
1961	Professional Archers Association established.
1962	Fred Bear appeared on "To Tell the Truth" national TV show.
1963	Bear introduced snapon bowquivers.
1963	Fred Bear Grizzly Hunt in British Columbia featured in *LIFE* magazine.
1963	Fred Bear hunted Bengal Tiger in India.
1964	Bear's Two Season Hunter advertising theme began.
1964	Bear Archery introduced the premier Sight as an integral part of a bow.
1964	Fred Bear awarded Compton Medal of Honor.
1964	Fred Bear African safari with Arthur Godfrey (elephant).
1965	Fred Bear received National Leadership Award from National Sporting Goods Association.
1965	Fred Bear's third African safari - Lion and Cape buffalo.
1965	Bear Archery introduced high compression handle material.
1965	Fred Bear Featured on ABC/TV's "American Sportsman."
1966	Fred Bear inducted into Sporting Goods Hall of Fame.
1966	Fred Bear took Polar Bear on third try.
1966	Fred Bear appeared on the "Tonight Show."
1967	Fred Bear Museum opens in Grayling, Michigan.
1967	Bear perfects take-down bow design.
1967	Archery Lane Operator's Association established.
1967	First U.S. Intercollegiate Championships (Tempe, Arizona).
1967	Bear introduces their Inertial Stabilizers.
1967	Bear produced a 48" Super Magnum hunting bow.

Fred and grandson, Taurin, in the Bear home in Gainesville.

Fred and Henrietta canoeing on the AuSable River in front of their home in Grayling.

1967	Fred Bear hunted Asian buffalo on Marajo Island, Brazil.
1968	Bear introduced Converta Point arrows.
1968	Fred Bear's "Secrets of Hunting" record with Curt Gowdy.
1968	Fred Bear received Michigan Governor's Award.
1968	Bear Archery sold to Victor Comptometer Corp. Fred Bear remains President.
1968	"The Archer's Bible," first of Fred Bear books published.
1969	Fred Bear appeared on Mike Douglas TV show with "Gentle Ben."
1969	First U.S. World Championship target tournament (Valley Forge, Pennsylvania).
1970	Bear's take-down bow marketed after extensive field tests.
1970	Beginning of Fred Bear Sports Club.
1970	Bear Archery film library has 20 film subjects.
1971	Introduction of magnesium alloy handles for take-down bows.
1972	Archery made Gold Medal Sport for Olympic Games.
1972	Astronauts Charles Duke, Jr., John Young and Thomas Mattingly take one of Bear's Razorheads on Apollo 16's fifth moon landing.
1972	Fred Bear inducted into the Archery Hall of Fame.
1972	National 4H Club archery program begun.
1972	Fred Bear Sports Club opened to the public.
1973	Fred Bear inducted into Hunting Hall of Fame.
1976	Fred Bear's second book, "Fred Bear Field Notes" published.
1976	Bear plant produced a record 360,000 bows in one year.
1976	Fred Bear received NSGA's "Lifetime Career Award."
1976	Fred Bear received Winchester/Western's "Outdoorsman of Year" Award.
1976	Fred Bear receives "Regent's Citation of Honor" from University of Michigan.

Fred with great grand-daughter Anna MacKenzie McGrath, in Fred's Gainesville office, 1983.

Papa Bear instructing Christopher Heath in archery. July, 1972.

1977	"The Good Earth" filmed with astronaut Jim Lovell and Fred Bear.
1977	Fred Bear Sports Club helps launch "The American Outdoors" TV project.
1977	Fred Bear receives NAA's "Maurice Thompson Medal of Honor."
1977	Walter Kidde & Co. takes over Victor Comptometer Corp and Bear Archery.
1978	Bear Archery introduces Super Razorhead.
1978	Bear Archery plant moved to Gainesville, Florida.
1978	Fred Bear Sports Club and American Archery Council aid in distribution of 26 "American Outdoors" segments on nationwide TV.
1979	Fred Bear's third book published, "Fred Bear's World of Archery."
1979	Bear began design and construction of prototype fiberglass automotive springs.
1980	Fred Bear appears on Glen Lau's Sports Afield television series.
1980	Fred Bear Signature Bow announced.
1981	Subsidiary plant opened in Williston, Florida for producing glass springs for automotive and other nonarchery applications.
1981	Fred Bear Sports Club membership reached 30,000 (in USA and 44 other countries).
1981	Bear introduces stainless steel Razorheads.
1981	Bear introduced the Delta V – the World's Fastest Bow.
1982	Fred Bear's 80th birthday celebrated.
1983	Bear Archery celebrates its 50th Anniversary.
1987	Fred Bear inducted into Safari Club International Hunting Hall of Fame and Bowhunting Division Hall of Fame.
1987	Fred Bear receives Conservation Career Achievement Award from National Wildlife Federation and Minnesota Conservation Federation.

EPILOGUE

Over the past 50 years literally hundreds of articles have been written about Fred. They have appeared in small local newspapers with circulation in the hundreds and in major national magazines reaching millions. Each time such an article has appeared, from the very early 1930's up until the present, the result has been promotional exposure for archery and bowhunting. We began this book with an excellent story by John Mitchell entitled, "PAPA BEAR". We would like to end it with excerpts from one of the finest articles ever written about Fred. The author was Dr. Rob Wegner and it appeared in the October 1982 issue of Deer and Deer Hunting Magazine. It is reprinted here with the permission of the author and the publication.

THE MAN WITH THE BORSALINO HAT
Excerpts from an article by Dr. Rob Wegner

Robin Hood wore a felt hat in the Sherwood Forest in the 12th century. William Tull wore one in the Swiss forests of the 14th century. Saxton Pope and Art Young wore felt hats on their adventurous bow hunts in Tanganyika during the first decade of this century. Though the style and color may have changed, it seems appropriate that Fred Bear should wear one in the deer forests of the 20th century, more specifically a Borsalino felt hat, made in Italy.

The man whom we inevitably associate with the felt hat trademark is now 80 years old. While some 80-year-olds might have difficulty seeing deer, let alone shooting them with a bow, Fred Bear, as the Kansas City Star outdoor editor recently remarked, "keeps things in perfect focus when it comes to deer hunting." Just mention the very words "deer and deer hunting," and he is a youngster at heart again.

"I still get the same thrill out of deer hunting that I did when I started at the age of 10." He says, "I think the reason I have always loved the sport of deer hunting so much lies in its inherent challenge, for the whitetail is the smartest creature to walk this earth. It has eyes for anything that makes the slightest movement, it has a nose that can pick up just about any scent and it has ears that act like radar, warning it of any sound that is out of place. To outwit a creature as well-tuned to its environment as the whitetail takes some doing. They know where every tree, stump and twig is. We're definitely the ones at a disadvantage."

Despite the disadvantage, Fred Bear continues to hunt whitetails with all the vigor and enthusiasm of a 10-year-old boy. Indeed, he still finds time to leave Gainesville, Florida, the new home of Bear Archery, to head north to Michigan where he enjoys bow hunting deer along the banks of his beloved AuSable River. This fall we will surely encounter this long, lanky individual tramping the jack pine plain of northern Michigan as he pursues whitetailed deer with his bow and arrow in hand, a passion that Bear, still looking lean as a strip of venison jerky, has indulged in for the past 50 years.

While Fred Bear enjoys the camaraderie of bow hunting camps and actively participates in deer drives, he prefers to solo hunt. Like T.S. Van Dyke, Francis Sell and George Mattis, Bear finds still hunting and stalking to be most gratifying methods of bow hunting. These methods of hunting allow him to pit all of his skill against the instinct of the deer he seeks. In Fred Bear's World of Archery (1979), he clearly distinguishes between these two methods of hunting: "Still hunting is the process of walking quietly and slowly through game habitat, trying to see an animal before it sees you. Stalking is the culmination of the still hunt, wherein the hunter, having located an animal, attempts to close to within bow range. This is the real essence of hunting and requires more skill than driving or blind hunting. It is by far the most difficult and the most satisfying way to hunt, for it places the bowhunter on more even terms with his quarry."

The essence of Fred Bear's character emerges most sharply in his weather-worn, battered notebooks that he tirelessly updates in the tradition of the classic outdoor writer. From the "dogeared, rain-soaked pages" of his journals, we find a warm, humorous and compassionate man who at the end of the trail greatly enjoys eating fried venison tenderloins smothered in onions, beans, hot biscuits and jam; always finishing the meal with tea.

After eating such a delightful deer camp meal and with a tarp stretched above him and a lantern swinging overhead, he reflects and writes about his adventures in his notebooks. At times, snow blurs the ink on his notebook; ink freezes in his pen. As he thaws his pen out and stokes up the fire, he thinks to himself, "It's my wife's birthday and as always I am hundreds of miles away..."

The very remoteness of the wilderness in which he finds himself kindles the imagination of this adventurous bow hunter who "likes to think that he is perhaps the first white man to have climbed a certain ridge or looked down into a deep, glacier-carved canyon." As a confirmed climber, he always anticipates the view from the next ridge. As he writes in his notebook, "from the top of any mountain the challenge extends, far and wide, until the mountains meet the sky." As soon as he plans a deer hunt, anticipation gets the best of him: "My legs are suddenly too long for my desk and I usually find myself on my way several days ahead of schedule."

At the end of a successful deer hunt, it's not uncommon for a great celebration to take place outside the Bear's den. Even in a midnight rainstorm, Bear will participate in a shooting match by gas lantern, with the winner being the first to extinguish the flame of a candle, a candle protected with a tarp overhead. When he arises the next morning to fix his favorite blueberry pancakes, the bushes around his camp bloom with arrows.

Regardless of the name brand of the bow hunting equipment you use, it is more than likely based on principles which Bear discovered and implemented many years ago.

When asked some time ago how he would like to be remembered, he retorted, "that I was honest with myself and with others. And that I did my best at what I thought was important in my life. I am happy that I was able to grow up and live as a free man and to have the opportunity to work at what I enjoyed doing the most...hunting and fishing. It has always given me a great deal of pleasure to introduce new people to the outdoors and I am happy to have been able to do so over the years, as well as having been able to simply expose so very many people to the outdoor life through our films and books and travels. Anything else that I am remembered for will have to be decided by others."

Others, like Dick Lattimer, a long-standing personal friend of Bear's, have decided that "Fred Bear's world is one of wood smoke, pawed acorns, the sweet smell of decaying leaves, the twitch of a deer's tail and ragged birch bark blowing in the wind. He is a man of the forests and mountains; a man who is equally at home with a prince of India or a nervous new bow hunter on opening day. It is said about some men that they do not walk where the path leads. Rather they go where there is no path and leave a trail. Fred Bear is such a man."

When the Hunter's Moon rises above the deer shack this October like a huge, orange ball of fire, many of America's 2 million bow hunters will be in the deer forest with Bear equipment in hand and with romantic images of the old master in the back of their mind. Actually, Bear bows and razorheads are as common in the deer forests as Fisher Bodies are on the American freeways that lead to them.

As long as the Hunter's Moon returns in the October sky, our thoughts will turn to Fred Bear, the man whom *LIFE* magazine once referred to as a cross between Natty Bumppo and Robin Hood.

Even though he has shot a four ton bull elephant with a single arrow as well as polar bears in the Arctic and Bengal tigers in India, he still believes that "the wariest, craftiest and the hardest game of all to hunt is the whitetailed deer of North America." I agree. Why does the man with the Borsalino hat hunt whitetails? He answers this question for us in a classic essay entitled Thoughts on Hunting:

"I hunt deer because I love the entire process; the preparations, the excitement and sustained suspense of trying to match my woodslore against the finely-honed instincts of these creatures. On most days spent in the woods, I come home with an honestly earned feeling that something good has taken place. It makes no difference whether I got anything; it has to do with how the day was spent.

"Life in the open is one of the finest rewards. I enjoy and become completely immersed in the high challenge and increased opportunity to become for a time a part of nature. Deer hunting is a classical exercise in freedom. It is a return to fundamentals that I instinctively feel are basic and right.

"I have always tempered my killing with respect for the game pursued. I see the animal not only as a target, but as a living creature with more freedom than I will ever have. I take that life if I can, with regret as well as joy and with the sure knowledge that nature's ways of fang and claw or exposure and starvation are a far crueler fate than I bestow."

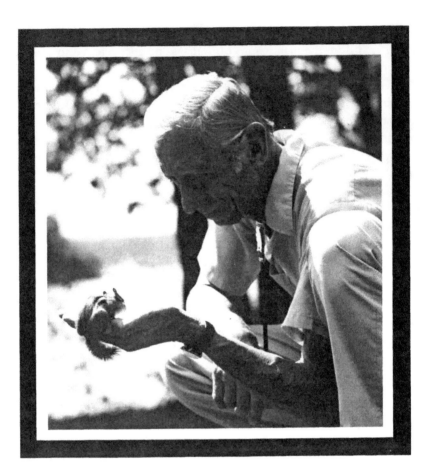

Fred Bear
1902-1988

Fred Bear passed away just as this book went to press. Matter of fact, just two days before he died he helped clear-up some photo identifications. Fred was looking forward to seeing the book in print, yet true to form, he was humbled and more than a bit embarrassed by all of the attention he knew its publication would bring him. Fred Bear was always the same genuine person, whether you were alone with him in a tarpaper hunting shack on the Alaskan peninsula or in a crowd of two-thousand bowhunters. We shall all miss him terribly.

(Dick Lattimer spoke at Fred Bear's Memorial Service of the way it might have been in the northern woods near Grayling on that Wednesday afternoon when Fred passed away.)

It was quiet in the forest.

The final snow of winter had just melted. The arbutus and wild violets were beginning to put on their annual show and the popples had just begun to burst. Both the birch trees and the maples were starting their rebirth for the year and the red oaks were finally giving up on winter and deciding to drop their rich brown leaves. Suddenly the quiet was torn by the plaintive caw of a solitary black crow as it skimmed over the tree tops toward the cedar and tamarack swamp. Deep within its soft island mounds the deer looked up from their daytime beds and wondered at the call. For the crow did not usually come to alert them while the sun was yet high. Along the crystal clear river the otter and the mink also looked up, wondering what had changed. The Rose-Breasted Grosbeaks, the Chickadees and the Nuthatches all heard the cry.

Finally, all of the creatures of the forest understood. For they knew that the crow had come to tell them of the death of the gentle bear. No longer would his huge soft feet walk down their worn trails. Nor would he pause to look under the low-hanging branches at what might lie ahead. And no longer would he move quietly through the forest with such great dignity.

But all of the creatures of the forest soon remembered that it was a time of renewal on the earth. Soon the persistent young Bracken Fern would work its way up thru the forest floor, the Indian Paint-brush and the Lady Slippers would mingle with the Wintergreen and the last few patches of snow would disappear deep within the Swamp, leaving behind an occasional tuft of deer hair from their winter beds. Soon the does would drop their fawns on the fragrant new grasses along the stream's edge and the eagle young would work their way through their protective shells.

Overhead the moon and stars would continue their pirouette around the Universe and star dust would continue each day to fall upon the earth.

But all would remember having seen the bear and watching his slow, but sure, movement through the forest. And all would remember that nothing had changed in the forest and never really would. The wonders of life and death would continue.

This was Fred Bear's world, a world of woodsmoke, pawed acorns, the sweet smell of decaying leaves, the twitch of a deer's tail and ragged birch bark blowing in the wind.

It is said that some men do not walk where the path leads, rather they go where there is no path and leave a trail. Fred Bear was such a man. We shall all miss our Papa Bear.

Eulogy By Brig. Gen. Joe Engle, Retired Astronaut, Commander of Space Shuttles Columbia, Discovery and Enterprise

What do you say about Fred Bear? What do you say about the mountains, the streams, the wildlife, the whole outdoors? All those things that defy description with mere words. My dad died in 1966 and I met Fred a couple years later. Fred filled a big void in my life. Like Dick and I suspect like so many others, Fred became my adopted dad. And he knew it and he accepted it.

Fred was a very humble person. He'd get embarrassed anytime you gave him any well deserved praise or recognition. So Fred, why don't I just say thanks — thanks for sharing your precious time with us — for sharing your invaluable thoughts and experiences — thanks for teaching us to be unselfish, to be kind and above all to be honest. You showed us that to be successful in life is to be respected. I saw you swallow your pride and bite your tongue, but you never gave up your integrity. You taught us that a man's word, that his handshake was worth more than any legal document that we've ever come up with. And in your magic way you got us all involved in the outdoors so we saw the importance of living in harmony with our natural resources and with our wildlife, to respect them and to love them.

We're going to hang up your bow Fred, but we won't hang up what you taught us. Every time we go into the woods, you'll go with us. We'll treat the outdoors and its inhabitants with the love and respect that you taught us. Every day we'll live our lives better because of you.

You've been held up a bit Fred, with that oxygen cart. I know there were some mountains a little to steep to climb, some trees a little too tricky to get up into, some streams a little too deep and swift to cross.

But, by God – no more.

You can go with us everywhere now. We won't climb a mountain, we won't build a campfire, we won't tell a story, or draw an arrow that you're not there with us. Thanks for showing us all of this.

Henrietta, thanks for sharing your Fred with us. And Lord, thanks for giving us Fred. Take good care of him, Lord. Give him his bow, his fly rod. Give him your best mountain, your best trout stream, give him your best campsite...because he always did this for us. And Fred, as you wrote on our bows and told us so many times as you sent us off on our adventures...from all of us...Happy Hunting, Fred Bear.

Memorial Service For Fred Bear

May 2, 1988

Fred's friend and employee for 48 years, Frank Scott, gave the following eulogy at the Memorial Service.

I have the honor of sharing some feelings and experiences about this very special man that we lovingly remember in our hearts today, Fred Bear.

It has often been said that each of us mean different things to different people and we will be remembered for different reasons by different people.

*To some, Fred will be remembered as a self made man, an industrialist who starting with little more than a dream, strong desire and determination created a company that provided employment for hundreds and recreation and enjoyment for millions.

In the process of creating Bear Archery he unselfishly shared his experience, knowledge and encouraged other members of our infant archery industry, he did this with the knowledge and confidence that everyone could benefit.

*To others Mr. Bear will be remembered as an inventor. Inventions that changed an industry and again he willingly shared with others for the benefit of all.

*He will be remembered as a conservationist and ecologist who was concerned about our natural resources and environment long before it was a popular crusade.

*Some of us will remember Fred as an outdoorsman, a hunter, fisherman and especially a bowhunter whose success and the promotion of this success encouraged millions of people to try this most challenging of sports. A bowhunter who became a legend and a role model for all of us.

*While he was many things to many people, there is one thing he was to all of us and one that we all shared in common and one that perhaps we never even thought about. Fred was above all else "A Teacher" and he taught us many things.

*He taught us to hunt, but to hunt for the right reasons. To hunt with respect for the game we hunt and to respect the land upon which we tread.

*He taught us that the success of the hunt should not always be measured by the fullness of the game bag but by the life long friendships made and treasured and the lessons learned by becoming one with nature.

*He taught us to be industrious and to take pride in the products we produce.

*He taught us there are many ways to do a job but there is only one right way and to always look for this right way.

*He taught us to be honest in our dealings with others, but most of all to be honest with ourselves. We can often fool others but we can never fool ourselves.

*He taught us to honor our commitments both business and personal, because honor is our most valuable asset and without it we are nothing.

*He taught us to laugh and most of all to be able to laugh at ourselves. To look for the humor in life because it often makes difficult things easier to handle.

*He taught us to lead and manage. He stated to me at one time to always remember we lead people and we manage things. The wisdom of the supervisor is measured by the ability to know which is which.

*He taught us that salesmanship and sales integrity is a company's most valuable asset. To give good value for good value received and that a salesman in the field *is* the company as far as the customer is concerned and it is here that a company's image is admired or destroyed.

Fred was proud of Bear Archery and all that went on within it and the Bear Archery sales force was always Fred's pride and joy, except for an occasion that I was involved in. In the early days I was the only salesman we had and a lot was riding on me. If I didn't write the orders they didn't get written. I came back to the office after a week on the road without an order in my briefcase. I was totally demoralized. Fred asked me how I made out. My answer was "Fred, I tried. I would lead the horse to water, but I couldn't make him drink." His reply was that "There were two things wrong, number one, we don't call our dealers horses and number two as a salesman, it is not your job to make the horse drink, it is your job to make him thirsty." In that one sentence he summed up the complete philosophy of salesmanship. That sentence changed my life.

*He taught us to share. To share our friendship and our love.

Dear Mrs. Bear, we pray that by our sharing your grief and by our sharing our love with you and your family, it will make this time easier to endure. May God Bless You All.

In the past I have worn this bolo tie as a symbol of Bear Archery. From this day forward I will wear it in honor of and in memory of Fred, my friend of 48 years.

Each of us will have our very own memory of something that happened that will keep Fred in our thoughts. A special place or special time that will remind us of the fine man that he was.

I will use a quotation from a man that Fred greatly admired and was greatly influenced by. Although, I don't think they ever met. That man was Ishi the last member of the Yana Indian tribe in northern California. In the Yana or Yahe language there were no words for goodbye. Ishi would simply say "You go - I stay." So to you our dear friend Fred we say to you - "You go - we stay" and by the grace of God we will meet again in a happy place where the environment will be pure and our joys will be boundless and our game bag will overflow with happiness and love.